P9-EAJ-549

[EVERYONE ELSE MUST FAIL]

ALSO BY KAREN SOUTHWICK

*High Noon: The Inside Story of Scott McNealy and
the Rise of Sun Microsystems*

*Silicon Gold Rush: The Next Generation of High-Tech
Stars Rewrites the Rules of Business*

*The Kingmakers: Venture Capital and the Money
Behind the Net*

[EVERYONE ELSE MUST FAIL]

THE UNVARNISHED TRUTH ABOUT
ORACLE AND LARRY ELLISON

KAREN SOUTHWICK

CROWN
BUSINESS
NEW YORK

LIBRARY
CLACKAMAS COMMUNITY COLLEGE
19600 S. MOLALLA AVENUE
OREGON CITY, OREGON 97045
WITHDRAWN

Copyright © 2003 by Karen Southwick

All rights reserved. No part of this book may be reproduced or transmitted in any form or by any means, electronic or mechanical, including photocopying, recording, or by any information storage and retrieval system, without permission in writing from the publisher.

Published by Crown Business, New York, New York.
Member of the Crown Publishing Group, a division of Random House, Inc.
www.crownpublishing.com

CROWN BUSINESS is a trademark and the Rising Sun colophon is a registered trademark of Random House, Inc.

Printed in the United States of America

Design by Lauren Dong

Library of Congress Cataloging-in-Publication Data

Southwick, Karen.
    Everyone else must fail : the unvarnished truth about Oracle and Larry Ellison / Karen Southwick.—1st ed.
        1. Oracle Corporation—History. 2. Ellison, Larry. 3. Computer software industry—United States—History. 4. Businessmen—United States—Biography. I. Title.
        HD9696.63.U64O728 2003
        338.7'610053'092—dc21   2003012044

ISBN 0-609-61069-4

10   9   8   7   6   5   4   3   2   1

First Edition

To my journalistic colleagues who, like me, have been seeking new endeavors in this economic downturn. May they all find projects as interesting as this one.

CONTENTS

[EVERYONE
ELSE MUST
FAIL]

INTRODUCTION

["IT IS NOT SUFFICIENT THAT I SUCCEED.

EVERYONE ELSE MUST FAIL."]

The saying "It is not sufficient that I succeed. Everyone else must fail" has been associated with Larry Ellison so often that most people think it originated with him. Actually, it came centuries ago with Genghis Khan. Ellison has referred to the quote in conversations, then laughed rather unconvincingly and tried to distance himself from the sentiment. But it sticks nonetheless. For Ellison, the founder and chief executive of Oracle Corporation, is like a modern-day Genghis Khan who has elevated ruthlessness in business to a carefully cultivated art form. His weapons are not the marauding hordes but his company's possession of a key technology platform, his willingness to exploit it, and his disdain for anyone who gets in his way. That includes subordinates, whom Ellison runs through and discards with unusual ferocity. He cannot tolerate executives who dare to stand up to him and has systematically purged Oracle's senior ranks of much of their talent. Many of the departed, among them Tom Siebel and Craig Conway, are running Oracle competitors, while others, such as Ray Lane, have notable second careers. But Oracle remains in their veins. Siebel is head of Oracle competitor Siebel Systems, Conway of PeopleSoft, and, as a venture capitalist at famed investment firm Kleiner Perkins Caufield & Byers, Lane is busily searching for the next Oracle.

Ellison named his company after ancient Greek prophecies that came from the gods and were spoken by persons in a trance. He does seem to lead in mystical fashion, proclaiming visions that others must follow for Oracle to move forward. These visions often prove to be profoundly insightful, as when Ellison, ahead of nearly everyone else, decided that software would trump hardware and, later, that his company's technology must encompass the Internet. He has come a long way from the college dropout who started at the bottom rung financially and socially. The bastard child from a tough neighborhood in Chicago is now among the richest men in the world, with a net worth in the billions. Ellison bootstrapped a tiny company with two friends and a few thousand dollars; he was the force who willed it to succeed and handpicked talented people who could help him achieve his dream. Today that company is the second-largest software vendor in the world. Along his way to the top, Ellison pursued and courted women by the dozens, marrying three of them and getting sued for sexual harassment by one of them. He learned to fly fighter planes, sail maxi-yachts, and collect Japanese art. He can discourse on everything from ancient samurai soldiers to modern biotech investing. Ellison is a throwback both to the early days of Silicon Valley and to the robber barons of the nineteenth century, when colorful visionaries founded companies in their own image and governed according to their whims.

Indeed, in mid-2003 Ellison again showed his capacity for reinvention and surprise by launching a hostile bid for Conway's PeopleSoft, which had just announced a plan to merge with a smaller competitor and displace Oracle as the number-two player in business software. Although Ellison has toyed with the notion of acquiring companies such as Apple Computer and Netscape, Oracle had never done a major takeover in its twenty-five-year history. The CEO believes firmly that Oracle's technology is the best in the business, and anyway, the company's culture doesn't lend itself to easy accommodation by outsiders. However, Ellison, who is now proclaiming that the number of players in the technology industry will shrink dramatically in coming years, evidently decided that bidding for PeopleSoft was worth the risk. Hostile takeovers have been rare in the software industry, because talented programmers, salespeople, and marketers can leave as soon as their stock options vest. But with a declining economy and a slump in technology purchases, hostile takeovers—seeking market share alone, not talent or intellectual property—may again become popular. And if they do, it was Ellison who led the way.

By turns brilliant and intolerant, inspiring and chilling, energetic and disinterested, Ellison is one of the most intriguing, dominant, and misguided leaders of a major twenty-first–century corporation. He cofounded Oracle, the leader in database software, and has been its chief executive for more than twenty-five years. That gives him the longest tenure at the top for any of the technology revolutionaries, including his onetime peer, Microsoft's Bill Gates, who has stepped away from day-to-day management. Ellison's uninterrupted leadership, coupled with the fact that he still owns nearly one-fourth of Oracle's stock, gives him a tight grip on one of the most powerful forces in the twenty-first century, controlling the means to information at thousands of major corporations. Oracle is, in effect, the largest public company that remains "privately held." Its dominance in the database, which resides at the center of corporations, has been compared to Microsoft's hold on the desktop, although the market share figures for the monopolist Microsoft are much higher. Still, as of year-end 2002, Oracle held 60 percent of the market for the Unix databases most large companies use and 39.4 percent of the overall market, according to market researcher IDC. More than half of the *Fortune* 100 cited Oracle as the preferred database vendor.[1]

As Oracle enters its second quarter century, its rollercoaster history reads like an ancient tragedy, with a flawed, yet fascinating hero at the center. The company almost ceased to exist in the early 1990s, thanks to superaggressive sales tactics that eventually backfired and left it virtually bankrupt. Ellison was forced to bring in outside executives, consultant

Ray Lane and veteran CFO Jeff Henley, and together the three of them repositioned Oracle for its most spectacular growth during the decade of the 1990s. Ellison, whom one business psychologist refers to as the ultimate narcissist, refuses to acknowledge that at least part of Oracle's recent slide in revenue and profitability may be due to disillusion with his leadership—on the part of employees, shareholders, and customers alike. As the singular immanence from which Oracle's culture radiates, he is responsible for the contradictions that exist at the company: its independence, its ability to innovate in the face of wholesale skepticism, its often-callous disregard for the needs of customers, and its brutal competitiveness. When you interview competitors, partners, users, and executives of Oracle, two emotions are invariably expressed: respect for what the company has accomplished technologically, especially with the database, and irritation at how poorly it has handled just about anything that involves human interaction.

It's not clear yet what the fate of Ellison and Oracle will be, because the drama is not complete. In the pages of this book, we see the humble beginnings of the man and his company, watch as they emerge as great powers, then marvel as history takes its revenge upon a leader who won't acknowledge his weaknesses. The book opens with the scene in which Ellison eliminates his second-in-command, Ray Lane, because the CEO feels himself undermined by Lane's growing power. It then returns to Ellison's own roots, taking us back to his rough childhood and his serendipitous journey to Silicon Valley. We see Oracle become the fastest-growing software company in history for a time, even outpacing archrival Microsoft. We watch Oracle run aground and manage to right itself. With the development of the Internet, Ellison moves to a national stage with his drive for a cheaper alternative to the personal computer. We hear from Oracle customers, fed up with the company's disregard of their needs, and from competitors, who are taking advantage of that frustration. The book closes with an examination of Oracle's unique culture, derived from the DNA of its flamboyant chief executive, and a projection of its possible future—with or without Ellison.

Regardless of what happens to Oracle, the journey through its history and psychology is well worth taking, for Ellison is one of those irresistibly compelling characters whom we are unlikely to see again. The technology industry today is outgrowing the individualistic, mercurial CEO whose company solely reflects his grandiose personality. Ellison may be the last of his kind, but he is unforgettable. Long after Oracle's fate is decided, the legend of Ellison and the kingdom he created on the shores of San Francisco Bay will live on.

1

DAYS OF THE DEPARTURES

[
"THE PEOPLE WHO GET CLOSEST TO LARRY
THE FASTEST ALSO FALL THE FASTEST."
]

Out of all the technology powerhouses that sprouted in the late 1970s and early 1980s, like Microsoft, Apple, and Sun Microsystems, Oracle Corporation probably remains closest to its entrepreneurial roots. That's thanks to its charismatic, dominating founder, Larry Ellison, who runs the company as if it were still a start-up, with himself at the center, making decisions on everything from advertising to executive recruitment or, more likely, firings. "Larry was a classic entrepreneur, all over every detail of the company," says Tom Siebel, who should know, because after becoming Oracle's top salesman, he later founded his namesake company, Siebel Systems, an Oracle competitor. "In the early days, Larry made every decision, controlled the board of directors, approved every large sales contract." Siebel remembers that in 1985, when Oracle was barely scratching $20 million in sales, Ellison was predicting it would soon reach $100 million. "We all thought he was a little overenthusiastic," recalls Siebel, but they went along for the ride and were handsomely rewarded. Oracle stock options eventually made many of its early employees millionaires or multimillionaires.

Even today, when Oracle has forty thousand employees and around $10 billion in sales, Ellison's emotional impact is immense, in keeping with the huge Orwellian-like image he projects on-screen at company trade shows while he strides up to the stage. Ellison, a true ham, loves to perform—no matter how large or small the audience. Executives who know him say that in one-on-one forums, he can be persuaded to adopt a point of view other than his own as long as you're intellectually prepared. But in front of even a few people, "Larry feels compelled to perform," says Gary Bloom, a former executive vice president and onetime heir apparent who left to run a company of his own, Veritas, in 2000. "He gives the gospel of Oracle through these nonstop performances. . . . He'll give the same message ten times with the same lines," at trade shows with thousands of customers and at executive and product development meetings with half a dozen executives. The "gospel of Oracle," according to its primary interpreter, Ellison, is that (1) we have great technology; (2) our competitors (whom he names and disses repeatedly) will never catch up; (3) you should be buying from us because we can do it all—give you everything from the database to business applications.

Nobody can overshadow Ellison. Anyone who even tries is out the door. "The people who get closest to Larry the fastest also fall the fastest," says Bloom, who decided to leave Oracle after it became clear to him that Ellison would never step away and leave the top job to anyone else. Another case in point: Ray Lane, who jousted with Bloom for the role of Oracle's second-in-command and wound up leaving a few months before Bloom did. The "cult of the personality" that Oracle has become enchants a few and alienates many more, among them Siebel, Bloom, and Lane, and virtually all of the other Oracle executives who helped the company achieve its spectacular growth in the 1980s and 1990s.

Lane became the most celebrated example of Ellison's inability to share the limelight. On June 30, 2000, Lane was enjoying a well-deserved vacation, his first in more than two years, at his Oregon farm. The fifty-three-year-old president of Oracle could look back with satisfaction on what he had accomplished over the past eight years. When Lane, who's tall, with a trim build, thinning reddish brown hair, and clean-cut features, joined Oracle in 1992, the company was reeling from a $12 million loss, layoffs and defections, and widespread distrust among customers because of its reputation for selling products that weren't ready for prime time. Lane, a mild-mannered former IBM executive and Booz Allen consultant, had stood toe-to-toe with Ellison and helped convince him that Oracle had to change from a fly-by-the-seat-of-your-pants company into one on which customers, and Wall Street, could depend.

The pairing of Ellison, the visionary who loves his own hype, and Lane, the conservative consultant, worked brilliantly. By 2000, Oracle was a $10 billion company—the second-largest software maker after Microsoft—with a market cap of $220 billion. Its databases—storehouses of information—powered the majority of the world's biggest and most powerful companies. It had diversified into services and application software that runs a company's internal functions, reaping 50 percent annual growth rates. Best of all, Oracle had achieved respectability, and Ellison was feted as one of the founding fathers of the technology revolution. His personal wealth even briefly surpassed that of his nemesis, Microsoft's Bill Gates. Lane hadn't done too shabbily, either. He already owned nearly twenty million shares of Oracle stock and in a few weeks would vest another round of stock worth about $70 million at the time. So all seemed well in the gleaming, green towers of Oracle-land on the edge of San Francisco Bay in Redwood Shores, California . . .

Not quite.

That Friday at his farm, Lane got an unexpected phone call from Ellison, who was apologetic for bothering him on his vacation. "I was just about to go out on a rafting trip on the Rogue River with two friends and [wife] Stephanie," Lane recalls. But when Ellison called, he knew something was up. "I went downstairs and told them to go without me."

Then he came back up and had the conversation with Ellison, the one that Lane had known would come someday. After all, he'd watched a succession of other executives, mostly the ones who dared to disagree, leave. Still, he had to play out the game, asking Ellison what was so urgent that it couldn't wait until he got back. Ellison finally spilled it: he wanted the president's title back to add to the CEO and chairman titles he already had. "That's interesting. Why?" Lane responded.

"I want to consolidate authority," Ellison said. "There are two of us with authority, you and me. I can't risk having any confusion about who's in charge. So I want to consolidate that into one office."

"Are you telling me you want me to leave?" Lane asked incredulously.

"That's entirely your decision." Ellison, in his typical pattern, never liked to fire anyone directly.

"But," Lane protested, "I can't imagine your taking the title back and expecting me to stay."

"If that's your decision, we need to announce it to the world."

The thrice-divorced Ellison proceeded to describe the breakup in terms he knew well: "The marriage has gone sour," he informed Lane.

Lane, with a sinking feeling of inevitability coupled with relief that it was now in the open, asked Ellison to send him the press release, in which Oracle would break the news to the world, and to come up with a severance agreement that dealt with the additional options. Ellison never did any of that, part of a pattern that explains why Oracle is the target of several wrongful-termination lawsuits by other executives, although Lane has not joined them. "I never got a callback from Larry," Lane recalls. "The next morning, my mother reads it [the news of his departure] in a newspaper." Lane never went back to his office at Oracle. A secretary forwarded his personal belongings.

Tellingly, when I did a search for Ray Lane on Oracle's Web site, looking for that fateful press release, all reference to him had been completely expunged, as if Ellison were revising history. Through the grapevine, Lane says he heard that Ellison blew up at a company meeting one day, complaining that "all I hear is Ray Lane," and ordered the name stricken from Oracle's site. More than two years after the fact, Lane is still angry, not because Ellison wanted him to leave Oracle but because of how it was handled. "If you want to fire me, be a man and fire me face-to-face," says Lane. "Larry could have told me, 'I think you ought to leave the company, here's a package, take three to six months to transition out, go kiss all the customers . . .' Instead," says Lane, "he does it on the phone."

Ellison was careful not to tell his fellow executives that Lane was being fired. As had happened repeatedly, he was ousting someone coincidentally just before he was to vest in lucrative stock options. "I was two and a half weeks from vesting about $70 million worth of stock," says Lane. The forced departure, he believes, "was obviously timed to avoid paying that stock, even though it doesn't cost the company anything." Ellison allowed Lane to resign, avoiding the vesting and any severance. Lane felt that he had no choice but to resign rather than be stripped of his title. "He clearly went in with the intent to have me resign," says Lane. "He knew exactly what I would do. At Oracle, he's a master of games playing. There's no way I could play his game."

Lane has considered litigation, a route that a number of other ousted Oracle executives have chosen through the years. "Certainly I have the right to litigate, but so far I've decided not to because I don't want to go through two years of hell." Besides, he did end up with those twenty million shares of Oracle stock, making him, for a while, one of the richest men in the country. (Lane was number 338 on the 2000 *Forbes* 400 list, with a net worth of $850 million, although he dropped off the list the following year with the decline in Oracle's share price. In early 2002, the value of Lane's Oracle stake had dropped by more than half.) And while at Oracle, he married his former administrative assistant, Stephanie; the couple now have two young children. They also have three homes: a one hundred–acre farm in Grants Pass, Oregon, where Lane can hunt and fish; a place in Southern California's Palm Desert at Big Horn, where he can play golf; and a home in the exclusive San Francisco Bay Area town of Atherton. A few months after his ouster from Oracle, his operating experience at one of the most important technology companies helped him land a plum job at one of the premier venture capital firms, Kleiner Perkins Caufield & Byers, as a general partner. Several of Kleiner's top partners, including the man who was then the best-known venture capitalist in the world, John Doerr, personally recruited Lane.

CORPORATE POWER STRUGGLE

Thanks to Oracle, Lane is rich beyond his wildest dreams, richer than anyone in the world except a few thousand people. He also has a wife with whom he's made a successful marriage, several beautiful homes, and a reputation as a strong operational executive that could get him just about any job he wants. So why is he so bitter that his feud with Ellison spilled over into nasty arguments in major newspapers such as the *Wall Street Journal* and *New York Times?* Where once the headlines spoke about how well Ellison and Lane's complementary abilities served Oracle, now they dished up a disturbingly public spat between two of the most powerful men in technology. Lane accused Ellison of surrounding himself with yes-men and selling products before their time. Ellison responded that much of Lane's chosen team remains intact at Oracle (although that was no longer true by 2002). "He is the soul, the conscience of Oracle, and the other 45,000 of us are criminals?" Ellison commented.[1] "What I'm really bitter about," Lane confided, "is his breaking up a team that was working."

About a year after he left, Lane upset Ellison and alienated many of his former coworkers when he gave a keynote address at the annual conference of Oracle's biggest rival in the business application software business, the German company and market leader, SAP. Lane says he accepted the invitation because of his new role at Kleiner. SAP had changed its strategy in a way that would benefit Kleiner's funding of "best-of-breed" start-ups, "and I wanted to support that," he says. In his speech to about nine thousand attendees, Lane criticized Ellison's strategy of pushing companies to buy all their important enterprise software from Oracle. "I don't think one company can provide everything, and so I think we have to live in a world of best-in-class applications that are integrated together," he told the group. In effect, he endorsed SAP's approach over that of his former company. That leaves a lot of people shaking their heads. As another former Oracle executive, Marc Benioff, sees it, everyone who leaves Oracle has a "charge" surrounding the company. That charge can be either positive or negative, or maybe both. Lane's charge is clearly negative. "Larry's like a spiritual guru, and Oracle is like a cult," says Benioff, a junior Oracle executive who worked his way up into several different marketing and product management positions at the company. He is now CEO of a small but feisty Oracle competitor, Salesforce.com. "What you don't want to do," he says, "is get stuck on that charge," because it can mess up your brain. Once you've worked for Ellison, you're never the same again.

Lane has had no interaction with his former boss since he resigned from the company and left the board of directors. "I've never talked to him since that phone call in Oregon," he says. If he did talk to Ellison, "I would try to explain how stupid he was in throwing away a fantasy team. Ray and Larry together made people trust Oracle. He threw that away because of his ego." Although Ellison has complained both privately and publicly that he had to get rid of Lane because operationally things were getting out of control, Lane believes it was because ultimately he had become too powerful and Ellison couldn't bear it. "History was being written that Ray Lane saved the company, produced $10 billion worth of sales," he says, while Ellison wanted the credit for building the most valuable software company in the world. "What stood in his way was Ray Lane. It was probably inevitable that it was going to end up this way. He was already using his standard MO, undermining me to the board and the employees." Ellison has said on a number of occasions that he'll never have a designated number-two executive again. "Once someone perceives themselves as number two, they get blinded by the limelight and become less effective," he maintains, without naming names.

It's fair to ask whether Lane wasn't merely on the losing end of a corporate power struggle that was bound to happen. He admits he still has a chip on his shoulder when it comes to Oracle and Ellison. "I have very mixed feelings about Oracle today," he says, "because I can't separate Larry from Oracle. At the end of the day when I go to my closet and see those Oracle T-shirts, I can't throw them away. But I won't go out in public wearing them either." On the one hand, he's proud that he helped build one of the most powerful companies in the world. "It's a great legacy." On the other hand, he thinks about all the missed opportunities and what Oracle might have been had it held on to the talent that's washed into, and out of, its gates. "Oracle is dirty. Oracle is a Larry Ellison company," he says. "A part of me is purely mad at Larry. He blew up something that was working."

And yet, even though Lane has an obvious ax to grind, there are too many others who tell the same story to dismiss him as a sore loser. Oracle has run through enough executive and managerial talent in its twenty-five–year history to seed literally dozens of start-ups. The names are storied, and they've often become key rivals of Oracle: Tom Siebel, founder of Siebel Systems; Mike Fields, who formed Open-Vision; Craig Conway, who now runs PeopleSoft; Terry Garnett, a venture capitalist who funded Siebel; Gary Bloom, CEO of Veritas; Gary Kennedy and Jeff Walker, the pair who drove Oracle's growth in its first decade of success, . . . and Benioff and Lane. "There's a long history of these love-hate relationships with Larry," says Benioff. Ellison lavishes opportunities upon his favored executives—giving them almost free rein to grow—until he tires of them for one reason or another, or feels threatened by them, and finds a way to get rid of them. Ellison demands fanatical loyalty and will sacrifice anybody he perceives as incapable of such devotion. Since almost no one can really meet his standard of perfection, each person at Oracle becomes expendable, and in the end, he winds up with very few whom he can trust. This is the paradox that Ellison has created for himself and can't seem to break out of. It is also the paradox that afflicts Oracle itself, a great company with a tragic flaw—its inability to retain talent in an industry that runs on talent.

PUBLIC HUMILIATION

Mike Fields is a prime example of Ellison's use-'em-and-dump-'em relationship with his executives. One of the first African-Americans to rise to a position of prominence in the software industry, Fields was second-in-command to Gary Kennedy, president of U.S. sales, when Oracle blew up in 1990 (see Chapter 4). After Kennedy's departure, Fields was handed the top U.S. sales job. The consensus among other executives who were there at the time is that Fields was a placeholder until a more permanent successor to Kennedy could be brought in. With Oracle's sales force in disarray, Fields, rather like Jerry Ford when he became U.S. president after Richard Nixon's resignation in 1974, was viewed as the kind of square-deal guy who could calm things down. Says Geoff Squire, who was Fields's peer as head of Oracle's international sales, "At the time, Mike did an excellent job. The company needed somebody who was honest, stable, and a great communicator and motivator. He has those assets."

But Fields was not the kind of take-no-prisoners leader whom Ellison admired. Fields was an expedient choice for Ellison, for whom the sales force always took a backseat to technology. A programmer himself, Ellison preferred the technical wizards in development to sales and support people. Craig Ramsey, a former Oracle sales executive under both Kennedy and Fields, believes that Ellison expected Fields's tenure to be a short one. "I don't think Larry thought Mike could do the job. He put him into it knowing he was going to get rid of him," Ramsey says. That in itself is no surprise. Many top executives elevate someone into a job knowing that he or she is only a caretaker. But it was the way Ellison went about ousting Fields that rankled his coworkers. Ellison did not approach him directly but rather chose to humiliate him at public meetings of Fields's own staff and sales force.

Ramsey remembers attending a sales meeting that Fields was leading. "Larry came into the meeting, took control, and said, 'This is the most disgusting display of sales management I've ever seen in my life. This is the worst sales organization in the U.S.—no, correct me, in the world.'" Basically, Ramsey says, Ellison has little use for salespeople and thinks they're dumb. "This is part of Larry's heritage. There has never been somebody heading up sales at Oracle who's left as a friend," he adds. Mike Hagan, who worked in sales administration, recalls that Fields's approach was to emphasize selling solutions and developing relationships with customers, who had been sadly neglected during the hard-charging 1980s. But Ellison disparaged that approach, directly contradicting Fields in front of his own sales team. "Larry came into the meeting and said, 'The problem is that you guys are all focusing on relationship building and selling solutions. We sell databases. It's not that hard.'" Hagan estimates there were four hundred salespeople attending what was supposed to be a morale-raising session at a local hotel. "Mike got up and said one thing, and Larry said something completely different," Hagan recalls. Ellison's words of advice: "Just go out and sell the technology. This is great technology. Anybody could sell this."

In a later meeting of sales management executives, Fields was describing his plans to have a boot camp at nearby Stanford University for some of the staff. "Larry came in unexpectedly," recalls Paul Hoffman, who was one of Fields's managers, "and looked for his opening." He attacked Fields for planning the boot camp. "Who signed this contract?" he demanded. Fields replied that it was his assistant. "Your assistant signed this contract?" Ellison asked. "On my behalf," Fields said. That triggered a tirade that lasted nearly an hour in which Ellison berated Fields for bringing the company to its knees. "This was at a roundtable with about thirty of us who reported to Mike," says Hoffman. "Mike wasn't the strongest leader, but for Larry to do that in front of his team ruined his team. Mike just took it." In fact, Fields would soon leave the company, replaced by the incoming Ray Lane in mid-1992. Fields, like several other ousted Oracle executives, declined to talk about his former company. Communicating through his personal assistant, Fields, who became an entrepreneur (founding OpenVision) and investor, said he simply doesn't want to remember those days at Oracle.

ORACLE REFUGEES

By all accounts, former Oracle marketing executive Terry Garnett was something of an Ellison wanna-be. He was chief of corporate marketing at Oracle in the early 1990s, reporting directly to Ellison, who adores publicity. Garnett and Ellison were both ambitious, hard-driving, and not afraid to alienate other people in pursuit of their own goals. Ex-journalist Alex Vieux, who now runs the European technology conference ETRE, remembers how Garnett came to the press in late 1990 to try to salvage Ellison's reputation, tarnished when the company was forced to restate earnings. Garnett wanted to reposition Ellison from the impulsive CEO who didn't pay much attention to trivialities like accounting requirements to a somewhat chastened, more responsible leader. "When Larry found himself in the accounting snafu in October 1990, Terry went to see all the reporters, including me, and talked to us about not creating a snowball effect that would push Larry out," Vieux recalls. "He led a campaign to create a new Larry. Terry helped Oracle recover its financial reputation." But Kate Mitchell, an ex–Oracle marketing manager who worked for Garnett, saw another side of him. "He was tough to work for because he was so manipulating. He'd do anything to get his way," she says. However, for the time being, Garnett had a powerful ally in kindred spirit Ellison, to whom he gave total loyalty. "Larry gave Terry a lot of responsibility that other people were saying he shouldn't have. He was like a one-boss guy—no one else mattered," Mitchell says. Other executives started teaming up against Garnett. Mitchell recalls telling Lane in late 1993, "Something's got to give. I can't work for Terry." She recalls that Garnett was just too political. "He was always behind the scenes causing trouble."

Ellison finally tired of Garnett, as he has of other Oracle marketing executives, and abandoned him, so Lane wound up firing him. "Terry was brilliant at marketing, but he'd pissed everybody off, including Larry," says Lane. On the plus side, Garnett had put together the launch of Oracle 7, the version of the database that "saved the company" in the early 1990s, Lane recalls. Garnett convinced the analysts and press that Oracle was coming back, so it was worthwhile covering the launch. But then, according to Mitchell, Garnett leaked information to the press about Ellison's investment in an outside firm called nCube, which made parallel processing systems for video on demand, at the time a hot field. After Garnett's ouster in mid-1994, the dispute pitting the chief executive against his previously staunch ally turned public. Garnett filed a $30 million wrongful-termination suit, claiming that he was the victim of Ellison's treachery. Like Ellison with nCube, Garnett had also invested in an outside firm, Human Nature Interactive, an electronic home-shopping venture. Garnett's suit said he was fired because he refused to funnel business from Oracle to nCube, while Oracle countered that Garnett was spending too much time on his personal business. Garnett's lawsuit said Ellison had ordered Garnett to form Human Nature Interactive without the approval of Oracle's board of directors.[2] In early 1995, for reasons never publicly disclosed, Garnett dropped the lawsuit. Although he won no settlement, he did walk away with one hundred thousand shares of Oracle and $1 million in cash, according to court documents. In 1994, Garnett put $100,000 into Siebel Systems, giving him a stake valued at $10 million by the end of the decade. That, in turn, helped him and his wife, Katrina Garnett, also an Oracle alum, bankroll their own company, Crossworlds Software. Despite his success as a venture capitalist and an entrepreneur, Garnett's bitterness against Oracle remains. Through a spokesperson, he told me that, like Mike

Fields, he never talks about the company. From Vieux's vantage point, "Terry became disposable when Larry didn't need him anymore."

Geoff Squire, who had helped build Oracle's international sales to the half-billion-dollar level, was another executive who became disposable. The British native was an Oracle distributor, then its first country managing director, and wound up Lane's counterpart in Europe. But when Ellison gave Lane the title of head of worldwide operations in late 1993, he decided Squire must go and flew over to London, ostensibly to break the news. "Larry's never been trained to fire people," says Squire, rather charitably. Over breakfast at Claridge's in London, "we were talking about general things," among them Squire's desire to hire a new chief financial officer for Europe. "I don't think I'm going to do that. I want Ray Lane to take more responsibility," Ellison replied. Squire got the message. "Are you telling me to go?" Ellison inclined his head slightly. "I could tell by his eyes and the way he looked away and shook his head," Squire says, even though nothing was ever stated directly. (Lane says he had to confirm the termination.)

Squire would have gone without protest until he saw the release agreement that Ellison wanted him to sign. "I went through one of those bizarre periods when Larry wanted to screw me out of a bit of money," says Squire. According to him, the release agreement specified that he had been terminated on October 28, which meant that he was ineligible for vesting about $2 million worth of additional stock options that would have been earned by November 17. In November, Squire says, he was helping Oracle negotiate the possible acquisition of rival Ingres. "Even though I was in a room in November negotiating a deal and people were still sending me E-mails about it in December, Larry wanted me to say October 28 was my termination," Squire says. So he refused, based on the advice of his lawyers.

Ellison was prepared to take it to court, but Lane worked out a deal under which Squire got part of his options. At one point before Lane's arrival, Squire was generating such strong sales in Europe that he was virtually carrying the whole company, Lane recalls. "The rest of the company was slipping away, but Geoff was running a pretty good show." Squire's reward was getting shafted on his options. After Lane did damage control, "I signed the release about a month or so later," Squire says. Seven years later, he can still tick off the events as if they had happened yesterday. "Larry has an absence of generosity," Squire says. "At one stage, I was so mad, I almost rang up [Oracle cofounder] Bob Miner to tell him, 'Larry screwed me out of $2 million when I've made him $500 million. Would you give me $2 million of yours?' " What Squire didn't know at the time was that Miner was ill with the cancer that would soon kill him. "I'm glad now I didn't talk to him," says Squire. He didn't see Ellison again until several years later, at a function in Washington, D.C., where Margaret Thatcher was speaking. "There was a short hello," recalls Squire. In early 2000, Ellison sent him an E-mail saying, "Let's catch up." By this time, Squire had joined another company, Veritas, which makes storage and security software. "We wound up getting a deal with Oracle," he says, helping to mend fences with Ellison. "I'd say our relationship today is amicable," allows Squire.

THE SADDEST STORY

Wayne Harvey was one of those high-strung individuals who seem to be inevitably drawn to high-strung companies like Oracle. Gary Kennedy, who ran sales for much of the 1980s, credits Harvey, "an incredibly brilliant guy," with managing Oracle's product development effectively for perhaps the first time in the company's history. "We'd gone through several development vice presidents," Kennedy says, after cofounder Bob Miner, who had met Ellison when both were employed at another company, decided he didn't want responsibility for day-to-day operations anymore. Ellison may have been Oracle's prophet, but Miner was the guy who sat in the back room and wrote the product code that made the first database operational. "Bob [Miner] was very technically competent but a poor manager," Kennedy says. "We couldn't find anybody who was good at both." Joining Oracle in the mid-1980s, "Wayne was as technical as any of the programmers yet superorganized. For a while, he was our salvation."

While running development, Harvey was also a member of the executive committee that met regularly with Ellison on strategy. Other members at the time were Kennedy, Miner, CFO Jeff Walker, and another sales executive, John Luongo. "Harvey had too big a job [at development] for one man to do, and he was on the EC, too," says Kennedy. He recalls that many of the EC meetings "turned into Wayne-bashing sessions," in which everyone else would pile on Harvey for not meeting deadlines or failing to add some new functionality to the database. "Wayne was not a good debater," Kennedy says. "Jeff [Walker], John [Luongo], and Larry were all good." Of the other three, Kennedy and Miner managed to insulate themselves from criticism, even though, Kennedy says, "we weren't as good at debating." At that point, Kennedy was meeting his sales quotas, and that's all he was asked to do. Criticism just rolled off Miner, who had pulled back from managing anyway. "Bob would say, 'Shit, Larry, I don't want to be here anyway. I'll go off and do my programming,'" Kennedy recalls.

That left Harvey as the target, and one day he just blew, according to Kennedy. "He told me, 'Gary, I can't take any more.' Then he looked at Miner and said, 'You are the worst fucking manager.' Then he pointed at Larry, 'You're the second worst.' Then he decides to walk out of the room. He walked out, opened the door, and the door won't slam. He pushes it several times, it won't slam. We all break out laughing, completely inconsiderately. He goes red in the face and storms out of the meeting, cursing." Kennedy adds that it was the first time he'd ever seen Ellison speechless. Harvey was of course fired, "which was tragic for the organization," Kennedy says. It proved to be even more tragic for Harvey. A few months later, in November 1987, having also gone through a separation from his wife, Harvey, then thirty-six, killed himself and their five-year-old son, who was visiting at his home in Woodside, California.

No one can know for sure what went through Harvey's mind that day, but Kennedy believes that his ouster from Oracle contributed to his depression. Harvey was bereft of his wife and son, who was living with his mother, and "Oracle became his whole life. He worked harder than anybody there," says Kennedy. Although he joined a start-up after leaving Oracle, a month later Harvey was dead. Luongo remembers seeing Harvey "go ballistic" at a quarterly off-site meeting in London. "I thought he was going to hit me," says Luongo. "I used to say he was held together by rubber bands and I wouldn't want to be there when they snapped."

Most of Oracle's executives attended Harvey's funeral, except for Ellison, who never showed up.

MOVING ON

Even executives who leave Oracle on relatively good terms experience the stress of disengaging from Ellison. One of Oracle's earliest employees (number twenty-six), John Luongo came in through sales like Siebel and Kennedy. Unlike them, he stayed on after the accounting disaster of early 1990 but left later that year when the position he thought he'd been promised went to another executive, not an unusual thing at the highly politicized company. "I told Larry I'd leave," says Luongo. "I'm the only one of that era who left on amiable terms. I could read the signs and know when Larry was start- ing the process. *If you want to leave in a healthy way, go now.* There were a couple of senior people I told that to, but they didn't leave." He pauses and then adds, "I still like Larry. You have to take him for what he is," totally dispassionate when it came to sacrificing anyone to make Oracle successful.

"Larry would start running through people because they had passed the point where they were qualified to do what they were doing," says Luongo. "My belief is that people have a talent appropriate to a certain size range. Larry recognized when they needed to move on. There were very few people Larry let go who didn't need to be let go." On the other hand, he adds, "you never wanted to be the next in line for succession because Larry would feel threatened." Two early executives, U.S. sales manager Mike Seashols and international sales manager Geoff Squire, "both thought they could be the CEO, and Larry got rid of them." Luongo left voluntarily after Ellison handed the top sales job to Squire. "I could have made more if I had gotten [Ellison] to fire me," he says. "I got no severance, but I got [the options] I was entitled to."

Two other ex–Oracle executives, Gary Bloom and Marc Benioff, left on relatively good terms to found their own respective companies. Bloom departed unexpectedly in November 2000, a few months after Lane. Widely considered to be Ellison's heir apparent, Bloom, who was an executive vice president, came to realize that the CEO was nowhere near ready to step down. Bloom and Lane were allies in restoring Oracle's operational organization but rivals, as were all the executives, when it came to Ellison's favoritism. After Lane was ousted in mid-2000, Bloom became the second-in-command. "I believed I had the possibility of someday running Oracle," Bloom acknowledges. "I did want to be CEO." But ultimately, he realized that Ellison, who's in his late fifties, "wasn't going anywhere soon enough." Bloom, forty-one, didn't want to wait for what could be another decade, or more, to get the top job, so he resigned to become chief executive of Veritas.

Bloom had previously toyed with the idea of leaving Oracle in 1998 but stayed when Ellison gave him a million stock options and elevated him to executive vice president. "I thought in the 1998–99 time frame that Larry would start thinking about stepping aside," Bloom says. But Oracle's huge success in the late 1990s—its market cap surpassed IBM's for a time—had Ellison believing he could achieve his old dream of overtaking Microsoft to become the world's biggest software company. "That possibility caused him to completely reengage in the company and drive it forward," says Bloom. "So I said it's time for me to move on. I'd been at Oracle fourteen years. Emotionally it was a difficult decision, but practically it was an easy decision." He remains on good terms with Ellison, and Veritas has a tight alliance with Oracle.

Benioff joined Oracle straight out of college and never knew any other career until he left in 1999 to start his own company, Salesforce.com, which offers sales force automation software on an on-line, or hosted, basis. In the late 1990s, says Benioff, he was getting burned out at Oracle, where he'd held a succession of jobs, starting in the customer service call center and finishing as a senior vice president. Benioff talked to Tom Siebel, who offered him a job doing Siebel Systems' on-line offering, but Benioff had no desire to work for another strong-minded executive. Instead, he developed his idea for on-line applications while he was still at Oracle, with Ellison's permission. In fact, Ellison invested $2 million in Salesforce.com and joined the board of directors. Says Benioff, "I left Oracle because it was time and I'd done everything I could in the company, working for Larry for thirteen years. One experience I didn't have was doing my own thing." But in mid-2000, Oracle launched its own hosted applications business, in direct competition with Salesforce.com. Benioff promptly fired Ellison from his board of directors, reaping a marketing bonanza. "Larry built a competitive service while he was on the board," says Benioff. "He forced us to fire him, and we got a huge amount of press. He told me, 'You're using me to your PR advantage.' I said, 'Of course, you taught me how to do that.'" (In 1995, Ellison brilliantly exploited the computing world's increasing distrust of Microsoft by proposing a cheap, easy-to-use alternative to the personal computers that were nearly all powered by Microsoft's operating systems. Ellison mined the resulting PR relating to the "clash of the Titans," himself and Microsoft head Bill Gates, to make then-unknown Oracle a household name.)

Today, says Benioff, unlike most of the other ousted Oracle executives, he still counts Ellison as a friend. "Larry was very gracious and generous in helping me get my company started. Without Larry, we would not be where we are today." Echoing

Luongo, Benioff says, "My attitude is, 'Larry is Larry.' Getting mad at that is a fundamental error." If you let Ellison rattle you, whether you work for him, compete with him, or partner with him, you've lost, Benioff maintains. "You need to stay on course regardless of what Larry is doing. Bill Gates has always done that. He never got rattled by Larry."

SOFTER SIDE

Ellison seems either to love people or to hate them, with no shades of gray in between. He can also shift abruptly from love to hate, but his relationship with Bob Miner, a fellow programmer who cofounded Oracle and died of lung cancer in late 1994, is emblematic of the former. Miner and Ellison were the "old men" at Oracle, years older than most of the other employees. An important quality that Miner brought to Oracle was caring about the people who worked for him, something that Ellison would find hard to maintain once Miner left. "Bob was probably the nicest guy I ever met," says Ellison. "Our personalities were very different. . . . Bob loved the people in the company and was almost an irrational advocate of the idea that people are far more important than the business. . . . That [attitude] was clear to everybody, and he was very popular." One time Miner came to him to lobby for more stock options for an employee who was getting divorced. His wife would get half his stock options in the settlement, and Miner didn't want him to be shortchanged. Responding to Miner's concern, Ellison raised the employee's salary to cover child support. He still feels Miner's loss, comparing the cofounder to Apple's Steve Wozniak, who left that company early but had a lasting influence. "Our friendship was tremendously important, and the history we had together was very important," says Ellison. "I loved Bob a lot; I really miss him as a friend."[3]

When he died, Miner was worth $300 million to $500 million. But that wasn't what animated most of the 250 coworkers, friends, and family who attended his memorial service, held in San Francisco's Herbst Theater just after the Thanksgiving weekend in 1994. Many of the people there, including Ellison, rose to share their favorite "Bob stories." Luongo recounted how Miner went to a bank to make a deposit shortly after Oracle went public in 1986, and he was rich for the first time. He filled out a deposit slip for $500,000, stood in line, handed it to the teller, and asked for $100 back. The teller, a Russian woman, threw up her hands and screamed, "God I love this country!" Ellison's response to the incident was to tell Miner that lines are for other people. "You're a huge success; you don't have to stand in line anymore."[4] Even after he was rich, Miner still felt as if he was one of the common folk, whereas Ellison, who had sprung from the common folk, thought he was above them.

"Everyone liked Bob," recalls Oracle's first employee, Bruce Scott. "He was a man of high integrity and he was very smart."[5] Unfortunately, although he was a great code writer, Miner was a poor manager, and at Lane's urging, Ellison had removed him from direct managerial responsibilities in the early 1990s. Recalls Lane, "Bob was an entrepreneurial kind of guy" who was in over his head as Oracle grew. "He wasn't capable of managing several thousand developers. He'd come to management meetings in 1992–93 completely unprepared. I'd be asking him for dates for the next product release. He had no schedules. It was all seat-of-the-pants management." Miner, who lived in San Francisco, opened up an Oracle skunk works there in 1992 with a few handpicked developers, and he and Ellison grew distant geographically and socially. But Ellison never bashed him the way he did other people. "We used to have a rule at Oracle to never hire anybody you wouldn't enjoy having lunch with three times a week," Ellison recalls. In the early days of Oracle, he sought not just talented people but ones whom he could like and trust. As he explains it, he wanted to surround himself with people like Miner, "so when [they] succeed, that will not annoy the hell out of me. In fact, because I have so much affection for you, when you succeed, I will say, 'Look what Bob did. Isn't that fabulous.' I'll get as much joy—or almost as much joy—out of your achievements as my own."[6]

THE GOOD, THE BAD, AND THE UGLY

Ellison is not the first or last chief executive who uses people and then fires them. Some observers would say his continual restirring of Oracle's executive mix is a good thing, bringing in new blood, banishing complacency, forcing everyone to stay on their toes. In interview after interview, people praised Ellison's vision, his charm (when he wants to be charming), his intelligence, his charisma, and his motivational ability. "If you have to have anybody in a company, it had better be Larry," says Benioff. "As an entrepreneur, I'm in awe of his twenty-five years of being at the top." Lane agrees, to an extent. "You have to take the whole package with Larry, the good with the bad. He's a great innovator, very visionary, but he can also make you feel lower than dirt. If you decide to work at Oracle, you accept that you've made a pact with the devil."

John Luongo praises Ellison for his intellectual rigor. "If you give in to Larry, he'll dismiss you as a wimp. If you tangle with him and you don't argue persuasively, he'll dismiss you as a moron." However, Ellison respects people who "can argue with him in a rational way. He won't hold to an idea that turns out to be incorrect just because it was his." The trick to "winning" an argument with Ellison: never show him up in a public setting and let him think something is his own idea. "I was secure enough to know that Larry enjoyed debate for its own sake. I would argue with him, and three days later, he would say this is what I'm thinking." Luongo recalls that his peer on the executive committee, Gary Kennedy, wanted to go to a higher level of security at Oracle, which would have required armed guards, to win more government contracts. "The thought of these guys walking around the halls with guns terrified me," Luongo says. "I told Larry, 'You realize these are the guys who failed the police academy tests. Rent-a-cop with guns.' Larry thought about it, and we didn't go to the next level." Even Lane, who had his share of arguments with Ellison, says that the CEO could be convinced, for example, not to drop support of an Oracle product because customers were still using it and the replacement wasn't ready. Ellison has always been drawn to bright people and will listen when they disagree with him, as long as they publicly defer to him and allow him to appropriate any good ideas.

Kennedy, who left in bitterness, scapegoated for the 1990 debacle, acknowledges, "The further I get away from Larry, the more my respect grows." When he was a chief executive building his own company, Kennedy realized that some of the things that used to annoy him about Ellison now made sense. For example, Ellison had "inconsistent organizational structures" that forced two executives to compete with each other, such as Luongo and Squire on the international front. "I now know why it was in Oracle's best interests to pit Luongo and Squire against each other," says Kennedy. Both had talents the company needed, but neither would work for the other. "If Larry had taken a firm position, one or the other would have left." Ellison is also notorious for showing up late or not at all. "Larry was never on time, and it used to bother the hell out of me," says Kennedy. "But when you're a CEO, your time is the most precious thing in the company. If your mental energy is so crucial to the success of a company, I understand why you finish a project and let others be damned. Sometimes fifteen extra minutes of Larry's thinking turned out to be worth millions."

The problem is not so much what Ellison does as how he does it. You can send executives on their way without wounding them so deeply that they become permanent enemies, lashing out against you at every opportunity or suing you for wrongful termination or just clamming up entirely. Stephanie Lane, Ray's wife and a former Oracle employee, says she was very relieved when the end finally came. "It was Ray working himself to death for someone who was telling him, 'You're on your way out,'" she says. "It needed to stop for both of them. I was happy when it ended, but he was very hurt about the way it happened. He deserved more respect than that."

As Lane noted, an Oracle executive makes a Faustian bargain with Ellison: great opportunities and huge monetary rewards in exchange for being used. "Larry has an acute sense of when he doesn't need people anymore," says former journalist Vieux. "He's like a juicer. He squeezes people dry and then discards them. I've seen it with Gary Bloom, Ray Lane, Gary Kennedy, Terry Garnett. At the same time, he gives them good money and exposure they would never get without him. They get a springboard to do whatever they want with their lives. He fulfills his part of the bargain, but he does it in a very devilish way. It's not necessary to have so many hurt feelings."

If you could bottle the emotions that Ellison has created in interacting with just his own executives, you would have a very heady mix indeed, including anger, resentment, envy, vengefulness, distress, and grudging admiration. Of course, any chief executive has to rid himself or herself of deadwood. But the question is, why does so much of what Ellison sees as deadwood turn up alive and well at other companies? Oracle has a lot riding on the answer.

First of all, no longer is it truly dominant even in the Unix database market that it pretty much created. IBM, which owns the mainframe computer database market and recently snapped up Oracle competitor Informix in the Unix arena, now runs neck and neck overall with Oracle. With its long history and status as the biggest technology company, Big Blue has a considerably more benign reputation than Oracle. IBM is trading on its powerhouse size and customers' dissatisfaction with Oracle to make significant inroads against the database market leader. Meanwhile, Microsoft, which bought database technology from another Oracle competitor, Sybase, is sneaking up from below. Although Microsoft's database is not powerful enough yet to challenge IBM and Oracle at the top, Microsoft can offer midsize and smaller companies a compelling combination: a relatively cheap database and all the desktop PC technology they need.

In its second major line of business, enterprise application software, Oracle has never been the market leader. The German company SAP, formed by a team who left IBM, pioneered the enterprise application market and has retained its grip as the leading vendor. Oracle is also seriously challenged by such competitors as PeopleSoft, which Ellison was trying to buy in mid-2003, and Siebel Systems, both headed by ex–Oracle executives. Ellison dismissed applications as secondary to database for years, relegating a potential growth area to the backseat. Prodded in part by Lane's interest in applications, Ellison rather belatedly decided they were important and stunned competitors with a brilliant repositioning of applications from a client-server to an Internet modality in the late 1990s. But the transition left customers fuming over a succession of technical glitches. That, coupled with the economic fallout when the technology bubble burst in 2000, left Oracle with severe problems. Between fiscal 2001 and 2002, its revenues shrank by a billion dollars, from nearly $11 billion to under $10 billion. Analysts did not expect revenues to approach the $11 billion mark again until 2004.

Even as Oracle's fortunes were peaking and then slipping, Ellison continued the purge of executive talent detailed in this chapter. He has made it very clear who's leading Oracle; for better or for worse, it's the guy who got them there in the first place. But like many a great entrepreneur, Ellison may not possess the requisite skills to guide an established company whose markets are now mature and in some cases shrinking. Many of those qualities of his that were positives in Oracle's early years—absolute dedication to leading-edge technology, fixation on growth, driving ambition, visionary brilliance, and impatience with customers and executives who don't want to move so quickly—are at odds with the somber mood of the early 2000s. Ellison is a cocky, defiant Peter Pan when the world cries out for the nurturing Wendy. He may have out-lived his time.

2

WHO'S LARRY?

HE LIES AWAKE LATE AT NIGHT THINKING
HOW TO MAKE ORACLE—AND HIMSELF—
NUMBER ONE, BIGGER THAN MICROSOFT,
BIGGER THAN ANYONE.

It's not possible to understand Oracle without understanding Larry Ellison. No other large company is as dominated by a single individual. Ellison cofounded Oracle in 1977 and has been the CEO for its entire quarter century of existence. Among seminal figures in the computer industry, he is unique. Microsoft's Bill Gates, a perennial rival, comes the closest to being like Ellison, having cofounded his company in 1975. But Gates stepped away from day-to-day operations in January 2000, handing over the CEO job to Steve Ballmer while retaining the title of chairman. Sun Microsystems' Scott McNealy, a sometime partner, and Apple Computer's Steve Jobs, a close friend of Ellison's, also come close. However, McNealy didn't actually start Sun and didn't become its chief executive right away. Jobs's tenure at Apple was interrupted when he was ousted in favor of John Sculley, although he later returned. So Ellison stands alone in having founded his company and continuously run it for twenty-five years.

Ellison has created Oracle in his own image. Now in his late fifties, tall and trim, he has kept himself in excellent shape. His hair is still dark, running to reddish; he has brown eyes and a short beard, which helps to camouflage his long jaw. Not conventionally handsome, with rather coarse features (he had his nose fixed after he moved to California), Ellison radiates enthusiasm and charm. He's animated and engaging onstage, at his best in informal question-and-answer sessions where he can rap with the crowd. A fan of, and an expert on, Japanese culture, he sees himself as a samurai warrior. He also likes to quote Genghis Khan (although others attribute the saying to Attila the Hun or La Rochefoucauld): "It is not sufficient that I succeed. Everyone else must fail." The glistening green-glass towers of Oracle's headquarters in Redwood Shores, California, which remind many of Oz, are actually intended to be "huge monolithic shapes set in the middle of a Japanese garden," according to Ellison.[1] Inside they sport a collection of Japanese artifacts as well as a large fitness center and a cafeteria that wins raves for its fine cuisine. As an employee of Oracle, you can work out, swim, play basketball, relax in a sauna, get a massage, or eat anything from sushi to steak prepared by expert chefs.

For years, Ellison personally interviewed every job candidate at Oracle, seeking those who reflected the qualities he wants: bright, entrepreneurial, self-motivated, able to handle the rough-and-tumble Oracle culture. Anneke Seley, the twelfth employee of Oracle, remembers Ellison's peering at her résumé when she applied for a job as administrative assistant. "It looks like you did socially responsible things," he told Seley. "Why on earth are you interested in a for-profit business?" She responded, "I'm here to learn new things." Evidently the right answer, for later that same day, she got the job. "Ellison liked the idea of overqualified people in every area of the company. He also liked young, very attractive people," says Seley. Ellison still signs off on employment offers today, although with tens of thousands of employees, Oracle is too big for him to meet with everyone personally. Former and current employees of Oracle, to a person, told me that "Larry is Oracle and Oracle is Larry." Ellison made Oracle into the giant it is today, by means of his vision, his personality, his determination, his choices. But Oracle also made Ellison what he is today: wealthy, famous, able to proclaim his views on a world stage. So if Larry is Oracle and Oracle is Larry, the question becomes, who is Larry?

LIVING LONGER . . . AND BETTER

While Ellison spends a lot of his time with the press knocking rivals and boasting about Oracle's "unbreakable" database, occasionally he stops the act, which he's learned very well, and lets the mask slip off for a moment. By identifying so completely with Oracle, Ellison has insulated himself from other realities, like his difficulties in relating one-on-one with other people. You wonder what Ellison would have become without the money and power afforded by Oracle. Catch up with him on topics outside of Oracle—like sailing (he's an avid participant at the world-class level) or biotechnology (he's a big investor)—and you find the humanity. The Ellison Medical Foundation, which he endowed, funds research into diseases of the elderly. He's a majority owner in Quark Biotech, an Israeli company aimed at curing cancer. He talks quite knowledgeably about that fact that people are living longer and suffering more and that he wants his research to make a difference.

During a major Oracle trade conference in late 2001, Ellison sponsored an overlapping Life Sciences Conference at a nearby San Francisco hotel. It's a tribute to how seriously Ellison regards biotech—and it him—that he's managed to snag Craig Venter, known as the discoverer of the human genome, as the guest speaker. Indeed, Venter, who shares Ellison's love of the limelight, speaks for twenty or thirty minutes extra while attendees wait for the characteristically late Ellison to show up. When he does, he grabs the microphone up in front and launches into a brief monologue: "We've been expanding the life span for a long time. But if we dramatically expand the life span, what does that mean?" He asks the audience to ponder what the implications would be for Social Security or for marriage. With his well-known history of marital discord—he's been divorced three times—Ellison gets a laugh when he jokes, "How about a ten-year marriage license with an option to renew?" The reason his foundation is investing in aging research is because it's been neglected, he asserts, although many pundits have speculated cynically that he's in search of a Fountain of Youth for himself. But here, before a friendly audience of scientists, students, and biotech press, Ellison wins respect and admiration, soaking in the esteem he so obviously craves, for his intelligence, his understanding of an arcane subject, his demonstrable wit.

He opens up the floor to questions and responds candidly. Ellison is good in these informal give-and-take sessions, like a stand-up comedian ad-libbing, although his public relations staff hold their breath. Someone asks him if he'd ever become an entrepreneur again, perhaps in biotech. "I'm an entrepreneur in the sense of taking risks with ideas," he says. "I'll never again be an entrepreneur who risks his personal fortune. There's just too much there. Besides," he adds with a twinkle, glancing at his PR team, "I've got to worry about the Oracle stock price. I haven't been doing a very good job there." Another question concerns government funding of research. "In general, I don't think government is very good at anything, but there are a few things it should do . . . like spending on intelligence gathering. You wouldn't like to have Oracle run the army." He confides that he's a "lifelong Democrat" raised in a liberal tradition. "I haven't shaken it yet [although] I am with Republicans on cutting taxes rather than spending more."

On the final question, Ellison gets serious and reveals something about himself in the process. The questioner wants to know what he looks for in funding biotech companies. "I fund companies if they're clever, either nonprofit or for-profit," he says. "My [adoptive] mother died of cancer. I don't think she would have cared about the motives of the person doing the research before she died. If they're good scientists with good ideas, I don't discriminate." He finishes with a comment that epitomizes his own approach to life: "Who's the better person? Someone who spends forty-five years doing cancer research that fails or someone who wants to make a buck, starts a company, and cures cancer?" For Ellison, it's success that counts, regardless of the endeavor.

SUNRISE OVER TASMANIA

In his personal life, Ellison, who boasts that he's never been ill as an adult, is a risk taker on all fronts, not just business, having once broken his neck, his collarbone, a few ribs, and punctured a lung in a 1991 bodysurfing accident off the Big Island in Hawaii. "This enormous wave showed up, and I was in the perfect position to catch it," he says. "For the first half second, it was very exciting; after that, it was terrifying. . . . The wave took me down to the reef and buried me in the reef." He adds, "There was something in me that wanted to ride that wave," no matter what the consequences.

When you listen to people like Ray Lane who, generally with cause, fiercely dislike Ellison, it's easy enough to dismiss him as a "Darth Vader" who has gone over to the dark side of Silicon Valley's testosterone-fueled culture in his obsession with making money and building the biggest company in the world. (Not that Ellison is the only one possessed by this goal, but he is one of the longest-surviving and most notorious.) But then you hear him rhapsodize over the sunrise that followed the dangerous 1998 Sydney-to-Hobart yacht race that could have killed him, and you realize that Ellison is an extraordinarily complex individual. He runs the emotional gamut from poet to driven genius, from frat boy to insightful visionary, from aging athlete to thoughtful philanthropist.

At Oracle's big trade show in late 2001, amid all the exhibition booths pushing software and computers, sits a large model of the boat that Oracle Racing will sponsor in the America's Cup challenge the following year. It is actually a one-third replica, according to the brochure, built exactly like the real thing. Ellison stands next to it as he lays out his vision, and his passion, for yet another arcane subject: maxi-yacht racing. Ellison has most members of the racing team assembled for the press conference. He tells the audience that they've had to build four life-size boats like this one, gesturing at the model, in order to do all the requisite training. "Not a single dime from Oracle Corporation has been spent on this," he says. "It has all come out of my pocket, personally." The amount is breathtaking: $85 million. (And alas, the effort falls just short, as Oracle's boat loses in the semifinals. Ellison promptly challenges the eventual winner.)

He first began racing when he moved to the Bay Area, sailing fourteen-foot sailboats. "That's all I could afford." As he was getting Oracle started, he almost wound up living on a thirty-four-footer to conserve cash. Finally, after he made his fortune, a friend asked him, "Why aren't you sailing anymore?" So he took it up again, purchasing a maxi-yacht called *Sayonara*, which would prove to be almost prophetically named, in 1995. "I enjoy it so much in terms of racing and meeting people," he says. "If you're the owner of the New York Yankees, you don't get to play baseball. I actually get to sail with these guys."

Sailing with the guys resulted in a life-and-death experience that Ellison relishes recalling. "I'll never forget the race down to Hobart when I had the wheel. I couldn't handle it. There were no stars, you couldn't even see the sails, I didn't know what to steer by. I had to turn the wheel over [to someone else]. You discover your own limits." He chokes up, in a manner that doesn't seem fake, when he talks about it. Six sailors on other boats and several yachts were lost when hurricane-force winds battered the participants in the December 1998 race from Sydney, Australia, to Hobart, Tasmania. After the hurricane, as the Ellison team's boat limped into the river that leads to Hobart, "everybody on board was completely quiet," Ellison remembers. "We had been through a terrible hurricane, with one hundred–mile-per-hour winds sweeping the deck." The hull of their boat, *Sayonara*, had begun delaminating, which meant it could break up into pieces. Somehow, though, it held together. "We got to the end of the race, and . . . it had gone from a terrible hurricane to a glorious sunrise of amber and rose and Prussian blue," he says. "I was just filled with wonder at the beauty and glory of life . . . and how short and fragile it is. We knew sailors had died, and here was this perfect sunrise and everyone was just glad to be alive. These sailors were tough guys, but when we got to the dock, they were so moved, there wasn't a dry eye on the boat." He sums up, "Life is the only miracle."

ROUGH BEGINNINGS

For Ellison, life could have been very short indeed. Born August 17, 1944, to an unwed teenager in New York City, he contracted pneumonia and nearly died when he was nine months old. "I'm sure it was very traumatic," he says, especially for his mother and grandmother, who were taking care of him. At that point, they turned him over to be raised by relatives in Chicago: his grandmother's sister and her husband, Lillian and Louis Ellison. Louis Ellison, a Russian Jew who emigrated to the United States in the early 1900s, was by all accounts a rather remote and disapproving father who gave his adopted son little emotional nourishment. While Ellison describes Lillian as loving and committed, he found Louis scornful and authoritative. He told his adopted son that he would never amount to anything. "That was his form of greeting, as opposed to, 'Hi' or, 'good morning,'" Ellison says.[2]

Ellison didn't learn he was adopted until he was around twelve years old. Once, he recalls, his parents took him on a trip to New York and introduced him to a relative of theirs named Florence. No one told the boy that this was his biological mother. It wasn't until he was an adult, after he'd founded Oracle, that Ellison managed to track her down and talk for the first time to the woman who bore him. He didn't do it until both Lillian and Louis had passed away. In speaking to Florence, "the result was surprising to me, because I really found out who my family was, and it was the people who raised me, not the people who I was biologically related to."[3]

Ellison is prone to exaggerate the toughness of the South Side Chicago neighborhood where he grew up. After all, "rags to riches" makes for a better story than merely lower middle class to riches. He laughingly admits, "The richer I am now, the poorer we were as kids." Then he acknowledges that his neighborhood, although filled with struggling immigrants like his parents, wasn't really crime-ridden nor poor. "It wasn't rough by today's standards. It was a series of ghettos, an Hispanic ghetto, a black ghetto, a Jewish ghetto. . . . 'Ghetto' in those days was a pretty nice place to live, compared to today, when it's absolutely scary."[4]

Ellison attended South Shore High School, where his grades, he says, were "checkered." He also didn't take kindly to authority. "I remember correcting a math teacher and getting into a big argument," he says. "I had a very difficult time with people who said, 'Do what I say—I'm the adult. You're the kid.'"[5] At age fifteen, he had a girlfriend, Karen Rutzky. They were together for five years, attended proms, and wore matching shirts. Lillian gave Ellison money so he could take Karen out, but her parents didn't like him and she turned down his marriage proposal while he was still a teenager. *Washington Post* reporter Mark Leibovich, who culled these details on Ellison's early life from interviews with him, Rutzky, and others, writes that "no subject animates Ellison more than Rutzky. For all his success, her rejection—and her parents' dislike—seems a lingering embodiment of all that made him feel unworthy." Ellison bragged to Leibovich about how he made the list of *Playboy*'s top ten best-dressed people. "I think my journey from those stupid matching shirts with Karen Rutzky to *Playboy*'s best-dressed list is a more heroic journey than going from the South Side of Chicago to running Oracle."[6]

After he graduated from high school in 1962, Ellison was admitted to the University of Illinois, where he planned to major in physics. His real interest was biology, but as he said in a speech to a group of biotechnology researchers, "unfortunately when I was going to college, biology was more like home economics than the understanding of molecular science that it is today, so I ended up in physics." At the end of his sophomore year, his adoptive mother, Lillian, died of cancer (a disease that would also claim his biological mother), and he left school. Although later he enrolled briefly at the University of Chicago, Ellison, like Bill Gates, never obtained a college degree. It must seem to Ellison as if he's been chasing Gates most of his life, ever since they founded their respective companies, Oracle and Microsoft, in the same time period of the late 1970s. Oracle became a stunning success, but Microsoft surpassed it, as Gates also surpassed Ellison in some ways—including personal wealth.

GO WEST, YOUNG MAN

Even his admirers admit that Ellison has at times embellished his personal history. The more tactful of them say that he mixes up the future and the present, creating a world that he wishes would be rather than the one that actually is. No doubt that stems partly from his childhood, which was scarcely ideal, although he was close to his adoptive mother, Lillian Ellison. As is the case with many great men, separating the myth from the reality is difficult, compounded by Ellison's tendency to remake the world to bring it closer to the one in his head. Thus, his childhood neighborhood became a tough, crime-ridden area, when in reality it was a rather quiet enclave of lower-middle-class Jewish immigrants. Or he was able to graduate from a prestigious university and get accepted to medical school, when in reality he dropped out of two different universities. Once he thinks something, it becomes true, at least in his own mind. One example of this "wishful thinking" apparently occurred after Ellison told people he'd been accepted into medical school in California. He showed a couple of friends, including Rutzky, an acceptance letter from the University of Southern California, but the document didn't appear to be legitimate. Ellison says he doesn't remember showing anyone an acceptance letter. "It just couldn't be," he maintains.[7] To customers' chagrin, he has been known to do the same thing at Oracle. Once Ellison anticipates something, such as an Internet-ready application suite, to him it's done. Customers may be frustrated by the gap between the chief executive's pronouncements and the actual delivery date, which can be years away, but Ellison is serene in his conviction. It's a quality that has enabled much of his success as well as his difficulties with the rest of the world.

In the mid-1960s, the San Francisco Bay Area radiated a powerful siren song for young people all over the world. It embraced the beginning of the free speech movement in Berkeley, the rise of the hippie culture across the bay in San Francisco's Haight-Ashbury district, rock music, love beads, free love, dropping acid . . . Out in cold, windy Chicago, living with a loveless father, Ellison heeded the call and drove west to Berkeley in the summer of 1966. "California is where it's all happening," he says. "But I never wore beads. I'd like to get that straight now. My friends who were all wearing beads in those days in the '60s would try to get me to put on my love beads, and I'd say, someday . . ."[8] Even in his early twenties, Ellison had a firm notion of who he was and where he was going, and love beads didn't fit with that image. He would always be well dressed at Oracle, favoring Armani suits. He saw himself as a dapper, polished executive, and Oracle gave him the means to become one, superficially at least.

Growing up nearly side by side with the hippie movement was Northern California's burgeoning technology industry. Ellison had proved himself a decent computer programmer of IBM mainframes in one of his physics classes at the University of Illinois, although he was largely self-taught. "I was a very good programmer, and programming was an absolute meritocracy," he says. "You could be a high school dropout, and if you could code, it didn't really make any difference. You didn't have to wear a tie, or have enormous academic credentials. If you were a good programmer, you got the job."[9]

And so Ellison launched his career as a contract programmer, moving from job to job, making it on his own for the first time in his life. He scratched out enough of a living to attract Adda Quinn, a young woman whom he met at a San Jose employment agency. She had graduated from San Jose State University, majoring in Chinese history, and wanted to be a teacher. She worked at the employment agency to make a living. Although he often didn't have enough money to put gas in his car, Ellison was never boring. "I agreed to marry him because he was the most fascinating man I'd ever met in my life," she says.[10] In 1967, both in their early twenties, they married, although no one from Ellison's family attended. They moved into a tiny apartment in Oakland, where Quinn worried about paying the bills and Ellison held various jobs. Even then, he had a taste for the lavish, buying an expensive bicycle and his first sailboat, having a nose job. The burden was all on Quinn to make ends meet, and after seven years, she got tired of it and left him. At one point, he promised to make her a millionaire. She did not take him seriously. But he had "made a commitment to himself that he was not going to be a failure," she says. "I said, 'why don't you just go on and become a millionaire and make yourself happy? Because you're never going to make anybody else happy until you're happy.'"[11]

In an example of the extreme charity of which the mercurial Ellison is capable, he brought his aging adoptive father, Louis, out to live with him in 1971. Louis had to move into a nursing home in a few years and died soon after, apparently without ever reconciling with his son. Ellison also bought Quinn a car after their divorce, gave her second husband a job when he battled cancer, and paid the mortgage on her house. He and Quinn reportedly remain on good terms; he even called her up to talk about it when his second marriage ended in divorce after only eighteen months. With his brilliance and charm, Ellison never had a problem attracting women, just staying in a lasting relationship. Quinn was probably the closest he ever came to the latter. Ellison acknowledges that he has always felt like an outsider, even within his own family, who were hardly truthful with him about his origins. His inability to adjust to things as they are, especially as they apply to his image of himself, makes for a fascinating human being from afar, but not one who's comfortable to live with for long.

THE JAPANESE LINK

In the early 1970s, Ellison was hired to work at Amdahl Corporation, run by one of the early geniuses in high technology, Gene Amdahl, who had helped develop the mainframe computer at IBM. Amdahl's ambitious idea was to outdo the reigning mainframe computer maker with cheaper machines that could run the same software. Since Ellison had learned his programming skills at the University of Illinois on an IBM mainframe, he seemed like a natural at Amdahl, where he was supposed to teach the programmers about the relatively new machine. Although Ellison didn't last long at Amdahl, which laid him off during a period when it was struggling, the company instilled in him two important things: a lifelong interest in Japan and a considerable respect for an entrepreneur who would bet everything on a seemingly crazy idea.

Making mainframe clones was a capital-intensive endeavor, so Amdahl turned to Fujitsu Limited of Japan as a partner and an investor, unleashing a storm of criticism for selling out American technology to the Japanese. (Although Ellison would later be forced to do something similar himself, he was careful not to give away too much. See Chapter 5.) At any rate, the deal allowed Ellison to make a business trip to Japan, his first, where he visited the beautifully ornamented city of Kyoto. He quickly fell in love—not so much with the actual city but with the idea of it. Visiting Kyoto, "I was stunned; it was one of only two times I was stunned," says Ellison. "The first time was when I first saw Yosemite Valley. I simply didn't know such a thing could exist. The same thing with Kyoto."

Kyoto, says Ellison, "wasn't on the messianic scale of Yosemite Valley and other creations of God." However, Kyoto used the same natural "design" as God, but on a smaller, more human scale. "There were these wonderful gardens that were designed to promote intimacy between the viewer in the garden and the garden itself." The gardens also were the essence of tranquillity; what Zen Buddhism—and indeed, "what the entire Japanese culture—seems to do is intelligently pursue tranquillity." The Japanese Zen garden was a miniature reproduction of a forest, where humanity first evolved. "We really have become adapted to living in the forest and its nature, much more adapted than living among concrete buildings and highways and glass and steel and all of this stuff and its attendant noise," says Ellison. The Japanese Zen garden, which he would later reproduce in his own living environment, symbolized a return to man's natural habitat.

He can also wax poetic about the "minimalist nature" of Japanese music, which is meant to replicate the sounds of nature, like wind going through bamboo or water traveling across stones. "Japan is like going to another planet," he sums up. So much so that when he visited Europe for the first time, he was disappointed, because it wasn't much different from the United States except the buildings "were a little older." In Japan, "I learned so much from the insights of that culture, insights unavailable, for the most part, to us in the West." Among those insights: The Japanese "are at once the most aggressive culture on Earth and the most polite. There is this incredible arrogance combined with unbelievable humility; a magnificent balance."[12] When Ellison would try to replicate those values at Oracle, the balance tipped decidedly toward arrogance, as in his treatment of subordinates and customers, although he is capable of humility when it's necessary, as it was to save the company in the early 1990s.

The schizophrenic nature of "incredible arrogance combined with unbelievable humility" is evident in Ellison. On one hand, he loves the tranquillity and naturalness of Japanese settings. But his own personality is just the opposite: bombastic and over-the-top, with a flair for showmanship. The Japanese culture generally encourages subservience of the individual to the collective good, although there is an exception: the ancient samurai warrior, destroyer and transformer, fighting on behalf of the "little people." It is here that Ellison reconciles the seemingly incompatible aspects of his personality; he is a modern-day samurai, slashing his way through his enemies yet adhering to a specific cultural imperative.

(Ellison displays a gorgeously detailed set of samurai armor in his office at Oracle.) One of his heroes is the sixteenth-century samurai Miyamoto Musashi, who was orphaned as a child of seven and left in the care of an uncle. Musashi was strong-willed and boisterous; at the age of thirteen, he killed an older man, a samurai, by defying the rules, throwing him to the ground, and beating him with a stick. Wrote Musashi in *A Book of Five Rings*, "Strategy is the craft of the warrior. . . . There is no warrior in the world today who really understands the Way of strategy. . . . It is said the warrior's is the twofold Way of pen and sword, and he should have a taste for both Ways." Again, this reflects the contrast that exists within Ellison, who is a ruthless warrior while at the same time a learned and cultured expert in the arts.

Ellison also found heroes closer to home. Watching Gene Amdahl at Amdahl Corporation and his subsequent company, Trilogy Systems, Ellison developed an admiration for the intrepid nature of the entrepreneur. "That's the nature of risk-taking . . . you're driven to see if you can solve the next problem, just like [Sir Edmund] Hillary was driven—was curious if he could climb the mountain," Ellison says. Amdahl pioneered the notion of large-scale integration in chip technology—putting lots of transistors on a single chip. That worked, but his next idea, putting the whole computer on an enormous chip, failed. Sums up Ellison, "That's what innovators do. They try to move to the next fascinating problem; and not all the problems are solvable. It doesn't mean you don't try to solve 'em."[13]

THE GOOD THINGS OF LIFE

It's not exactly clear when, or why, the man who was charmed by the tranquillity of a Japanese Zen garden became fixated on the notion of becoming the world's richest person. Ellison was definitely interested in running his own show, being his own boss. "I think I always would have gone out and started my own business," he says. "But it might have been in construction. I know, as a kid, I wanted to be an architect." But then he realized, in part by reading Ayn Rand's *The Fountainhead*, that an architect hardly makes any money and is not his own boss. "Even school teachers make more money than architects," he says disparagingly. But he likes architecture because it embodies the act of creation, "the most profound act we can have as living beings." Since men cannot have children, "our creation has to be our art or our engineering." His goal, then, was to work in a company that built things. "If I needed information to build something, I was relentless. I could not stop thinking about a problem that had to be solved in order to build something."[14]

When he cofounded what became Oracle, Ellison's definition of success was employing fifty people whom he enjoyed being with, working on interesting projects, and controlling his own environment. He also acknowledges that he started a company because the kid from the hardscrabble background wanted to live comfortably and buy some nice things. At the time, "financial success was buying a house," he says. "I lived in an apartment on the south side of Chicago. Living in a house in California and driving a new car was success. Everything beyond that has not been as big a deal. In my wildest dreams, I never intended to build a big company. It just happened."

But once it happened, along a path very similar to Microsoft's, Ellison became obsessed with overtaking Bill Gates on the *Forbes* 400 list of the world's richest people. "Bill wants to be the world's largest technology provider. Larry wants to be the richest man in the world," says Tom Siebel, a former Oracle sales executive and now CEO of competitor Siebel Systems. For a few heady weeks in 2000, Ellison achieved that goal. In April of that year, Ellison's 24 percent share of Oracle was worth on the order of $77 billion, slightly more than Gates's piece of Microsoft. "I was almost surprised when for something like sixty days last year, [Ellison] was richer than Gates," says longtime Oracle observer Alex Vieux. "He mentioned it so often. He had it and he lost it." Because when the *Forbes* 400 survey was published in October, Gates was by then number one again and Ellison was number two. "Forbes spots Bill as many billions as he needs," Ellison sighs.[15] By the next survey in 2001, Microsoft had shaken off the Department of Justice lawsuit while Oracle was battered by loss of business due to the dot-com fallout and slowing growth in both its primary markets. Too bad for Ellison, he slipped to number four on the *Forbes* list, with a measly $21 billion in net worth, behind not only Gates ($54 billion) but also Warren Buffett ($33 billion) and Paul Allen ($28 billion), another Microsoft-created billionaire.

Ellison has everything material that anyone could ever need and then some. For starters, he has three beautiful homes, including the replica of a sixteenth-century Japanese village he's building on twenty-three acres in Woodside, California, for a reported budget of $100 million, double the $50 million Gates spent on his waterfront mansion near Seattle. The project includes an eight thousand–square-foot main house along with five guest residents, plus an artificial lake, streams, waterfalls, and a forest. In addition to his own maxi-yacht, Ellison spent $85 million to finance an America's Cup challenge. He has a private jet—a $38 million Gulfstream V—wears Italian suits, drives a Mercedes, and once dangled an offer of a $50,000 Acura sports car to get a woman to date him. Yet it's not enough. He still wants to overtake Gates, maybe to show Louis Ellison once and for all that he has amounted to something: he's on top of the world's-richest list. If Ellison is relentless in pushing subordinates, he is even harder on himself. He lies awake at night thinking about how to make Oracle—and himself—number one, bigger than Microsoft, bigger than anyone.

A NATIONAL STAGE

As he built Oracle into a major company, Ellison, with his willingness to make outrageous statements, thrust himself onto a bigger stage. He first achieved national prominence in the mid-1990s for his idea of inexpensive network computers that were supposed to provide an alternative to the PCs dominated by Microsoft (see Chapter 7). More recently, in the wake of September 11, 2001, Ellison, who describes himself as a liberal Democrat, unleashed a storm of criticism from civil libertarians when he called for a national ID card, catching even his own public relations people off guard. In a September 21, 2001, interview with a San Francisco TV station, he said, "We need a national ID card with our photograph and thumbprint digitized and embedded in the ID card."[16] Ellison said Oracle would provide the underlying software for such a system "absolutely free." He later reneged, after everyone from an American homeowners group to the Electronic Privacy Information Center dissed the idea.

At the trade show COMDEX Fall 2001 in November, Ellison said flatly, "I have never been for a national ID card." Instead, he suggested that existing ID cards, such as credit cards, driver's licenses, and the like, be made more efficient by embedding biometric information. He did say a large national database was needed to keep track of all these IDs, presumably with software supplied by Oracle. In an op-ed piece for the *Wall Street Journal*, Ellison wrote, "Do we need one national ID card? No. But the IDs that the government issues—such as Social Security cards should use modern credit card technology." And those IDs should reside in a single national file, making life tougher for terrorists.[17]

At Oracle's OpenWorld conference in December 2001 at San Francisco's Moscone Center, Ellison announced that Oracle had delivered the database to create such a file, although he coyly wouldn't specify which government agency received it. In a follow-up press conference, Ellison chastised a reporter who asked about the national ID card. "Have you read my piece in the *Wall Street Journal*? Obviously you haven't," he said. "I didn't call for a national ID card. We should have a set of national standards around our IDs. You need a license to get married or catch a trout or drive a car. All I proposed is having a single standard for those. Why doesn't the government adopt a credit-card ID standard, which would make IDs more difficult to duplicate?" He added that one of the World Trade Center skyjackers shouldn't have been able to "come waltzing through passport control when he's wanted in Florida." Said Ellison, "All the bad guys are listed in hundreds of databases around the country. Let's keep a list of the people who are wanted in one place." He also suggested airlines could require people who didn't have one of the nationally verifiable ID cards to undergo a different search procedure. The database for these cards should store biometric data as well so identities can't be duplicated. "If you want to visit this country, you should have a digital ID," he maintains. "Fifteen million people are in this country illegally. We should admit we've looked the other way. There's so much pretense in all of this."

All this is vintage Ellison. First, float a seemingly radical idea that has a nugget of common sense at its base but probably goes too far for most people to stomach. We do need some way of better identifying the potential terrorists and criminals within our borders, but Americans have never much cottoned to the idea of a single, government-issued identification card. It's too totalitarian for our freewheeling culture. Second, as criticism flames, back off from the over-the-top idea and refine it into something more palatable. Make sure it's to Oracle's advantage by agreeing to supply the needed technology. Milk the ensuing publicity in numerous forums, from a prestigious newspaper to COMDEX to OpenWorld. Finally, deliver the technology and stoke the mystery by not naming the agency that got it, while making a teasing reference to Oracle's long-ago project for the Central Intelligence Agency.

Even though he complains about the way the press tears down heroes, comparing the media to lions at the ancient Roman Colosseum, Ellison seems to take a gleeful joy in creating controversies, like a small child building a bonfire. *I'm doing something the adults wouldn't like, but boy am I having fun!* Take his feud with the San Jose International Airport. Ellison wanted to fly his Gulfstream V into and out of the airport anytime he wanted, defying nighttime curfew restrictions. The city of San Jose wrote Ellison threatening letters but never took any other action. Finally, Ellison forced the issue by taking the matter to court in January 2000, charging that the city "gratuitously attacks Mr. Ellison" because of his wealth. The city retorted that Ellison is not above the law and shouldn't be allowed to thumb his nose at the curfew rules. In June 2001, more than two years after the dispute first came to light, the court ruled in Ellison's favor, calling the city's curfew law "unreasonably discriminatory" against private jets. In his ruling, U.S. District Judge Jeremy Fogel, in urging a compromise, wrote, "It is regrettable that a dispute about one airplane has consumed so large a quantity of human and economic resources. . . ." That Larry Ellison penchant for bonfires again!

He also hired Bill Clinton's press secretary as a communications guru, although Joe Lockhart, who had to deal with Monica Lewinsky, impeachment, and the Elian Gonzalez incident, evidently couldn't deal with Ellison. In May 2001, he left, six months after he was hired, although he has declined to comment on why. As we'll see in subsequent chapters, Ellison has tapped private investigators to snoop through Microsoft's trash; won a sexual harassment suit in which he admitted sending an assistant whom he was dating a "playful" E-mail message promising to buy her a sports car, a house, a jet, a diamond, and General Electric Company; and played off Harvard and Stanford Universities against each other by dangling a $150 million offer to fund a center that would study the effect of technology on economics and politics. The words most often used to describe Larry Ellison, like *outrageous*, *flamboyant*, and *colorful*, somehow seem inadequate.

THE EXTREME NARCISSIST

The analysis of Ellison that comes closest to the mark resides in a *Harvard Business Review* article entitled "Narcissistic Leaders: The Incredible Pros, the Inevitable Cons," by Michael Maccoby, an anthropologist and psychoanalyst who runs The Maccoby Group, a management consulting firm in Washington, D.C. Maccoby has since written a book about the same subject, *The Productive Narcissist*, published in 2003, so he has devoted considerable time to thinking about the seeming conflicts that allow self-absorbed men like Ellison, Gates, General Electric's Jack Welch, and Enron Corporation's Jeff Skilling to change the world. "People of this type impress others as being 'personalities,'" Maccoby writes. "They are especially suited . . . to take on the role of leaders, and to give a fresh stimulus to cultural development or damage the established state of affairs." Along with Ellison and many corporate chieftains, including Apple Computer's Steve Jobs, Maccoby says other narcissistic leaders include Napoleon, Mahatma Gandhi, and Franklin Delano Roosevelt. What Maccoby calls productive narcissists can be extraordinarily effective. "Throughout history, narcissists have always emerged to inspire people and to shape the future."[18]

In corporations, he says, "productive narcissists are not only risk takers willing to get the job done but also charmers who can convert the masses with their rhetoric. . . ." But there is a bleaker side to narcissism, which "can turn unproductive when, lacking self-knowledge and restraining anchors, narcissists become unrealistic dreamers. They nurture grand schemes and harbor the illusion that only circumstances or enemies block their success. This tendency toward grandiosity and distrust is the Achilles' heel of narcissists. Because of it, even brilliant narcissists can come under suspicion for self-involvement, unpredictability, and—in extreme cases— paranoia."[19] They have thin skins, akin to the fairy-tale princess who could feel a pea underneath many mattresses. That makes them intolerant of dissent and abrasive toward or dismissive of subordinates who fight back. Maccoby singles out Jobs as a CEO who publicly humiliates subordinates, but certainly Ellison also fits that bill.

Although Maccoby has never met Ellison, he says he interviewed enough people at Oracle to label the CEO as "an extreme narcissist," albeit also an extremely productive one. Based on my description of what I'd learned about Ellison, Maccoby says the lack of a father figure in his early life suggests that the Oracle founder never developed a strong conscience, or superego. "Narcissists don't have a built-in system of right and wrong. They have to create their own system," he says. "They have a strong need to make whatever their vision is real, even if they have to lie to do it." That's why, he adds, Ellison promises products that he hasn't yet developed and pushes the rules as far as he can. Sometimes these traits pay off—in Oracle, Ellison has built a great company but one that's in danger of foundering because the very qualities that build a great company can also tear it down. The time, as Maccoby acknowledges in his own book, may have passed for productive narcissists.

Another consultant who studies CEOs and leadership, Rich Hagberg, of Hagberg Consulting Group in Foster City, California, generally agrees with Maccoby. Ellison ranks high as a "visionary evangelist," one of Hagberg's three pillars of leadership. The others are "builder of relationships" and "manager of execution," where Ellison ranks low. Ellison is good at setting direction but poor at "investing in people so they're willing to trust you and follow you," says Hagberg. A leader who's strong in all three pillars has confidence in himself, knows his strengths and weaknesses, and can attract and admire people who fill in those weaknesses. "That's where Ellison falls way short," notes Hagberg. "His personal insecurity means that he doesn't know himself or manage himself very effectively." Ellison makes up his own world, seeing what he wants to see. "He's not open to input. If you agree with him, he likes you. He can't tolerate people who disagree with him," says Hagberg. Like former president Clinton, "he uses people." Ellison can't truly care for or love someone else because he's the only one in his self-absorbed world.

However, the label of a narcissist is a bit too neat to summarize Ellison entirely. The man doesn't fit into a single box, although the elements of narcissism in his personality are undeniable. But he is also an artist, a consummate actor, a visionary, even a good friend on occasion, as with Bob Miner. Denied any strong male role models in childhood, Ellison fashioned himself out of the clay of all his experiences and came up with a grandiose, deeply flawed, yet extraordinary, human being.

VICTIM OF CIRCUMSTANCE?

It's hard to feel sorry for one of the richest men in the world, but probing beneath the surface offers at least some reasons for why Ellison is the way he is. With a distant adoptive father and a biological mother who gave him up, his difficulties in establishing relationships with women—indeed, with any-one—become more comprehensible. After divorcing Quinn, Ellison married twice again: in 1977, to Nancy Elizabeth Wheeler, who was with him for a year and a half before she filed for divorce, and in 1983, to Barbara Boothe, an Oracle employee who became the mother of his two children, a boy and a girl, now teenagers. That marriage lasted nearly three years. Then there was the famous appearance on the *Oprah Winfrey Show* in 1996, in which Ellison admitted to the talk show hostess that he was looking for love again after the end of his third marriage. Future wife number four should be someone exciting, funny, smart, and of course, good-looking. He appears to have found her: in 2001, he was engaged to a freelance writer and would-be romance novelist more than twenty-five years younger than he is, Melanie Craft. (Her novel, amusingly entitled *A Hard-Hearted Man*, was published in 1998 to less-than-sterling reviews.)

Because of his childhood, Ellison feels vulnerable whenever he feels himself growing dependent on someone else. He can't stand the thought of abandonment, so he abandons other people before they can do it to him. He also views money as the penultimate sign of achievement and uses it to protect himself and to manipulate others. Both his vulnerability and his attachment to money were evident when he offered Ray Lane 2 million additional stock options to keep him at Oracle when he was contemplating the top job at another company, Novell, in 1996. "Then Larry went to the board and increased it to 2.5 million options," Lane recalls. "That was a sign to him how vulnerable he was. He felt that he was vulnerable to me because he had to beg the board for stock." The knowledge of his dependence on Lane continued to fester, until Ellison finally found a way to end the relationship.

Alex Vieux, who wrote about Oracle for years as a journalist before becoming an entrepreneur, suggests that Ellison should be judged charitably. "In the end, Ellison's achievements overshadow the rest of it," he says. "What he has built and the way it has served the industry should be the prominent part . . . not Larry trying to bang his receptionist." Vieux, who is black, calls Ellison "the blackest of white executives" because of the environment that shaped him. "His road to success was paved with many more obstacles than Bill's," he says, referring to Bill Gates, who was raised by his biological parents in a comfortable, upper-middle-class setting in Seattle. Vieux adds, "That the man [Ellison] has been able to rise above his environment is a tribute." Maccoby's psychological reading is that Ellison has to be top dog to overcome the feeling of low self-esteem stemming from his childhood. "The bad things he does exacerbate that feeling," Maccoby adds. "Even though he doesn't have much of a conscience, he's smart enough to know what he's doing is not right, so he has to be the best to justify himself to himself."

No doubt some of that is the impetus for his investments in biotech. If Ellison's research yields a cure for cancer or Parkinson's or Alzheimer's, surely that will balance on the scale of his deeds and misdeeds. But Oracle remains his greatest achievement. By being true to his own superb instinct for how the technology revolution was unfolding, he was able to create a singular force that helped to mold that very revolution. The problem is that the revolutionary period has ended, and we're now at a time that demands consolidators and synthesizers, not builders and rebels. Ellison is unsuited to the current era, but he refuses to let go, believing that he can still remake the world. Perhaps he can. But history will judge him by how well Oracle fares when it is ultimately separated from its creator.

ADVENTURES IN LARRYLAND

An old television show used to talk about eight million stories in the *Naked City*. At Oracle—or "Larryland," as it's called by many wags—there are almost that many about Larry Ellison. Here are just a few of them:

In the late 1980s and early 1990s, Ellison drove a red Ferrari that became infamous among the Oracle employees. One time, he drove the car so fast that the grease and oil on the back ignited. Another time, as Ellison arrived at Oracle's old headquarters in Belmont, California, he was followed by a police car with siren sounding and lights flashing. As he pulled into the driveway, the police officer came up beside the car, but Ellison refused to get out, until the company's then general counsel, Ray Ocampo, came out of the building. Ellison exited the car, passing by the police officer, and told his general counsel to deal with the matter. The employees were all standing in front of a window, watching this unfold. As he stepped out of the car, Ellison turned around and grandly waved to them. Disdain for following the rules and showboating have long been part of his personality.

Ellison's pickiness and attention to detail are legendary. Once, in Oracle Europe, a consultant suggested a change to the red Oracle logo, which consisted of adding a box around it to make it more visible. "Don't fuck with my logo," Ellison responded, and walked out of the room. "It was a two-second presentation, the shortest I've ever seen," says Fred Janssen, a former sales executive for Oracle Europe. He has another story. At one of Oracle's famed Quota Club meetings, which celebrate the top sales performers, the legal counsel from Europe had flown to Maui to attend, along with his wife. They were sitting at Ellison's table for the *Top Gun*–themed presentation that featured Tom Cruise in his plane shooting down Oracle's database rivals. "I'm not sitting with fucking lawyers at my table," Ellison told the couple. "He decided he only wanted salespeople at his table," says Janssen. Having come some ten thousand miles, the legal counsel and his wife were banished to another table.

Nimish Mehta, a longtime Oracle engineer, knew that the young product manager wasn't doing a great job with her presentation on a new product that Oracle was planning to introduce. Ellison, who has zero tolerance for presentations that run off track, did, too. "She was talking about her vision of where she thought the product should go," says Mehta. After a few minutes, Ellison stopped her and graciously thanked her. Then he turned to her boss, Sohaib Abassi, who was also attending the presentation, and said briskly, "Sohaib, fire her." Abassi did as he was told: "You're fired." The young woman broke down in tears and ran out of the room.

Alex Vieux, whose company, Dasar, oversees the major European technology show, ETRE, remembers how Ellison cavalierly picked up one of his female floor managers at the conference. "Ellison told her something like, 'Alex is my friend. He won't mind if you go with me. Come and fly in my plane,'" Vieux recalls. The pair left the conference in France and flew to Italy, returning around three o'clock in the morning. "Everybody at the conference saw him go with her. I had to fire her," says Vieux. He felt bad about it. "She got caught by Larry's talk. He conned her into thinking it was OK because I was his friend." Only a few hours after firing his employee, Vieux found himself onstage introducing Ellison, who was giving one of the keynote speeches. "I had this moment of hesitation where I thought about telling the whole story," says Vieux. He resisted, merely telling the crowd, "Here's one of the most controversial CEOs in the business."

All these incidents show Ellison at his worst—and best. He doesn't like authority or following the rules. People who don't follow the rules are the ones who do great things, or terrible things. One could imagine Ellison taking different paths in life, as a hard-charging scientific researcher or a military leader (if he could ever get through boot camp) or even a master criminal. Whatever path he chose, though, he would never have been ordinary.

3

THE EARLY YEARS

[HOW ORACLE GRABBED A NEW MARKET
FROM UNDER THE NOSE OF IBM]

I t's undeniable that Oracle, for all its contradictions, has become a great and enduring force in the technology industry. It once had almost as firm a grasp on the distributed (nonmainframe) database market as Microsoft does on desktop operating systems, although that grasp is now slipping. Oracle has also become a major player in enterprise applications, all-important software that runs financials, human resources, manufacturing, sales force, and customer interactions at top companies worldwide. Thanks to Larry Ellison's vision, Oracle is regarded as one of the leaders of the Internet age, and it rode the dot-com boom of the late 1990s to a onetime position among the three most valuable technology companies in the world (the others being Microsoft and Cisco Systems). Its annual OpenWorld conference in San Francisco is one of the biggest in the industry, attracting twenty-five thousand people to the 2001 event.

When Ellison and two others cofounded what became Oracle, there was no intent to create a dominant player in the technology industry. He just wanted enough money to live on, to own a house, to be his own boss. But his timing was serendipitous. In the late 1970s, the high-technology industry was poised to take off in a way that no one—not Ellison in his little contract programmer business nor Bill Gates and his cohorts fiddling with operating systems in Albuquerque nor the dreamy researchers at places like IBM and Xerox PARC, whose ideas would be largely exploited by others—could foresee. It was not just that new products would emerge and business processes would change. It was a movement from centralized mainframe systems, where closely guarded corporate knowledge resided in the hands of a powerful elite, to a distributed desktop computing world, which made information widely available to all employees and even outsiders. This presaged a fundamental, seismic shift in the business world comparable in impact to the industrial age.

Oracle, perhaps unwittingly, became one of the prime movers in that transformation. Although Ellison borrowed the original idea from an IBM research paper, Oracle's development of the first relational database helped to enable the information explosion. For if you can't deliver information to those within your organization who need it in timely, comprehensible fashion, all those billions of data bits that computers can hold are useless. Oracle's technology lets companies store their important information among different types of computers, such as minicomputers and workstations, while users can access it from their desktop PC. Relational databases also gave rise to a new generation of application vendors, which could concentrate on such functions as financials and human resources without worrying about the storage and retrieval of data. Oracle's technology became a *platform* on which these other vendors depended and that they, in turn, expanded. The relational database meant that nontechies, like salespeople and marketing managers and product analysts, could access and massage corporate intelligence in a manner useful to them, without having to rely on some geek to interpret the mysteries of a mainframe punched card. In a way, the name of the company is a misnomer for what its technology does, for in place of one great medium that consults the dieties, Oracle's database turns every user into a potential prophet.

FROM AMDAHL TO ORACLE

After he left Amdahl in the early 1970s, Ellison bounced around the nascent Silicon Valley (which had recently acquired its name), landing next for a brief stint at Ampex Corporation, which was working on storage of audio and video data. His boss there was Bob Miner, who had coincidentally also attended the University of Illinois. Unlike Ellison, Miner did graduate, with degrees in math and philosophy. Like Ellison, Miner largely learned programming on the job, having worked for the U.S. government, IBM, and Computer Sciences Corporation. One project the two worked on together at Ampex was a storage, or database, project for the Central Intelligence Agency with the code name "Oracle." Another programmer at Ampex was Ed Oates, who had known Adda Quinn, Ellison's first wife. The three men shared an understanding about the pitfalls of corporate life and quickly became friends, although they would soon go their separate ways. Ellison wound up at Omex Corporation, a now-defunct maker of optical storage systems.

In 1977, while Ellison was still working at Omex, the company put out a request for bids on software to manage its latest storage device. Ellison contacted Miner and Oates and convinced them to found a software development consulting firm to bid on the project. The trio came in with the low bid of $400,000 and won the Omex contract. The new company, called Software Development Laboratories, was split among the three founders: 60 percent to Ellison, who had negotiated the deal and recruited the other two, who each received 20 percent. (Oates, who left the company in 1980, sold his 20 percent for $20,000. Today, 20 percent of Oracle would be worth billions of dollars.) As a contract software house, SDL was profitable but hardly the stuff of Silicon Valley legend. In 1980, it had eight employees, a handful of customers, and less than $1 million in annual sales.[1]

The breakthrough came when Ellison, accustomed to keeping up on IBM's doings from his days at competitor Amdahl, read a published paper from IBM researcher Ted Codd about how to design a relational database. Up to this time, databases had stored their information in hierarchal tables, something like the old handwritten outlines you used to do in junior high school. To find needed information, you could read down from the top of the outline but had no way of directly relating data that were listed under different headings. Codd's paper described a new computer language, called Structured Query Language, or SQL ("sequel," for short), that would enable you to do that. Ellison and his small team at SDL, which they soon renamed Oracle, determined that they would outrace not only giant IBM but another research team headquartered at the University of California at Berkeley, dubbed Ingres, in developing the first relational database.

BEATING BIG BLUE

Ellison came across Codd's paper when IBM Research published it in late 1976, assuming that the arcane subject matter would be of interest only to academics. They didn't count on Larry Ellison. Upon reading it, he had what he describes as an "epiphany." For the first time, "someone has ascribed a mathematically consistent and complete way of managing and retrieving information," he says. "Never before had this been done."[2] But at the time, even IBM didn't think that a relational database could be commercialized, since it had let Codd's plan to develop one languish for eight or nine years. Big Blue created a prototype but took it no further, allowing Oracle and Ingres to slip in and grab the business. "Conventional wisdom was that relational databases would never be commercially viable, because they were simply too slow," says Ellison. Although relational databases were much easier to use and would run on computers other than IBM mainframes, no one believed that they could be turned into a real product. Universities, like the Ingres project at U.C. Berkeley, were creating relational databases as research projects, but no companies had committed. Oracle picked up the gauntlet.

"I saw the [Codd] paper and I thought that, on the basis of this research, we could build a commercial system," says Ellison. "And, in fact, if we were clever, we could take IBM's research . . . and beat IBM to the marketplace with this technology. Because we thought we could move faster than they could."[3] And that's what his four-man team (Ellison, Miner, Oates, and Bruce Scott, who had also worked at Ampex) did, proving once again the ability of small, nimble companies to exploit technology breakthroughs more effectively than large, bureaucratic companies. Silicon Valley exists because of the failures of companies like IBM and Xerox to harness the possibilities of their own research. Companies such as Intel, Microsoft, Apple Computer, Adobe, and Oracle, as start-ups, did it instead. As they, in turn, grew big and bureaucratic, newer upstarts like Palm and Google find and exploit new opportunities. (That's why the scary thing about Microsoft's dominant position in technology isn't its actual monopoly but the consequences if it's able to choke off or absorb small, innovative companies.) While Oracle was hard at work turning Codd's paper into reality, Big Blue didn't release a non-mainframe version of its database product, known as DB2, until 1993, nearly fourteen years after Oracle came out with its first product in late 1979!

"We did publish all of that information back in the 1970s, making it possible for others to grab hold of it," concedes Steve Mills, a longtime IBMer who's now senior vice president and group executive of IBM Software. In a sense, IBM created Oracle, in somewhat different fashion than it did Microsoft and Intel. The latter two became key suppliers of, respectively, the operating system and chip for IBM's personal computer, whereas Oracle merely seized technology research pioneered at Big Blue and ran with it. With IBM fixated on the mainframe market, Oracle saw the potential to run the more portable relational database on other platforms, like minicomputers and workstations based on Unix, an open operating system popularized in the 1980s as an alternative to proprietary mainframe systems. "Making information available to create an industry is not necessarily a bad thing," says

Mills. "Unfortunately, IBM was not very focused on Unix and workstation software. We didn't invest the way we should. We could have been the market leader." Instead, the market leader is Oracle, and IBM is playing catch-up. "We clearly lagged the market by a substantial amount of time and gave them plenty of time to build up a customer base," says a chagrined Mills.

THE FIRST CUSTOMER

It took Oracle two years to get the first version of its relational database out, during which the company had to support itself with contract jobs for Tandem, Amdahl, Memorex, and other computer firms. Unlike today, when venture capital investors fund start-ups in exchange for equity, back then entrepreneurial investing was just getting started, and software was not considered much of a bet. "We could not raise money," recalls Ellison. "No software companies could raise money at the time. That's why we had to take $2,000 of our own hard-earned money and start the company. . . . We did consulting work to fund our product development work. . . . We had no outside investment whatsoever."[4] Arnold Silverman, a venture capitalist who served on Oracle's board through the 1980s, agrees with Ellison that investors then were afraid of database software. "It was a real gamble, the kind of thing traditional VCs could see as a bottomless pit," he says. Neither the relational database itself nor SQL were yet established as a standard. "IBM had developed this but couldn't figure out what to do with it. And Oracle could have run out of steam way before they did," notes Silverman. Despite all the caveats, he joined the board in 1980, in exchange for stock options, because "I liked Larry and thought it was an interesting play."

At one point, Ellison mortgaged his house to get a bank credit line to keep the company going. When a cash-strapped Ellison stopped making payments, his lender filed to foreclose on the house where he was living and another he was building.

He was saved by a loan from another venture capitalist, Don Lucas. Although Ellison is not a believer in venture capital and routinely claims that Oracle never took any formal venture money, he acknowledges his debt to Lucas, who is still a close adviser and remains on Oracle's board of directors. The tiny company was then sharing space at 3000 Sand Hill Road, one of the early venture capital strongholds. "Bob Miner told Don that my houses were being foreclosed on, because I couldn't make payments. . . . I was president of the company, and I'd stopped paying myself first," says Ellison. Lucas wandered down the hall into the Oracle office and casually asked Ellison how things were going. The young entrepreneur lied and said everything was great. "Finally, I realized that Bob had told Don, and Don made me a loan." Lucas told Ellison, "You should just be worrying about the company. You have amazing potential with this company. You shouldn't be distracted by a personal financial crisis."[5]

Fortunately, unlike hardware, which requires expensive manufacturing systems, software is not a capital-intensive business, and in fact, most of the early software powerhouses started on a shoestring, just as Oracle did. Ellison recalls having a conversation with the branch manager of the local bank where Oracle kept its company money, around $200,000 built up from various consulting deals. With that amount of money in the bank, "we figured that we could stop doing consulting now, because this $200,000 would last us until we got our product out the door," says Ellison. "And we timed it, as it turned out, very, very close." The branch manager couldn't understand why Oracle was dumping its money-making consulting business and devoting its energy to finishing this weird thing called a relational database. Finally, close to insolvency, Oracle sold a database to its first customer, the Advanced Technology Division of Wright-Patterson Air Force Base. "Who but the federal government would buy database technology from four guys in California?" Ellison asked. He handled the installation of the technology and training himself.[6]

MARKET-SHARE PHILOSOPHY

Many promising software start-ups from the 1970s and early 1980s are now merely forgotten names: Computervision, Digital Research, Oracle's rivals Ingres and Ashton-Tate . . . As has been proved time and again in the industry, better technology does not guarantee winning or even surviving. By all accounts, Ingres's technology was more elegant than Oracle's. What carried the day for Oracle was having workable technology, picking the right hardware and operating-system platforms, and striving relentlessly for market share. Ellison's decision to go with SQL for its database programming language was a serendipitously brilliant choice, for IBM gave SQL its stamp of approval in 1981, making that the industry standard. Just as it had done with Microsoft and Intel, IBM's decision established Oracle as the leader of a new, small niche of software poised to take off in a big way. Although Ellison scoffs at IBM, saying it made a trillion-dollar error in giving the "keys of the kingdom" to Microsoft and Intel, Oracle's debt to Big Blue is incalculable. Not only did Oracle base its seminal technology on IBM research, but its market dominance was made possible by IBM's endorsement of the SQL standard.

If IBM gets the credit for the research, Ellison gets the credit for the hard-driving focus on defeating Oracle's enemies and aiming for domination. Geoffrey Moore, the consultant/author who invented a nomenclature to describe market dominators, calls Oracle a "classic gorilla" that was able to gain first-mover advantage and therefore benefit from what's become known as "increasing returns." That is, the company perceived as the market leader consolidates that position because, when buying technology, customers flock to the "safe buy"—the company that looks to be the long-term survivor and establishes a standard to which others must adhere. IBM did it in mainframe computers, Intel in chips, Microsoft in operating systems, Cisco in routers . . . the list could go on. Oracle did it in relational databases, and to this day, its gorilla position benefits it, not only producing tremendous profitability but providing a cash flow that allowed Oracle to move into other markets such as enterprise applications. Virtually all of the big winners in technology have been "gorillas" that invented a market and kept on growing both the market and their share.

But back in the early 1980s, none of this was evident. Ellison took his market-share dominance strategy straight from the Japanese. Ellison recalls a conversation that he had with a Japanese business executive in which he was defending free-market economics and the notion of multiple competitors. "In Japan, we believe our competitors are stealing the rice out of the mouths of our children," the executive retorted. "In Japan, we think anything less than 100 percent market share is not enough." It's not much of a leap from there to Ellison's notion that "everyone else must fail." He zeroed in on his competitors, like Cullinet, Ingres, and Informix, with targeted marketing campaigns focused on their weaknesses (for more on this, see Chapter 10). "Market share is everything," says Ellison. "In the long run, you will live or die [by market share]." Other successful business leaders in the United States, like Bill Gates and Jack Welch, were also fervent believers in the pursuit of market share. Even when Oracle overcame all its rivals to become the gorilla in database software, Ellison's primary goal remained increasing its market share.[7]

For the early companies that became major players in the technology industry, like Microsoft, Oracle, Sun Microsystems, and AOL, this market share *über alles* philosophy worked. Companies that concentrated on refining their technology (Ingres, Apollo Computer) or their organizational scheme (Digital Equipment Corporation) got left behind. With greenfield markets to reap, the key factor became obtaining customers, who could, in turn, be used as references for more customers. The winning strategy is less obvious today, when many technology markets are saturated and obtaining customers is a zero-sum game. As we'll see in subsequent chapters, Ellison's ruthless, take-no-prisoners approach also has its negative side, alienating not only competitors but customers and partners, but in the decade of the 1980s, when the relational database market was in its formative state, the strategy paid off in building a billion-dollar enterprise.

RECRUITING THE FUTURE

Ellison's approach to recruiting people was as single-minded as his hunt for market share: get the best and brightest young people from the top schools (the usual suspects like Harvard, MIT, Stanford, as well as the University of Illinois, which he and Miner both attended), throw them in, and let them sink or swim. Ellison may never have finished college, but he respected people who had, at least those who were at the best schools. Once Oracle got these people, experience didn't matter. What kind of match they were for the job didn't matter, for the job would change in a year or two. Employees could create their own opportunities by starting new departments and lines of business. No one was pigeonholed as just a secretary or just a phone clerk or just a salesperson. Take Anneke Seley, who joined as employee number twelve in 1980. In ten years at Oracle, she started as the company receptionist and became assistant to the vice presidents of sales, administration, finance, and software development. From there, she moved on to managing staff in contract administration, shipping and fulfillment, customer relations and events, and international sales services. She also started Oracle's inside sales department, now the Direct Marketing and Internet Sales Division. Seley's efforts verified that complicated software like databases could be sold over the telephone. "These well-paid and educated telephone-based sales representatives were among the first to qualify leads and sell complex, costly, and intangible products without face-to-face interaction," she says. And the internal sales department became the training ground for such renowned Oracle "graduates" as Marc Benioff and Tom Siebel, both of whom now head their own companies. Seley, who today runs a consulting service, was hired right out of school, like many an Oracle employee. Says she: "The culture was extremely encouraging of creativity, allowing people opportunities even if they didn't have the experience." Ellison personally taught Seley and other employees how to program in SQL, anticipating that they would seize upon larger opportunities.

It took Oracle a year and a half to grow from employee twelve to employee twenty-six in mid-1982. That was John Luongo, hired from Tymshare to oversee Oracle's international sales effort. "I almost didn't take the job," Luongo recalls, because Ellison, already cultivating the habit of keeping people waiting, was fifty-seven minutes late for the interview. "At Tymshare, no one would wait more than twenty minutes for anyone," says Luongo. "I was furious. At one hour, I was walking out." Ellison showed up three minutes before that deadline. "I learned," says Luongo, "that if you were going to see Larry, you didn't make any other appointments for the rest of the day." Nonetheless, he was drawn to Ellison. "There were things I liked about him: he was very smart, and he was ethnic." An Italian born and raised in New York, Luongo was worried about joining "all these WASPs in California." But Ellison "cursed like a truck driver. I figured I could be comfortable with Larry."

Gary Kennedy, who joined sales at about the same time as Luongo, says Ellison had to take risks hiring bright people who weren't necessarily knowledgeable about Oracle's technology. The database was so new, who would have been, at the time? Maybe Ted Codd himself. "I was a consumer packaged goods guy from Procter & Gamble with a little bit of hardware experience at Intel," says Kennedy. "Larry's strategy was, always hire the best we can, and two years from now, we'll be able to hire better people and trade them out." It turned out that people like Seley, Luongo, and Kennedy were able to grow in ways that Oracle needed them to. Ellison did have an uncanny knack for picking people from disparate backgrounds who would somehow find themselves at Oracle. Seley was a young, idealistic woman on her way to medical school. Kennedy was a deeply religious Mormon. Luongo was a wise-cracking New Yorker. Yet they meshed in the freewheeling, fast-talking start-up called Oracle. "We were cowboys beyond anything you ever imagined," says Kennedy.

Another early salesperson, Gary Bloom, had more experience than many of Oracle's new hires in that he was working at Chevron when his boss left to run an engineering project at Oracle. Bloom, who had worked at IBM's mainframe division, decided to look into this start-up, dwarfed by the huge companies where he had previously worked. In 1986, he had a ninety-minute meeting with Kennedy, precipitated by his sassy response to the question "Why do you think we should hire you?" Bloom snapped back, "I'm not sure you should, because I'm not sure I want to work here." Kennedy hired him to do technical sales support. Thirteen years later, Bloom had become Ellison's reputed heir apparent.

Craig Ramsey had outranked Ellison when they were both at Amdahl. Ramsey, who had come to Amdahl from IBM, was in sales while Ellison was a lowly contractor in development. "Larry and I never met at Amdahl," says Ramsey, but apparently Ellison knew of him, for in 1986, he sent a headhunter to find Ramsey. Kennedy, who by then was vice president of sales and marketing, needed an assistant. He and Ellison both talked with Ramsey. "Larry interviewed me, and I was very impressed with the way he talked about his business strategy," says Ramsey. At the time, Oracle's biggest success had come in making databases for Digital Equipment Corporation (DEC) minicomputers. "Larry wanted to move into Unix," a market that was then quite small and undeveloped. Ramsey bought into Ellison's take on Unix as the corporate operating system of the future. Then, as now, Ellison had the capacity to be utterly convincing because he was such a complete believer in his own vision. "Larry's ability to present complex ideas by summarizing the points and then hammering them through the company is a great skill," says Scott, who left Oracle in 1982. "Larry never gets stuck in the minutiae."[8] Like many great leaders, Ellison fixates upon a single idea and leaves it to others to fill in the details. He's an intuitive genius who seems to sense the future; he's been right on trends such as Unix, the predominance of software over hardware, and the importance of the Internet long before most other people.

THE EXCITEMENT OF A START-UP

In the 1980s, Oracle was a heady place to be if you were young, bright, and eager to make a name for yourself by giving everything you had to the company. "Larry always wanted to make sure everyone he hired really believed in Oracle," recalls Noosheen Hashemi, who joined as a sales administrator on June 10, 1985 (she still remembers the day). "He thought that any two people in the company, in whatever job they have, should be able to hold a fifteen-minute conversation and enjoy each other's company. Even people at the bottom were at a high level of intelligence and ambition."

Hashemi fit this profile perfectly. Three years after she started, she was a director of the company, at barely twenty-five years old. "I was managing sixty people around the country," she says. Many nights, she and Gary Kennedy would work until midnight. "I was married to Oracle," Hashemi says, the passion evident in her voice. "I had ten incredible years." Oracle attracted the kind of people who "astonish others by achieving their own impossible standards," says Hashemi. Another important cultural aspect was nonacceptance of authority just because it was authority. People would come into meetings and suggest a new organizational chart that had their peers reporting to them. "They would go to Larry and say, 'My boss is incompetent. Here's why,'" she says. In many cases, the outcome was that the boss was gone and the uppity subordinate now ran the division. (Terry Garnett, cited in Chapter 1, was a master of that kind of politicking, as were many others. Oracle seemed to draw them like moths to a flame.)

Marc Benioff was one of those kids who seemed born to be an entrepreneur. In high school, he had his own software business. In college, he was a programmer for Apple. In May

1986, he was trying to decide what he should do after college. He interviewed with Kennedy and Seley at Oracle's new offices in Belmont, California, a wealthy, little-known suburb on the San Francisco peninsula. Nearly all the cubicles were empty, Benioff recalls. "I figured they must be planning to expand." They didn't offer him the direct sales job he really wanted. Instead, they asked Benioff to answer the customer service line. "It wasn't the job I had in mind, but they were 'A' players, so I joined. My mother always said if you play with 'A' players, you become one." Benioff soon moved into telesales. (One of his coworkers was Stacey Brusco, who would later marry Tom Siebel.) But he was tired of the San Francisco Bay Area and wanted to move back to Southern California to be with his college sweetheart. So Oracle sent him to work under Craig Ramsey in Marina del Rey. Benioff started closing big transactions and, in May 1987, was named "rookie of the year" at Oracle's annual Quota Club honoring its sales force. "I'd done several million dollars' worth of orders," he boasts.

Kennedy and Luongo, who respectively headed U.S. and international sales, were avid coworkers in boosting Oracle's revenue and rivals for Ellison's cachet. "Larry is really good at recognizing a good idea and letting you run with it," says Kennedy. "If he likes you, he anoints you." That gave Kennedy virtually free rein to define the objectives for his sales staff and push them very hard. Even though Oracle's managers were all inexperienced, including Ellison, "we were able to take off and learn as we were flying," says Kennedy. That approach worked extraordinarily well in the 1980s, as Oracle grew from $1.2 million in revenue in fiscal 1980 to nearly $1 billion by fiscal 1990. But that unprecedented growth, as we'll see in the next chapter, came at a price that Oracle would one day have to pay.

LEADERSHIP BY LARRY

Although Ellison gave plenty of leeway to managers in whom he believed, he was clearly the leader in devising the strategy, setting the primary goals, and carrying others along with his conviction that the relational database would become a key technology for every major company. "Larry emerged as the alpha founder," says Siebel. "His word was pretty much law." Ellison was also incredibly charismatic in articulating his vision. Hashemi remembers attending Quota Club in 1987 in Hawaii, where Ellison gave a speech ostensibly warning against arrogance, or what he defined as "unwarranted pride." He went down the list of all Oracle's successes in the past year; in each case, the company had exceeded its goals, more than doubling revenue from $55 million to $131 million. As he listed each achievement, Ellison would ask with a smile, "Unwarranted pride?" At the same time, Ellison already was developing his formidable gift for humiliating those who didn't meet his expectations. "People got their hands slapped," says Seley. It happened to her. She was running Oracle's user conference and had to make a decision on what to charge attendees in order to meet her deadline. "Larry hadn't officially approved it, and he got very angry with me," she says. "I had a momentary understanding of why people feared him. It was his tone of voice and body language." He demanded of the cringing Seley, "Who approved this?" She adds, "I think I looked at him in horror. He decided it wasn't that big a deal and let it go."

Before his death from cancer in 1994, at the age of fifty-two, Oracle cofounder Bob Miner provided a much-needed balance for Ellison in puncturing his arrogance and combating his increasing tendency to treat people as disposable once he figured he'd sucked out their best days. Says Luongo, "The Larry and Bob interaction was a crucial part of the early days. Bob helped keep Larry grounded." He recalls a favorite story about the pair of them standing in line at Bank of America in the mid-1980s. "Larry was getting huffy because he hated to wait," says Luongo. "Bob raises his voice and says loudly, 'Can we order this line by wealth?' Larry turns beet red." Even though Miner and Ellison would engage in shouting matches, it was a match of equals. "Larry would listen to Bob the way he wouldn't listen to anyone else," says Luongo. "When Bob died of lung cancer, it was devastating to Larry."

GOING PUBLIC

In late 1985, Oracle started exploring the idea of an initial public offering (IPO) of its shares. But Ellison, surprisingly, was not sure the company was at the right level. Recalls board member Silverman, "Larry and I went to lunch at a Japanese restaurant to talk over the IPO. He felt uncomfortable and said, 'Do we have to go now?'" Silverman told him the event could still be called off, and it was. "He didn't think the company was ready," says Silverman. "I give him credit for having the courage to pull back. I thought that showed a lot of character and insight."

Six months later, Oracle had launched a new version of its database, and the board and executive committee voted in favor of an IPO. Luongo was the lone dissenter. "I was the only one of the executive committee who voted against going public," he says. "We were only around $25 million at that point, and I thought we were too small." Ellison, although he still had doubts, voted in favor. "His was the vote that really counted," says Luongo, "although I know he was worried about [the IPO]." Ellison spent considerable time educating Wall Street and the underwriters, Merrill Lynch and Alex Brown, about just what a relational database was, but he shielded his senior executives from the grind. "Larry told the underwriters they had no more than an hour with each of the senior executives," says Luongo. "I had almost no involvement in the whole process." On March 12, 1986, Oracle sold one million shares, priced at $15, and they closed above $20, a good return for those days. That valued Ellison's 34.8 percent of the company at $93 million. The very next day, Microsoft went out at $21 and closed at $28, valuing Bill Gates's stake at $300 million. The two companies appeared to be on somewhat different tracks: Oracle selling its database into the corporate information technology (IT) infrastructure, while Microsoft's customers were PC users. Still, Gates and Ellison jockeyed for position as to who would champion software as the predominant force in the technology industry.

"Oracle and Microsoft were rivals for who would lead the new era of software," says Silverman.

People who were there at the time remember the IPO from varying perspectives. Silverman felt that the IPO was an important event, but there was none of the euphoria associated with later public technology offerings. "It wasn't like we had made it," he says. "Going public was simply necessary to finance the company's continued growth." Luongo, who had just returned from a trip to England, went to the leased headquarters in Belmont, California, expecting to party. Instead, "it was more like a funeral," he says. "Larry and Bob Miner had had a huge fight. The opening price was fifteen dollars, and we closed at nineteen dollars [actually slightly higher]. Bob was outraged that it had gone up that much. He felt we were cheated out of the four dollars," since Oracle's proceeds came only from the fifteen dollars listed price. Siebel remembers getting an E-mail about the first day's market performance and thinking of the famous quote from Winston Churchill: "This is not the end. It is not even the beginning of the end but it is, perhaps, the end of the beginning." Oracle was embarking upon a new era that would bring great rewards and great temptations. For the next three years, its revenue and stock both jumped precipitately. "The IPO was a significant financial event for everyone involved," says Siebel. "The primary motivation for working there was making money. That's why people stayed; [over the years] I made millions of dollars." Seley, on the other hand, didn't quite realize what an IPO entailed. "I was naive," she confesses, and hadn't even asked for stock options when she joined the company. "A major in human biology had not prepared me for stock option grants," she says. Thanks to Miner, who had insisted that all employees get stock, Seley had five hundred shares at the IPO. (She would get more.)

ONWARD AND UPWARD

Although many people contributed mightily to Oracle's success in the 1980s, like Kennedy, Luongo, and the sales team, along with Miner and the development team, Ellison stood out as the driving force. In 1980, when Oracle began selling its database, software was a poor cousin of hardware. Companies decided what hardware they were going to buy and then found, or created, software to run on it. "Larry had a very clear vision of how that was going to change," says Silverman. "He was going to stick it in the ear of IBM and the other hardware vendors by letting people make the software decision first." That was why using SQL, which allowed Oracle's database to be portable and run on different hardware platforms, was important. "Larry wanted a portable database so that people could make the software decision first, then choose the hardware it would run on." In a day when software was an afterthought to the hardware vendors, "we were selling these guys on the idea that they needed to be compatible with our software," says Silverman. That shift was akin to the move to the Internet a decade or so later.

Ellison not only had the vision, he had the determination. Scott, who was Oracle's first employee (after the three founders) and cowrote the relational database with Miner, says Ellison willed Oracle not to fail, since failure was intolerable to him. Scott remembers the time when Oracle needed to get its terminals connected to the computer room, which was next door. "We didn't have anywhere to really string the wiring," he says. "Larry picks up a hammer, crashes a hole in the middle of the wall, and says there you go. It's just the way he thinks, make a hole, make it happen somehow."[9] Silverman agrees. "Larry had the force to make Oracle succeed. Without Larry, Oracle never would have gotten off the ground," he says. In 1988, Ellison had a five-year plan to reach $5 billion, Silverman recalls. At that time, "there weren't even any billion-dollar software companies." To hit that $5 billion figure meant Oracle would have to continue its spectacular 100 percent plus annual growth rate, which was faster than any other company's pace during the 1980s. "Larry was obsessed with the 100 percent figure. It became his whole mantra," says Silverman. It was a mantra that was about to turn into a nightmare.

4

On the Ropes

In the 1980s, Oracle lacked strong internal accounting standards, which wasn't a surprise, since the government didn't demand any of software companies. The oversight boards have always lagged in figuring out how to account for new technology. It wasn't until 1998, for example, that financial-accounting bodies decided whether software should be expensed immediately as a cost of doing business or capitalized gradually as an asset. They're still arguing over what to do with Internet sales. In such a vacuum, with a leader who regarded accounting management as trivial, the Oracle sales team basically ran amok. The entire emphasis was on making deals, selling software by whatever means necessary. If that meant promising the customer Oracle software in perpetuity, so be it. If that meant dropping the customer flat after the sale, because there would be no new revenue, hey, there were seemingly endless new customers out there. Everybody was going to need a database sooner or later. But when a company presells everything in its cupboard and then the cupboard runs bare, it runs into crunching reality, which is what happened to Oracle in 1990–1991. It dug itself into such a deep hole that it was teetering on the brink of bankruptcy. Then the federal government belatedly stepped in and assessed a few penalties.

The software industry in the United States was born with companies like Microsoft and Oracle, and one thing the two have in common is running afoul of the government. Microsoft was sued for being a monopolist, Oracle for overstating revenues. Both were aggressive in exploiting a new technology—software—in which they sold lines of code, not an actual product like computers or chips. The accounting rules were fuzzy as to when and how to book a software sale. In fact, at first, there weren't any rules, so companies tended to make up their own. If a customer buys a software license but the product is never delivered or, when delivered, doesn't work, is that a sale? Oracle would say yes, because it planned to make the product work eventually. Never mind that the customer might not get what was promised for months or years. If the customer license specifies that any number of people get to use the software, will that customer ever buy again? If a customer also pays for maintenance and enhancements, what exactly does that entitle it to and how should that be booked, especially if the customer later cancels the contract? If a vendor advances credit so a customer can buy a five-year software license, is all that revenue booked immediately or spread out over the five years? Companies answered these questions themselves, and the answers were nearly always to count revenue as soon as possible and let tomorrow take care of itself.

But for many entrepreneurial companies, there were no tomorrows—they ran out of cash and were forced to close their doors or be absorbed. Oracle came close to being one of the *desaparecidos.* It had expanded so fast that its growth outstripped its executives' managerial abilities. Throughout the decade of the 1980s, it succeeded in achieving the Silicon Valley dream of almost unbounded growth. Revenues in fiscal 1981 (Oracle's year ends May 31) were a measly $1.2 million, but from there on, they more than doubled every year to reach nearly $1 billion by the end of the decade, an astounding 83,000 percent growth rate! Oracle even paid its sales commissions in real gold at one point, just before the fall. Unfortunately for Oracle, the growth was achieved in part with methods that became insupportable: basically mortgaging the future to make the present look good, by booking revenues too early. As Larry Ellison put it, "I had no experience running anything this big . . . in growing a company this fast. This is all uncharted territory for me, personally, and in the history of commerce."[1]

The penalties for Oracle included the embarrassment of reporting a $36 million loss in the first quarter of fiscal 1991, being forced to restate financial results, seeing the market cap plummet by more than $3 billion (Ellison's own stake dropped in value by $800 million), ousting executives such as U.S. sales manager Gary Kennedy, and laying off four hundred employees, 10 percent of its U.S. workforce at the time. The company even temporarily stopped work on its showy new headquarters in Redwood Shores, on the San Francisco peninsula overlooking the bay. It was a bitter lesson in humility for Ellison, who had counted on doubling Oracle's growth until it became a $5 billion company. Oracle would achieve that and more, but not at the same record pace and only after a painful retrenchment that led to internal restructuring, imposition of new discipline on a company and culture quite unaccustomed to it, and a recasting of Ellison's role.

However, this down period—and the measures it compelled Ellison to take to recover—wound up setting the stage for Oracle's emergence as one of the "real companies" of Silicon Valley, in the words of investor and longtime board member Don Lucas. In the 1990s, Oracle became—like Microsoft, Intel, and a handful of others—a dominant force whose technology is the platform upon which many companies build. The crisis was inevitable, for Oracle could never have continued on the path that its leaders had set. Sooner or later, the blowup would come. Everyone knew it, but Ellison, as if he were "playing chicken" with history, kept the pedal to the metal until the last possible moment, barely avoiding annihilation. It's not that Oracle was alone. Practically every early technology market leader learned the same lesson: market share at all costs. Then savagely exploit that market share to enter new arenas and dominate those. Software is an industry in which customers practically demand dominance. It's similar to the telephone industry before AT&T was broken up. A telephone is only useful if it can communicate with others; hence, the need for standardization, which breeds a natural monopoly. Software is only useful if developers write programs to do things you want, and developers write for the market gorilla. Microsoft Windows wasn't the best desktop operating system around; it was just the most pervasive. Likewise, initially Oracle didn't have the best database from a technical perspective, but it got enough sales to establish first-mover advantage.

ELLISON MEETS HIS MATCH

In the 1980s, Oracle had, without a doubt, the most admired—and feared—sales force in the technology industry. In the United States, the person who got the credit, and later the blame, was Gary Kennedy. A big, soft-spoken man, Kennedy emanates the kind of commitment on which he insisted from his employees. A devout Mormon who is a former bishop (head of a congregation) and mission president (head of a missionary region for the church), Kennedy brought his religious conviction to Oracle as well. He was a young salesman at chip maker Intel in the early 1980s when Bruce Scott, a fellow Mormon, persuaded him to interview with Ellison. The first meeting, over lunch, was not promising. Kennedy thought Ellison was flaky; Ellison thought Kennedy, who had an MBA, lacked the technical background he preferred. At one point, Kennedy displayed a chutzpah that matched Ellison's own. Ellison asked him, "What would you like to do here?" Kennedy's response: "I'd like your job, Larry." The founder laughed. "If you're good enough to take it away from me, I'm ready to challenge you."

Ellison and Kennedy engaged in some cat-and-mouse before the latter came on board. Ellison waited six months after their first meeting, made Kennedy an offer, then rescinded it. "I want you to learn relational database first," he told Kennedy. For half a year, Kennedy dutifully learned how to program in the SQL language Oracle used for its database. Then, said Kennedy, "I called Larry and said I'm ready now, but he wouldn't return my calls for several weeks." Kennedy wrote Ellison a letter complaining that he'd spent six months of his life learning Oracle technology, but the letter arrived after Ellison finally told Kennedy he could be vice president of marketing. Marketing, where there's constant turnover due to Ellison's nitpicking, is the entry-level pathway for many an Oracle executive. It doesn't take technical skills but rather an articulate personality who can trade jabs with Ellison, as Kennedy did. "He received the nasty letter after he'd already made me an offer, and to his credit, he didn't rescind it," says Kennedy. Ellison has always had a great instinct for talent, and he will overlook a lot of things to get it. Few of these early hires were an obvious match for what Oracle needed, but they became what the company needed, through a combination of Ellison's relentless ambition and their own.

During the interview process, Kennedy had his first hints of the roller-coaster ride he would be in for at Oracle. In their first chat in 1981, Ellison had informed him that sales were around $5 million a year, maybe a little under. A couple of months later, Kennedy was invited to join Oracle's employees for a celebration in the cafeteria. "Larry was standing next to me, and another employee was on my right," he recalls. "I asked her, 'What are you celebrating?' She said, 'We just hit $1 million in sales.' I turned to Larry, and he just rolled his eyes." After he joined in 1982, Kennedy had only been at Oracle a few days when he learned that the job he'd been given, vice president of marketing, was actually held by someone else. Supposedly, Ellison had fired the other guy, but they were now reconciled, and he had returned. Ellison told Kennedy, "I think you can sell, so go to Chicago for me and open an office there." Kennedy went from vice president of marketing to running a ten-state sales territory where Oracle as yet had no accounts. He and his wife, Jane, moved to Chicago, where the first Oracle sales office was in their bedroom. After Kennedy started making some sales, he hired his first salesperson, a recent graduate of the University of Illinois named Tom Siebel.

Siebel had the technical background that Ellison loved: a master's degree in computer science. He was also smart, articulate, and driven. Kennedy, who had discovered Siebel by calling his thesis adviser, "told me they were looking to hire someone who was very strong technically and understood database technology," Siebel recalls. "I seemed to have what they needed." After he flew out to California to interview with Ellison and cofounder Bob Miner, Siebel found himself drawn to the energy of Oracle, even though at the time it was a tiny company. He liked working with very bright people committed to a single goal: making Oracle successful. (After he left Oracle seven years later as its top salesperson, Siebel founded a database competitor that he sold to Sybase. He used the proceeds to found Siebel Systems in 1993, which, like Oracle, grew a niche software market into a multibillion-dollar business. As Oracle also moved into the same business—sales force automation and customer relationship management—Siebel became one of its most formidable competitors.)

MOTORING ON

At first, it was tough going for the newly opened Chicago sales office. In nine months, Kennedy had not been able to close any sales, mainly because the current database product, version 2, did not work very well. Companies would set up the database, dutifully input data, and never be able to retrieve it, which is the whole point of a database. "We had a thirty-day clause that if it doesn't work, we'll cancel the contract, so in two cases where I made sales, I had to give the money back," he recalls. Kennedy had a ten thousand–dollar balloon payment due on his mortgage and figured Oracle was going to fire him because he hadn't brought in any money. He found a job in Salt Lake City and then flew to California to resign. He told Ellison, "I'm leaving because I'm the worst salesman in the group." Ellison, for once, was candid about the product's shortcomings. "Nobody could sell this piece of shit," he told Kennedy. "If you'll give me six months, either version 3 will work or I'll find you a better job than the one you've got." That, says Kennedy, "turned out to be one of the few true things Larry ever said."

In those days, customers were patient with Oracle because most software didn't work out of the box and required considerable tinkering to make it functional. Besides, the purchasers of database software were engineers themselves and didn't mind the tinkering; in fact, many of them relished the challenge. It would be different when Oracle started selling application software to end users like accountants, but at first, the fact that the database didn't work properly was not a particular barrier as long as it worked better than whatever else was out there, which wasn't much. While IBM labored internally for years to perfect its relational database, Oracle released flawed version after flawed version and grabbed the market.

With the slightly improved version 3 database, Kennedy started to score a few sales, mostly in government agencies. Then he made a significant sale to Ford Motor Company: the first contract was for $300,000 with an option for $2 million more. "That put us on the map," Kennedy says. "It was our first *Fortune* 100 sale." Ellison flew out to help close the deal. "We met with a very senior fellow [at Ford] who said, 'We're committed to IBM,'" Kennedy recalls. Ellison's rebuttal was impeccable: IBM's database, DB2, at the time did not run on non-IBM platforms such as Unix. So he told the Ford executive, "I don't think you've committed to IBM. It's a relational database you've committed to. So buy everything from us." To this day, Ford remains a major Oracle customer, for both the database and applications products. Once the automaker committed to Oracle technology, it was hooked. The switching costs of changing database technology are enormous. That's another reason why Oracle's strategy of reeling in market share even if it was with initially buggy software paid off. Customers almost always stuck with Oracle through the transition, so it took a long time for a company like IBM, even if its products were better, to make inroads.

By the mid-1980s, with Tom Siebel now a top salesman "closing million-dollar deals right and left," Kennedy recalls, Oracle's growth rate accelerated. In fiscal 1983, the company hit $5 million in revenue; by 1985, $12.7 million; in 1986, $23 million. Ellison asked Kennedy to move to Washington, D.C., and take over sales for the entire East Coast. By now a Mormon bishop in Chicago, with three young children at home, Kennedy didn't want to move. So he commuted to Washington from Chicago. Kennedy was named national sales manager in 1985, "and the whole country reported to me." Finally, in 1986, just before Oracle went public, Ellison promoted Kennedy to vice president of U.S. sales, terminating Mike Seashols, who had previously held the job.

"Larry just turns on people," says Kennedy, who would experience the same thing himself. "He turned on Mike." In typical fashion, Ellison started his campaign to oust Seashols by making snide comments about him to other people. When Ellison starts the bad-mouthing, it's as much to convince himself as anyone else. Kennedy remembers sitting in a cab in New York with Ellison "listening to him rail about how dumb Mike was," always a giveaway. "Larry would say, 'Mike looks nice in his suit, but what does that matter?'" To Ellison, Seashols was a "well-groomed former IBM executive without a brain in his head," Kennedy recalls. Seashols was smart enough to know that the end was near. Two days before the end of the quarter in February, he called Kennedy to tell him he was worried about losing his job and to ask him to pull in a couple of deals quickly to make the numbers for the quarter. Kennedy called Seashols over the weekend to assure him that he'd brought in the deals, but on Monday, Seashols was gone and Ellison offered Kennedy his job.

FASTER THAN A SPEEDING BULLET

Oracle's strategy in the rabid growth years of the mid- to late 1980s was simple: do whatever it takes to meet your number. For most people, that number doubled every year. "We had a

fundamental decision to make," says Kennedy. "If we were
going to double every year, we could hire twice as many salespeople, or we could give higher quotas and less territory."
Usually, he adds, Oracle would increase the size of the sales
force by 50 percent and also boost the quota and reduce the
territory of the holdovers. Salespeople who met their quotas—
which 70 percent to 80 percent did, according to Kennedy—
were well rewarded. In the late 1980s, the typical quota was
$3–$4 million for the year, compared with about $800,000
for the software industry in general, he recalls. A salesperson
who just met a $3 million quota would get a commission of
.75 percent, or $22,500. But once you got over the quota,
"your commission rate would double or triple to 2 percent.
You'd earn more on your next million than you did on the first
three," says Kennedy. Top salespeople were pulling down generous six-figure incomes, along with stock options.

Noosheen Hashemi, who held a number of sales administration jobs at Oracle from 1985 to 1995, is typical of the dedicated young people whom Oracle attracted with its promises
of high rewards for high commitment. "What was important
to me first and foremost was the company's success," she says.
"We were all focused on work, making a commitment and
making it happen. Come hell or high water, you would make
it happen. If you put your name down, you would make it
happen." Kennedy's view was, hire the cream of the crop, give
them their plans, and send them out to sink or swim, Hashemi
recalls. "The ones who could do it did great. The ones who
didn't got a few chances and then they were gone." She adds,
"There was never room for bullshit or sugaring it up. It was all
about producing results."

Salespeople who didn't produce, who missed their quota,
would be publicly embarrassed. Kennedy sent out an E-mail
every quarter listing the rank of the salespeople by name in
reaching or exceeding quota. "It was pretty much understood
you'd be out of a job if you didn't meet your quota," says
Anneke Seley, the twelfth employee of Oracle, who worked her
way up into sales from an administrative assistant role. She
remembers these "Hail to the Stars" E-mails vividly. "Every-

body was ranked based on their actual and assigned number," she says. "I was usually in the top, but it could be devastating if you were at the bottom. Usually, people would just quietly leave before they were asked." Another Oracle salesperson, Craig Ramsey, who would wind up as Kennedy's number two, thought the tactic misfired. "The problem with those lists is, you kill people's egos," he says. People on the bottom "would be so broken, they would have a tough time ever performing," so the list became a self-fulfilling prophecy.

To Kennedy, it was part of his "commitment culture," in which he asked people to publicly state that they would meet their numbers each quarter. "I believed that people had a right to know where they stood," he says. "They're all part of a team, so everybody has a right to know." He denies that people were summarily fired for missing their number for one quarter while acknowledging that the shame attached to being on the bottom of the list could encourage voluntary attrition. As an example of his "compassion," he cites a meeting he held with the Los Angeles sales office in early 1989. At the time, the L.A. office had the worst results in the country. "Everybody thought I was coming down to fire them," Kennedy recalls. But in the morning, he went through sales reviews and could see that people were doing the right things to turn it around. "I stood up in the afternoon and told them, 'You guys are going to make it. The results are going to come.' " Then he said, "Let's go play softball." The Los Angeles office went from the worst to second-best office the next year.

But Kennedy did not tolerate people who wouldn't commit. "I would tell one of my regional sales managers, 'You've got to do $10 million,' " he recalls. The manager would say, "Yes, I can do it." Of course, "If he said no, I'd get somebody new in there," Kennedy states emphatically. "Management is about influencing results. I learned that from [Intel founder] Andy Grove. Why the hell are you here if you can't influence results?" He wasn't afraid to do that himself. Oracle's board of directors was wary when Kennedy demanded that the company lease a floor in Manhattan for its first sales office in New

York. "They said, 'You must be kidding. It costs too much,'"
Kennedy recalls. Finally, the board said Kennedy could have
the space if he could guarantee the sales to support it. "I said,
absolutely, even if I have to make them myself." It took about
six months to get the board's approval, and at that point, the
single floor wasn't enough, so Oracle had to lease more space
in Manhattan. "By the time you get around to a decision like
that, the company's 50 percent larger," he notes.

DOING WHATEVER IT TOOK

Everyone who was at Oracle during this phase remembers
Ellison and Kennedy's relentless drive to make the numbers.
Although it was clear that the direction was coming from Ellison, Kennedy was the public face for the sales staff. He was
the one who held meetings in which salespeople stood up and
"committed" to their number for the year. He was the one
who sent out the E-mails letting people know where they
ranked. "Larry had a lot of input into what my number was,"
Kennedy says. "He would say, we want to do $100 million,
and 65 percent of that needs to be U.S. Then I'd go away and
figure out a way to make it work. The goal every year was to
double."

There's an obvious conundrum to this goal: going from $23
million to $55 million between 1985 and 1986 is one thing.
But soon Oracle was in the hundreds of millions. It grew from
$282 million to $584 million between 1988 and 1989. The
goal for 1990 was to burst through $1 billion, and the sales-
people were the first ones in the line of fire. To meet their
inflated numbers, they started pushing harder and harder.
Oracle played fast and loose with so-called revenue recognition, the point at which you can book the revenue for making
a sale. Ramsey remembers booking multimillion-dollar deals
for products still in development. "There was a $6 million
license deal for applications in the late 1980s where only a
minimal amount of code had been written," he says. Oracle
also started selling site licenses, offering the database and all

the existing applications in perpetuity, in exchange for a large up-front payment.

Near the end of a quarter, the pressure to close deals got even more frenzied. Salespeople would offer heavy discounts to get a customer to sign before the deadline. Customers could buy software under a so-called credit acquisition plan: Oracle would extend them several million dollars in credit to buy products, so the revenue could be counted immediately, even though the actual payoff might not come for years. Contracts negotiated after the quarter closed, but signed before, were counted. Kennedy says Oracle based that on an accounting opinion that "minor changes" in the contract were OK, even if they happened after the end of the quarter. "For years, there was some percentage of the contracts we were in the process of making minor changes to after the quarter was over," he says. "There was really no definitive way to determine what's major or minor. We'd still be negotiating things like the right to replicate software, which is a major term." As long as the customer's signature was on the title page before the quarter ended, the revenue would be counted.

"To make a deal bigger and bring it in sooner, you could do anything it took," recalls another former Oracle sales manager, Luke Little. His favorite approach was to establish a time limit, artificial or not, for getting a customer to sign a contract. "You can always generate a fever to meet a deadline. Then it's much easier to increase the size of the deal as the date draws near." At Oracle, "you ran your territory like your own business," Little adds. "You could be very entrepreneurial. If you were smart and had a good idea, people would follow it." For instance, he would learn that one client needed extra functionality in the database, so Little would propose that Oracle work with the customer to add the new tricks, whatever they might be. "That way, we got money now from that customer and we're adding something other customers might want that made it a more robust product going forward."

In an effort to milk more money from customers, Oracle would "build fences" around its deals. For example, if a customer told Little it could only spend $1 million, he would sculpt the deal to meet that. "You found out how much money they had to spend, and you take it all," he says. "Then you make sure you put enough boundaries around it that a discount doesn't hurt you with other customers." So, for example, if an automaker wanted to buy the Oracle database for managing the shop floor, it got just that: a database for managing the shop floor. But if it wanted a database to manage its dealerships, it would have to buy a new license. "We did a lot of deals like that: you can use it on Mars but not on Venus," Little says. "But soon it got to be a nightmare dealing with all the restrictions." In those early days, the goal was market share, not margins. "We wanted to get more customers using Oracle. The incremental cost of a database goes to nothing if you get enough people using it," he adds.

Ellison's goal was to make Oracle the number one software company in the world, says Seley. "If you worked for Oracle, you were expected to believe. To get into that sales rally mentality, you had to put your brain on hold." Once, in the mid-1980s, she asked Ellison, "Why do we need to double every year and send out tapes before their time?" referring to the buggy software that Oracle was distributing. Ellison's reply was classic: "There's no reason to be out there if you can't be number one. Do you know any other soft drinks besides Coke and Pepsi? You don't survive if you fall behind. It's not an option of fast growth or slow growth. It's survival or not."

GO FOR THE GOLD

The perfect metaphor for Oracle during the go-go years came in the fourth quarter of fiscal 1990 ending May 31, when Kennedy instigated the infamous "go for the gold" campaign. The last quarter is critical for any software company, because that's when the sales force goes all out to bring in any pending deals and stoke the numbers for the year. Oracle was looking to break into the billion-dollar club, and to do that, it would have to rack up something like $370 million in sales in the fourth quarter. So Kennedy devised the idea of paying the sales commissions in actual gold coins. "We had a campaign every year to provide fourth-quarter incentive," Kennedy recalls. Because 1990 was an Olympics year, that became the theme for the quarter, and the notion of rewarding people in gold was born. To explain the campaign, Kennedy enlisted an actor dressed as a forty-niner (the original, not the San Francisco football player). "I was in the middle of my speech for the fourth-quarter kickoff meeting, when this forty-niner guy walks in and starts yelling, 'Gold, there's gold in them thar deals,'" he says.

At another sales meeting, Kennedy recalls fondly, "we brought in a chest full of one-ounce gold Eagles [each worth about $400]. We passed it around, and people would run their hands through it." The salespeople were given the option of taking their commission in gold or the usual check. More than half wanted the gold. "There is something magic about gold," he sighs. When it came time for the payout, Oracle had to come up with millions of dollars in gold coins. "We started buying American Eagles and ended up having to buy Canadian Maple Leafs as well because there weren't enough Eagles available," he recalls. For the larger offices, "we had a Brink's truck pull up, and an armed guard would get out and distribute the gold," plus a check for any difference between the gold coins and the actual amount of the commission. Kennedy defends the campaign, which helped generate $340 million in sales for the quarter (later restated to $318 million). Oracle ended the year just short of $1 billion, at $971 million (later restated to $916 million). "From a sales and motivational standpoint, it was a very successful campaign," he says. Then he admits, "It was also like telling someone who has a problem controlling their sex drive to indulge in hedonism."

People who were there for this still have some of the coins tucked away in their closets. "It was a huge theatrical thing," says Mike Hagan, who worked in sales administration. He remembers that Kennedy often accompanied the Brink's truck guard (whom Hagan figures was an actor) to Oracle sales offices to distribute the coins. "He would pump everybody up about how this is such a great company to work for." And the gold wasn't just for salespeople. "Anybody in the sales organization, including office administrators, could get these gold coins," adds Ramsey.

KILLING THE GOLDEN GOOSE

With hindsight, everybody at Oracle says they should have seen the crash coming. Some tell me they did see it, tried to warn Ellison and Kennedy and other executives, but to no avail. At any rate, with typical Oracle bluster, they admit that the company pushed the envelope but didn't really do anything wrong. It's true that Oracle's misdeeds pale compared with the accounting scandals of 2002 involving companies like WorldCom and Enron, but Oracle did do some things wrong. It overstated revenues by about $55 million out of nearly $1 billion, mostly by billing too soon or incorrectly. In 1993, after an investigation by the Securities and Exchange Commission, Oracle paid a $100,000 fine and signed a consent decree in which it agreed to desist from such practices as double billing and booking premature or nonexistent revenue. By contrast, WorldCom misstated $3.8 billion in revenue and had to file for bankruptcy; Enron inflated earnings and revenues based on partnerships that it owned and filed for bankruptcy while its chief financial officer was indicted for fraud, money laundering, and conspiracy. "We aggressively approached the accounting rules and modified business practices to hit the goals," recalls Oracle's Ramsey. "What we did was accepted [by the accounting gurus] at the time, but looking back, it's not healthy for an industry to be able to do those things. It sets up this problem that everybody is booking revenue that has yet to be earned. Essentially, you're stealing from the future. At some point, that's going to catch up with you."

In the first quarter of fiscal 1991, ending in August 1990, the glory ride came to a screeching halt. Kennedy learned from his sales vice president, Mike Fields, that the domestic organization wouldn't make its number. First the shortfall was $5 million, then $20 million, finally $30 million. On top of that, the sales commissions on the "go for the gold" campaign had been miscalculated, and Oracle owed another $10 million. Then, too, the company was sitting on millions in bad or duplicated receivables that it wouldn't be able to collect. Of fiscal 1990 revenues of $971 million (before restatement), receivables were a whopping $468 million, or almost half of the total! In November 1990, receivables were a record 176 days old, meaning that Oracle hadn't been able to collect from some of its customers for almost half a year. It didn't help matters that Oracle's chief financial officer at the time, Jeff Walker, was really a developer (of the company's financial applications) pressed into service because of Ellison's known disdain for "bean counters." Says Ramsey, "Larry wanted a CFO he could control instead of one who should be a second opinion." Kennedy, who was at odds with Walker, set up his own financial organization inside sales.

Kennedy remembers meeting with Fields, who ran direct sales and accounted for 70 percent of domestic revenues, on the Friday before Labor Day. "It's really bad," Fields said. "How bad is it?" Kennedy asked. "I don't think we're going to end up with $35 million for the quarter. Everything just fell out," Fields replied. Since his "number" had been around $60 million, that was a pretty significant shortfall. Fields and Kennedy broke the news to Ellison, who seemed calm. "I guess we'll have to deal with it," he told them. Next day, he invited Kennedy for breakfast. Kennedy insists he was never fired by Ellison but elected to resign rather than give Oracle two years in another position. "After that, Larry blamed everything on me, including the California earthquake," he says. Indeed, in a subsequent press conference at an Oracle trade show, after Walker announced that the company would post a substantial loss for the first quarter, Ellison essentially scapegoated Kennedy and the sales organization for the debacle. "It was a very, very aggressive selling organization," he says today. "And there were no controls in place. Normally, you have a chief financial officer making sure that certain procedures and protocols are in place, so there are no abuses going on out in the field. And we had none of that. I didn't even know you're supposed to have that. . . . I was spending most of my time worrying about products."[2]

Siebel, who left shortly after Kennedy, describes Oracle in this period as "a disaster waiting to happen." There were no good financial controls, customer or information systems. "They didn't even know how much revenue they had," he adds. "Larry shot Gary Kennedy and blamed him for all the woes," although, Siebel maintains, Ellison has to bear the ultimate responsibility. "Larry's philosophy was that it's OK to do anything at all as long as you didn't get caught," Siebel says. "There were definitely things that were over the edge on his watch. His culture was, you could do anything to achieve the desired result, which was crush the competitors, make the numbers." Oracle salespeople would discount sharply to beat a competitor, even if it meant taking a loss on a deal.

Other former executives are a bit more charitable toward Ellison, saying his inexperience in leading a large organization and his eagerness to push fast growth blinded him to the problems. Says Ramsey: "We had a bunch of bright young people learning the business and being aggressive in an industry that was very immature. We were all making mistakes out of immaturity and aggressiveness, including Larry." Ramsey says that when Ellison announced Kennedy's dismissal, he was fuming about the gold campaign. And yet, "Larry let Gary run the shop. He didn't look into it," says Ramsey. He believes that Kennedy, as the sales manager, should have warned Ellison of the impending train wreck. But even if he had, "Larry just wants to hear what he wants to hear and stops the dialogue."

THE SILVER LINING

Amid all the gloomy news, international sales remained one bright spot for Oracle. In the 1980s, Oracle's growth in Europe and Japan was as spectacular as in the United States, although from a smaller base. By the end of the 1980s, Oracle ROW (rest of world) accounted for about half of the company's total sales. Geoff Squire, a British native who started as managing director of Oracle U.K. in 1984, when it consisted of nine people, remembers his relationship with headquarters: "I sent Larry checks that didn't bounce, and he sent me products that occasionally loaded [that is, worked]." In those days, Oracle managing directors ran their companies like individual fiefdoms, almost entirely free of any direction from the parent. As Squire, who eventually headed all of Europe, told Ad Nederlof when the latter became managing director of the Netherlands, "You run the Netherlands like it's your own company. Do whatever you want so long as you make your numbers." Nederlof says the charge to the country managers was similar to the charge to U.S. managers: double revenue every year. "The culture was, 'We don't ask questions. Do it your way and make your numbers.' If you made your revenue and your margin, you had complete discretion."

Squire, a heavyset, bluff Englishman with thinning brown hair and a hearty laugh, says he charted a different course from Kennedy in the United States. "I believed we could build an integrated company. I sketched it out for Larry: database, tools, decision support [later applications], with consulting and support and training to back it up." Squire can still produce the rumpled paper where he diagrammed his concept of an integrated Oracle for Ellison. A former consultant himself, Squire offered Oracle customers service along with the product license. "I was selling the whole model, with my own consulting people on the side," he says. "My sales compensation model encouraged people to put services in, where Gary's was purely on license." (Kennedy admits he didn't compensate people for ongoing support. "If a customer was going to buy more product, they got great support from the salesperson. Otherwise, they didn't." Entrusting salespeople with service "was like taking a bunch of trained killers and trying to convince them to be docile," he says.) Consequently, customers in Europe got more hand-holding and, usually, more stable products because most of the early adopters were in the United States. Ellison, according to Squire, loved to visit Europe "because everybody there thought he was a nice guy."

Squire says he translated the integrated U.K. model to the rest of Europe and Asia, with modifications to fit other countries. In four years, for example, he helped build Oracle Japan to $170 million. In contrast to Oracle U.S.A., Squire says, "I listened to what worked rather than try to tell everyone how to do it." Partnering with major Japanese computer vendors, like NEC and Toshiba, was what worked there. But even in Europe and Japan, growth slowed as the new decade dawned. International operations accounted for $479 million of Oracle revenue in 1990, compared with $282 million in 1989, which sounds great but fell short of the annual doubling of sales that had been customary and was now expected. Still, in contrast to what was happening in the United States, international provided "steady revenue" that didn't require all the restatements that occurred in the United States. "At one stage, we were 71 percent of the business," Squire says. "America had screwed up."

CLEANING UP

Kennedy, who after leaving Oracle would serve as a Mormon mission president in Brazil, now acknowledges that he gave his sales force mixed messages. "I told them, 'Make your number no matter what.' I also said, 'Play by the rules.'" But with all the emphasis on results, people dumped the rules in favor of making the numbers. "I bear responsibility for not being clear about the priorities," he says. "If I had to do it over, I'd say, 'No matter what, don't break the rules, even if you miss your number.'"

He and Ellison aren't exactly chummy today, although Kennedy professes no surprise at being the designated scapegoat. "That's Larry's MO. After you've seen it a dozen times, it establishes a definite pattern. That didn't bother me." What bugs him is the fact that Ellison failed to give him any credit for building Oracle into the $1 billion selling machine—albeit a messed-up selling machine—that it was in 1990. "If Larry had said, 'Gary built the organization, Gary was responsible for letting it get out of control,' I could accept that. But Larry's position was that he built it all, then Gary destroyed it. That part did bother me." A few years later, Gary and Jane Kennedy ran into Ellison at an event in San Francisco. Says Kennedy, "Larry told Jane, 'I'm not sure you and Gary ever recognized how appreciative I am for what Gary did to build Oracle. I'm not sure I ever told you.' That's as close as he's ever come to apologizing."

Recovering from the "do whatever it took" era of the 1980s would be painful, for Ellison personally and for the company. But Oracle, which became for a time the fastest-growing company in the world, had succeeded in putting itself on the map as a major database vendor. Pete Tierney, a former senior vice president of marketing, believes that Ellison pushed the company to the breaking point to achieve the market dominance it holds to this day. "I'm convinced that Larry would do anything to capture market share," he says. "We did that to the point of breaking the company. We were buying the [database] market away from the competitors. The financial terms [on some of our contracts] were a disaster." In the fourth quarter of fiscal 1990, Tierney remembers, deferred revenue was about 70 percent of the total. This was due to the credit acquisition plans in which Oracle basically paid for customers to buy its products by extending them credit for as long as five years. "These CAPs gave us tremendous revenue growth, but they exacerbated the cash-flow problem," says Tierney. The Financial Accounting Standards Board finally stepped in and told software companies they couldn't do CAPs anymore. "But it broke the competition's back," Tierney says. "Even though Oracle was wounded and had a burned-out management and burned-out customers, the competition was in worse shape. We won the database war."

What finally stopped Ellison was running into the wall. But he had the guts and determination to pick himself up, find some badly needed management expertise, and get Oracle off and running once more. It's this resilience that, more than once, has revitalized Oracle as a company and as an important force in the technology world. Were it not for Ellison's grit and intelligence, Oracle would probably have finished its existence as a minor consulting firm installing other people's software; IBM might have had time to perfect the relational database and dominate the market. Or someone else—Ingres, Ashton-Tate, or Sybase—would have been where Oracle is today. But none of them had Ellison, who has the sheer brilliance to recognize a new technology trend before practically anyone else (like the potential of a relational database) and the will to turn that recognition into reality. At the beginning of the 1990s, he had driven his company to its position atop the database market, even though the march came at great cost: shredded employee morale, dismayed customers and shareholders, implacable enemies among competitors. Now he would have to do something he'd never done before, and hated—retrench. But the objective was important enough— the very survival of Oracle—that Ellison swallowed his pride and did what needed to be done.

5

SAVING ORACLE

[LARRY GETS SOME MUCH-NEEDED HELP]

public company pays a high price for messing up. Not only did Oracle have to contend with its internal problems—a sales organization out of control, demoralized employees, executives pointing fingers at one another—but the press and analysts, sensing blood, began to speculate on the possible demise of the company and the fate of Larry Ellison as its chief executive. Ellison compares the period to taking the helm of a sailboat during a storm. Unlike the Sydney-to-Hobart race, where he had a professional crew to whom he could turn, at Oracle there was nobody. Many of his veteran executives either had been dumped, like Gary Kennedy, or had quit in disgust, like Tom Siebel, dismayed over the scapegoating of his mentor Kennedy. Overseas, Geoff Squire, perhaps the most experienced executive still left at Oracle, was too far away from the center of power to have any real shot at the top job. "I made the decision to tack the boat," says Ellison, meaning that he would steer his company into safer waters. He had decided that he was the best equipped to fix the problems, although that required shifting his focus from engineering to embrace all of the company, especially sales. "It was a horrible experience, because I had been paying no attention to the field [sales] or to finance."[1]

Yet this desperate period, perhaps more than any other, shines a light on Ellison's schizophrenic nature. Under considerable pressure from his board of directors, the chief executive was willing to do what was needed to save the company— bring in veteran management, beg for money—but at the same time, he was up to his usual tricks of ousting, in humiliating fashion, some of the very people who had helped Oracle get this far, like Mike Fields. He had to convince the skeptical board that he was still able to lead Oracle, while he was brash enough to shock Japan's Nippon Steel by insisting on renegotiating a deal to provide a much-needed cash infusion. It demonstrated once again how much Ellison had become intertwined with his company. He would not let it fail, no matter what he had to do, what steps he had to take that would have been anathema to him in any other situation.

What was abundantly clear was that Ellison's method of developing executives by letting them grow into the job wasn't viable with a $1 billion company. Oracle had to move beyond its entrepreneurial roots and its ad hoc management style. This is a transition that has come hard to nearly every Silicon Valley icon, from Apple to Sun, Netscape to Yahoo! Suddenly, you're not the feisty upstart anymore, nipping at the heels of the large, entrenched behemoths like IBM. Now you've become the large, entrenched behemoth, with customers depending on you, shareholders suing you if you miscalculate, and analysts and journalists watching your every move. The 1990–1991 financial crisis compelled Ellison to look outside Oracle for the leadership of the future: an experienced chief financial officer, Jeff Henley, who was still with the company in 2003, and an executive with badly needed operational management skills, Ray Lane. These two, along with Ellison, were the troika that governed another amazingly successful decade, in which Oracle grew tenfold to $10 billion and became the world's second-largest software company after Microsoft.

FINDING A FINANCIAL GURU

For Oracle, the first order of business was to recruit an experienced chief financial officer. Jeff Walker, who had been handling the financials, was a software developer, responsible for the company's nascent applications business. Ellison's decision to put him in charge of finance demonstrated his total lack of respect for what he called "bean counters." Former director Arnold Silverman, one of only four men then on the board, was a venture capitalist investor in Oracle and has been chair of the American Electronics Association. As a current principal in Discovery Ventures, he sits on the boards of numerous other companies. "It was a terrible conflict of interest for Walker, being CFO and head of applications," says Silverman. Walker was both controlling a chunk of Oracle's revenue and responsible for certifying the results. Yet Ellison wasn't too sure he wanted to bring in a new CFO. "Larry's attitude at first was, this was a blip, we'll come back next quarter," says Silverman. But the board felt the company was in jeopardy, and Ellison came to the realization that this was serious. "I suspect by Larry's demeanor that, for the first time since he took all the risks to get Oracle going, he was scared," says Silverman. "I saw fear in his eyes. I'm sure he finally recognized he could lose the company." In this time frame, Silverman, worn out by all the infighting with Ellison and the publicity surrounding Oracle's problems, left the board. "You wake up one morning and find your name on class-action lawsuits," he says. "It's a shock and a wake-up call." Coupled with that, "Larry wasn't listening, and he was exacerbating the problems. Larry viewed me as disloyal for leaving. We didn't talk for a year."

Silverman's departure left just three members of Oracle's board: Ellison, Bob Miner, and investor Don Lucas. (In the past, Ellison has preferred small boards because they're easier to control. In the late 1980s and early 1990s, Oracle's board had only four members. In the latter part of the 1990s, as Oracle became bigger and more important, it gradually expanded its board.) Lucas also sat on the board of what would become Cadence Design Systems and decided to recruit its president and chief executive, Joe Costello, for Oracle's board. Ellison had been instrumental in helping Costello land the top post at Cadence and sat on its board. Costello came in just after "the shit hit the fan," he recalls. Lucas wanted Costello for his strong opinions and his ability to stand up to Ellison. "I was the designated outside board member," says Costello. "It was a reasonable bet that Larry could tolerate me on the board. Larry suffered no fools. He would cut you to ribbons if he didn't respect your intellect." Ellison, who has always dominated Oracle's board because of his commanding stock position, at best treats his board as a "necessary inconvenience," in Costello's words.

It didn't take long for Ellison and Costello to clash—over Ellison's defense of Walker as the CFO. "Oracle was about a $1 billion software company with a CFO who's never been a finance guy," says Costello. "Larry's theory is, it's just bean counting and pretty much any moron can do that work." Ellison thought that having Walker build the financial applications and use them meant the company would be "eating its own dog food." To Costello, the strategy was doubly flawed, the "worst of both worlds." Over Ellison's objections, the board started an executive search to replace Walker. The search came up with Jeff Henley, an avuncular straight arrow who had been CFO at Pacific Holding Company and Saga Corporation and also had experience at two technology companies, Memorex and Fairchild Camera and Instruments. Walker "knew he was out as CFO," recalls Silverman. "We had no credibility on the Street or with customers. Larry went down to a users conference and couldn't find a single user who was happy with the company." A professional CFO was absolutely critical to restoring confidence. And the newcomer also had to have strong ethics and a mind of his own. The board found all that in Henley.

But Ellison remained stubbornly unconvinced. "The CFO thing was a long, protracted battle," says Costello. Even Lucas, who had a father-son relationship with Ellison and put up with an awful lot from his protégé, was dismayed by Ellison's resistance. "Don, to his credit, kept at Larry," recalls Costello. It was also fortunate that Henley, besides being deep in financial experience, "had worked for a wild man before," says Costello. "Not just anybody would work for Larry Ellison. Jeff had enough of that personal risk taking in him that he got on with Larry when they met." Finally, Ellison agreed to hire Henley, but the battle wasn't over yet. Lucas and Costello had crafted an offer that Henley had tentatively accepted. When he saw the offer, Ellison cut the options in half, telling the board something like, "We're not going to pay so much to a goddamned bean counter," Costello remembers. For once, the board got tough with Ellison. "We told him, 'We found a fabulous guy. Now you're hanging up over the stock. This is a test of your leadership. If you don't have the judgment for this, maybe you can't run the company,'" Costello says. Ellison "saw in our eyes how serious we were and changed the offer back." Henley got his five hundred thousand Oracle stock options.

In the March 26, 1991, press release Oracle put out announcing Henley's appointment, Ellison naturally put the best face on the new hire: "Jeff Henley brings a wealth of experience in finance and business management to Oracle, and has a superb track record in instituting and managing the financial controls and systems needed by a billion-dollar company." He also added that Walker "will be able to devote all of his considerable talents and energies to the profitable growth of our applications business."

DEALING WITH THE JAPANESE

In addition to hiring a real CFO, Oracle was in severe need of cash. Because of the way it had structured its contracts—offering future products in exchange for current payments—the company was unable to collect on millions of dollars' worth of receivables when buyers couldn't get the products to work. Customers were growing wary of Oracle's promises, especially now that the company was in dire financial straits. Oracle's syndicate of thirteen banks suspended its credit line until the company could come up with collateral to match $170 million in outstanding loans. It put up its receivables as collateral but, since a chunk of those receivables was suspect, had to increase its reserve for uncollectibles by $42 million, leading to another restatement of quarterly financial results. Oracle had no possibility of doing any public financing with the share price battered so much. After studying all the financial information, Henley came to the board and, "with his sly smile told us, very calmly, 'This is a little more serious than I first thought,'" Costello recalls. Until Henley delved closely into the balance sheet, no one had really known how bad things were. He was blunt about the situation. "We had to have cash to save the company," says Costello.

Fortuitously, just before Henley's hire in early 1991, Lucas and Oracle's investment banker, Morgan Stanley, had contacted Nippon Steel in Japan to talk about a possible cash infusion in exchange for Oracle stock. "The theory was that a Japanese company would love to get significant ownership in Oracle and Oracle Japan," says Don Keller, an attorney with Venture Law Group who served as Oracle's external counsel during this time period. Henley picked up the negotiations. In fact, "on his first day of work, he went to a significant meeting on Nippon Steel," Keller says. By June 1991, Oracle and Nippon Steel appeared to have a deal. Oracle issued a press release announcing a letter of intent related to a $200 million investment by Nippon Steel, $100 million in preferred stock and $100 million in convertible debt. But then Ellison scuttled the deal, deciding that Oracle could get by on less cash and he didn't want to dilute the stock by that much. The Japanese company would have owned 49 percent of Oracle Japan and nearly 10 percent of Oracle itself. Henley, Keller, and the Morgan Stanley representative delivered the bad news to Nippon Steel. Not surprisingly, the initial reaction wasn't favorable, but Nippon Steel was reluctant to back out on the deal because "they'd spent a lot of time on it and believed there was a huge opportunity for Oracle in Japan. They did not want to lose that opportunity," Keller says. Finally, new terms were hammered out: an $80 million loan to Oracle and a 25 percent interest in Oracle Japan, which was just getting off the ground. The deal, on which negotiations had started in March, finally closed in December 1991.

Keller believes that Ellison made the right decision in junking the first deal. "It was a very courageous call because the company needed cash so badly," he says. Already, though, there were signs in late summer and early fall of 1991 that Oracle was on its way to a rebound. Henley was putting financial controls in place, including writing off the bad receivables, and the market for database software was poised to take off. "Being able to walk away from Nippon Steel meant we renegotiated the deal to avoid significant dilution for Oracle shareholders," Keller says. "What Larry did was risky, but in hindsight, it was a tremendous judgment call." Costello disagrees. Even though the company was on its way to a turnaround, it was bad business to change the terms after they were publicly announced, he maintains, and would hurt Oracle's ability to do deals in the future. "That kind of stuff comes around and bites you in the ass," he says. As he told Ellison, "It's just a crappy way to do business." But Ellison, who figured he knew the Japanese way of operating, retorted, "You don't know how to deal with the Japanese. They'd do it to me." Says Costello, "Larry wanted to screw 'em. He didn't care if they were the bank of last resort."

FINANCIAL CONTROLS

With cash in hand from Nippon Steel, Oracle could focus on putting its house in order for the long term. Two men led that effort: Jeff Henley on the financial side and Ray Lane on the sales and operations side. Henley, who was hired a little over a year before Lane, started cleaning up Oracle's balance sheet and putting a series of financial controls in place almost immediately. "We weren't managing our receivables properly; we had profitability and liquidity problems. . . . So we went back to basics," the CFO says. That included instituting standard payment terms for receivables and eliminating extended contracts, going over all the lines of business to see which were profitable and which weren't, and instituting financial benchmarks. Henley says that turnarounds are simply a matter of refocusing on fundamentals. "At Oracle, it was paying attention to detail and convincing management that the business wasn't just selling software—it was being a well managed company."[2]

Noosheen Hashemi worked closely with Henley for a year and a half, about the time it took to complete the turnaround. "Jeff was one of the best things to happen to Oracle," she says. "He was a world-class CFO, technically extremely competent and very politically savvy." While he would go into the boardroom and bang on the table and tell an overreaching executive, "No, you can't have a private plane," Henley would be so cordial to that same executive out in the hall that no one would know anything had happened. Henley was also incorruptible, according to everyone associated with him. "He was never into the glamour and schmoozing of being an officer in a big company," says Hashemi, unlike many Oracle executives who got hooked on opulent perks such as lavish offices, stock options, and first-class travel.

While Henley tackled the phone calls to customers to bring in the receivables, Hashemi was assigned to go through all the contracts to verify what had been shipped, what was real revenue, and what might have been double-billed or not billed properly. She says Henley's "fix-it-now" approach contrasted keenly with Walker's laid-back nonchalance. "A real CFO would have had smoke coming out of his ears" over Oracle's revenue-recognition practices, Hashemi maintains. "One of the biggest accomplishments that Jeff [Henley] and I did was to bring the closing process [on contracts] from six weeks to six days." They also established a new infrastructure to oversee contracts and license management. That is, once the contract was signed, customers were supposed to pay Oracle annual fees depending on how much they actually used the products. The company had been lax in tracking that. "We were leaving money on the table," says Hashemi.

Another Oracle executive at the time, Mike Hagan, says that Henley could be quite emphatic about what everyone needed to do. "I remember the meeting where I first saw Jeff," he says. "He was talking to the accounts receivable group. He got pretty angry and started pounding his fist on the table, even jumped up on the table, trying to get these people fired up." Henley told the group, "These people owe us money. This is unacceptable." Hagan says the people in the room were wide-eyed, because no one had cared enough before to get angry about such matters. Henley's ire is always well directed, Hagan says. "He gets emotional at the right time, and it's very effective." Henley went after the receivables, wrote off bad debt, and got rules in place about spending money. "I credit Jeff for helping to save the company," says Hagan. "It very well could have failed if they hadn't brought him in." Keller agrees: "Jeff Henley came in right at the time he was needed. He's a very levelheaded, sensible executive who's not limited to simply having a financial vision. He's been a stabilizing influence on the whole company."

INTERSECTING DESTINIES

The other "stabilizing influence" was about to join Oracle. A couple of years younger than Ellison, Ray Lane had a completely different upbringing. Born in 1946 on the leading edge of the baby boom, he grew up in the Pittsburgh area, where his solidly middle-class family had a long tradition in the steel industry. Lane was always interested in math and science and got good grades in school. When he was twelve, though, the doctors diagnosed rheumatic fever and he was forced to stay in bed for three months, then confined to limited activities for three years. "To this day, I don't believe I had it," he says. That event "took me off my game plan." An avid sportsman today in his midfifties, Lane obviously resents the time he lost to the putative illness. He largely missed out on junior high and high school sports, although he did a little track and played saxophone in the band. Meanwhile, Lane's father became the first one in the family to go to college; it took him fifteen years to get his degree attending night school at Carnegie Mellon University. "All during my growing-up years, he was working and studying," says Lane. He attributes his strong work ethic to his father, who died of cancer at forty-three, when Lane was a teenager. Although Lane's father didn't spend a lot of private time with him, he instilled in his son definite values. "He believed that the harder you work, the better you do and proved it by example," says Lane. "My mother would reinforce what she thought my father wanted." In the 1960s, as Lane was preparing for college, it was expected that he would follow his father into the technical field of engineering.

But for the first time in his life, Lane was determined to get away from home. He wound up at West Virginia University, which had just built a new engineering campus. "They wanted me; they made me feel like a king," he says. "It wasn't my parents' decision. I felt like I could make this decision myself." He did, and it worked out wonderfully. "It was the best choice I ever made." Lane changed his major from aeronautical engineering to math and became president of his fraternity and senior class, throwing off his childhood shyness. "I went from being introverted to extroverted." He also learned that he could depend on his own intuition about what he should do. "I came out of high school well grounded but not very understanding of life in general," he says. "My mother was very protective," especially after the bout with rheumatic fever. Lane never spent any time away from home until he went to college. In his sophomore year, he met his future wife, Donna, whom he married in their senior year. After college, he interviewed both with General Electric, which promised him a deferment from military service, and IBM, which said it didn't believe in that. Lane doesn't believe in taking the easy way out either. He chose to join IBM; got drafted and served two years (1969–1971) in Fort Riley, Kansas; then returned to Big Blue and eventually wound up as a consultant for Booz Allen Hamilton after a stint at Dallas-based Electronic Data Systems.

At Booz Allen, Lane stayed on in Dallas, where he moved up to leading the worldwide information technology practice. "I was one of the top half dozen people," he says. "I loved the work, the business they were in, the relationships I could build with clients." He and Donna had three daughters by the late 1970s, but Lane was never home. "I was traveling all the time," he says. For him, the next step was either to become head of Booz Allen or to remain a member of the inner leadership circle. He was pleased with what he'd accomplished at the consulting firm because, unlike most of the top echelon, Lane didn't have an MBA. Booz Allen clients often tried to hire Lane, but he was content. As a partner, "I figured I'd retire after twenty years with $10 or $15 million." Then, in early 1992, a headhunter sent Lane a letter asking him if he was interested in heading Oracle's consulting business, which then had only a few hundred people. "I got this letter and threw it away," says Lane. The headhunter persisted, convincing Lane that it was at least worth chatting with Ellison. "I figured the worst that could happen was I meet Larry and sell him some consulting services," he says.

Lane decided to talk with Robert Shaw, then a partner in Booz Allen's San Francisco office. Shaw, who would follow Lane to Oracle, felt that the company was getting ready to jump-start database sales again and had a promising new line of business in applications. So when Lane called him, Shaw urged him to make the move, although he wasn't sure how the chemistry between Lane and Ellison would work. "If you're going to do something, this is the time to go in. They don't have any serious management," he recalls telling Lane. Shaw "was the only one I talked to who was positive about going to Oracle," says Lane. "Everyone else—clients, associates—told me I was crazy. They said it's a place customers won't buy from and Larry is a madman." Lane, however, had a gut feeling that he wanted to do this. "I believe in talking to people to test my resolve, but I make my own decision," he says. He flew to California and met with Oracle executives and board members, learning that financially, the worst was over. However, Oracle now had to address its languishing sales; competitors, especially Sybase, were outstripping it in growth, and U.S. customers were leery of Oracle. He also had a three-hour "meeting of the minds" with Ellison. "It was a battle of IQs," says Lane. "I love to be challenged." Lane talked about the misuse of technology by CEOs and top management. Ellison described his vision of relational databases, open systems, and the paradigm of the day: client-server, in which desktop clients access software via a network connected to a powerful server. "We were feeding each other's egos," says Lane. "We clearly had complementary points of view: mine from management, his from technology."

Ellison, who always decides swiftly whether he likes someone or doesn't, pushed the board to hire Lane. It was the opposite situation from Henley, on whom the board had insisted. "Larry was the first guy on the board to meet Ray, and he became the champion of Ray," says Costello. "He really liked him, liked his style. To Larry's credit, he found Ray and he supported him to the hilt." Ellison offered Lane not the consulting job but the position of head of U.S. sales, replacing Mike Fields, who was on his painful way out. And Ellison tripled the number of options Lane would get from one hundred thousand to three hundred thousand. "He told me, 'You're the guy. I want you here,'" says Lane. The Booz Allen senior management track didn't seem quite so compelling anymore, contrasted with the chance to complete the turnaround at Oracle and to become wildly rich if he succeeded. "It was a different slope than Booz Allen," says Lane, rather understatedly. In his midforties, "I knew that either I did this or remained a consultant the rest of my life."

He took a trip to meet with the head of Booz Allen, Bill Stasior, at the headquarters in Bethesda, Maryland. "I thought it would be a very difficult meeting, that he would try to talk me out of it," says Lane. He was not sure that he didn't want to be talked out of it. As he rode the metro to the Booz Allen offices,

"I was still thinking I could turn back." But then, as he came up the steps from the metro station and looked down the street to orient himself, "I saw a huge red Oracle sign right next to Booz Allen," Lane recalls. The Oracle "sign" sealed his decision, and Stasior proved to be very supportive of the choice. "I found out later he called Larry, who didn't know him, and said, 'You just hired one of the best guys I have. Don't screw with him.'" In June 1992, Lane joined Oracle, just as the company released version 7 of its database. The combination of a great organizational sales manager coupled with a much-improved product to sell proved to be the catalyst that Oracle needed.

FIRST IMPRESSIONS

Like every executive who came to Oracle, Lane would have to prove that he could deal with the hard-charging, free-flowing culture and make an impact. When he came, Lane was a complete unknown, and there was some skepticism as to whether a consultant, who had previously worked at slow-moving dinosaurs IBM and EDS, could do much for Oracle. "Nobody knew what to think when Ray came," says former longtime Oracle executive Polly Sumner. Oracle's ugly brand of politics—pitting one executive against another—reared up almost immediately. Over in England, Geoff Squire, who had assumed he would be running both international and U.S. sales, was particularly skeptical of the newcomer. "The reason Ray was allowed in to head [U.S.] sales is because I was too loyal to Mike [Fields] for too long," Squire asserts. Ellison believed it was time to replace Fields and his evangelical approach to the U.S. sales job with someone new. "In the end, he got rid of Mike himself and took the U.S. away from me and gave it to Ray," says Squire. Before Lane came on board, he and Squire had an edgy first meeting. "It was obvious that Geoff knew Mike was in trouble and that I was interviewing for his job," says Lane. He and Squire discovered that Ellison had led each of them to believe the other would report to him. "I told Geoff that my decision would be based on reporting to Larry," says Lane. Squire had to be content with the rest of the world, while Lane ran the United States. Eventually, as they worked to revive Oracle, the two men grew to respect each other.

"Geoff had established a great presence," says Sumner. "Mike had never established a presence; he was too far off the pendulum of what Larry cared about. Ray had to establish his presence very quickly." Lane was able to do that, as we'll see in the next chapter, by quickly assembling a team of people like Sumner and other executives whom he could bounce ideas off and use as a task force to address the daunting challenge of imposing organization on the seemingly untamable force that was Oracle. Says another member of that team, Paul Hoffman, "The minute you meet someone like Ray, you feel a calm aura about the guy. He had a certain presence that right away made you feel like he was a great guy for this company. It was a stroke of genius on Larry's part to bring him in."

Not everyone thought so immediately, though. In his first day on the job, Lane drove down to a now-defunct theater on Silicon Valley's Highway 101 to moderate a panel of financial analysts commenting on the future of Oracle. A number of employees attended the event, which was telecast in New York and accompanied the official launch of Oracle's newest version of its database, release 7. At the time, says Lane, "I knew nothing about the product." He stumbled through the presentation, with all those employees watching. In the audience was Stephanie Herle, whom Lane would later marry. "He was walking around the stage, looking like he didn't know what he was doing," she recalls. "I was sure he wasn't going to last. It's a bad idea to bank your future on any executive at Oracle, because they don't last. It's certainly not a good career move." She was decidedly unimpressed with her first glimpse of Oracle's newest executive and sure she didn't want to work for him.

DECIPHERING ORACLE

Lane had brought an assistant with him from Booz Allen but realized quickly that he also needed someone knowledgeable about the ins and outs of Oracle politics if he were to succeed. The company was still hovering dangerously near bankruptcy, and the responsibility for revving up revenue rested squarely on Lane's shoulders. He had to get off to a fast start. He turned to Ellison's own longtime assistant, Jenny Overstreet, for advice. Overstreet, since retired, was tough, bright, and thoroughly capable of handling Ellison. "She ran Larry's life," says Lane. "I told Jenny I wanted somebody just like her." Overstreet approached Herle, then in her late twenties, who had joined Oracle in 1987 and was running the company's user group conferences. Herle had started at Oracle as an assistant, and Overstreet felt she had the qualities that Lane needed. "She'll piss people off, but she'll do what you want and get it done," Overstreet told Lane.

Lane interviewed several candidates for the position and decided to hire Herle on the strength of Overstreet's strong recommendation. But Herle, who is slender and attractive, with dark hair cut into a pageboy that sets off her high cheekbones and big brown eyes, wasn't too taken with the idea. Not only had she witnessed Lane's bumbling performance at the Oracle 7 launch, but she didn't want to return to being an assistant, having worked her way up into facilities and events management. "Jenny came to me and said, 'I know you don't want to be an administrative assistant, but we have this new guy. You should talk to him. He's real good, and you might like it.'" Herle was noncommittal. "When you don't have your [college] degree, you're very wary of getting typecast at Oracle," she says. Nonetheless, at Overstreet's insistence, she agreed to meet with Lane. Overstreet told her that no way would Lane make it at Oracle without her. Herle brushed off Lane after the job interview: "If you want to hire someone else, fine, I've got better things to do. I have no desire to make anybody coffee." What she preferred was to do more of the "thinking work," handling projects like the business practices research.

Lane reassured her that she was not signing on for a menial role. "I wanted someone just like Jenny, with an IQ off the charts, who could understand all of my job, not just do calendaring. Who could make decisions because she knew the way I thought," he says. Evidently, he managed to convey this idea of a partnership, not strictly an executive-assistant relationship, to Herle, for she accepted the job. Besides, one thing Herle had learned in her five years at Oracle was that nothing was ever permanent. "It was like a soap opera working there," she says. "You did one thing for six months, and then you could move on. They put in that [six-month requirement] because so many people were jumping in and out of positions." The only constant: "You had to be smart."

COMPLEMENTARY SKILLS

Visionary leaders like Ellison must have someone like Lane in their corner, and perhaps deep down, Ellison sensed that when he courted the consultant so persuasively. He does seem to have the instinctive ability to identify people, even those from completely disparate backgrounds, who can do what Oracle requres. Psychoanalyst Michael Maccoby identifies Lane as an inner-directed "obsessive" personality, in contrast to Ellison's extreme narcissism. Obsessives are self-reliant and conscientious, create and maintain order, and make the most effective operational managers, according to Maccoby. They're interested in resolving conflict and creating win-win situations. "Obsessives are also ruled by a strict conscience— they like to focus on continuous improvement at work because it fits in with their sense of moral improvement," he says. But obsessives may also lack the "vision, daring, and charisma" it takes to turn a good idea into a great one, the very role that Ellison filled so effectively. "The most productive [obsessives] are great mentors and team players."[3]

Indeed, thanks to Lane's familiarity with mature companies as a consultant and also as an IBM engineer, he was able to soften Oracle's rough edges, to help fill the gap between Ellison's vision and what it actually took to get there. "Ray was like Larry's consultant," says former Oracle executive Marc Benioff, who worked with both of them. "Larry was comfortable fully delegating sales and operations to Ray." With Henley's steady hand on the financial side, Lane overseeing day-to-day operations, and Ellison providing the driving insight into where Oracle should be going, the company had a triumvirate almost unmatched in the industry. At Microsoft, Bill Gates was also building an impressive team, with the likes of Steve Ballmer and Nathan Myhrvold (now departed), but there were few other software companies that could match Oracle in leadership firepower. As Betsy Burton, an analyst who follows Oracle for the Gartner Group, sums up: "Ray Lane was a foil for Ellison just as much as Ellison was for Lane. It was a yin and yang sort of interaction." Sumner, another departed veteran now running her own company, asserts that without Lane and Henley, "Oracle would be an average software company today. Jeff did the right things financially—he fixed the bottom line, and Ray fixed the top line."

6

REMAKING ORACLE

[GROWING UP RELUCTANTLY]

R ay Lane faced a daunting task overhauling Oracle's
business processes. For the first decade or so of its
growth, "Do whatever it takes" had been the mantra at
Oracle, leading to such excesses as paying commissions in
gold coins, offering site licenses that gave away too much, and
selling products that did not yet exist. Everyone knew that the
company was out of control financially—Jeff Henley was taking care of that—as well as operationally. From his years as a
Booz Allen consultant, Lane was ideally suited to come up
with a plan to remake a troubled company, but nonetheless
one with enormous talent and potential. Despite the political
battles at the top, Oracle had within its ranks a solid base of
dedicated salespeople, consultants, developers, and others
who truly believed in the company and its future. At events
like user group conferences, the Quota Clubs for salespeople,
and internal pep rallies, the fervor and passion came through.
It was Lane's challenge to rein in the bad behavior that was
getting Oracle into trouble—with customers, the government,
and partners—without extinguishing the flame.

After joining Oracle in mid-1992, Lane spent the first three
months "assessing everything," including the management
team, customer attitudes, distribution channels, lines of business, products, analyst opinions. "The second three months, I

changed what could be changed, did away with overlapping organizations, fired a number of people, changed business practices, especially with regard to the license contracts," he says. "We put together a team of smart, experienced people who went through each business practice and came up with the best." For example, Lane embraced with enthusiasm the Oracle penchant for lavish productions to kick off the new sales year; among the various roles he played at the events were characters from *2001: A Space Odyssey*, *Braveheart* (Lane's favorite movie), and *Apollo 13*. But he eliminated site licenses, which front-loaded all the revenue with no further payoff, and toned down commission practices that had encouraged salespeople to go for big deals and ignore the customers after that.

To form his team, Lane drew many people from his contacts with the consulting world, including Robert Shaw, the only one who had urged him to go to Oracle. After six months of concentrating internally, Lane could shift his focus outward, to competing with Sybase and regaining the market share that Oracle had lost in the previous three years. Despite internal conflict, "to the outside world, it looked like we picked one direction and marched in that direction [fixing the sales problems]," says Polly Sumner, an executive who worked closely with Lane. "Part of Ray's leadership style was always questioning how we could improve. He believed you have to be in the game and swing the bat. You were not crushed if you made a bad decision. You were crushed if you wouldn't change."

Ellison was enormously supportive in the early years of the partnership, Lane recalls. Even when he fired several of Ellison's protégés, including Executive Vice President Craig Conway (who now runs PeopleSoft), "Larry was behind me 100 percent," Lane says. In fact, he tested Ellison's resolve with some of those early personnel decisions, figuring that if the chief executive balked, he could always walk. "I decided to test my authority: if Larry gets in the way of some of the decisions I make in the first three months, I'll go back to Booz Allen." That didn't happen. Ellison and Lane developed a live-and-let-live kind of relationship that let each emphasize his own interests. For Ellison, that was products and, to a certain extent, marketing. For Lane, it was sales, consulting, customer service, and operations. He could make a difference, he says, because he came in at the top and had Ellison's backing. "I tried to help Oracle grow up," says Lane, by throwing in some of the traits of his former companies: IBM, EDS, and Booz Allen. "They all have seasoned management and play by the rules," he says. "Oracle was still the Wild, Wild West."

TAKING THE PULSE

One of Lane's first steps was hiring an outside consultant to listen to Oracle's customers and find out why the company was so disliked. Interestingly, he chose McKinsey & Company rather than his former firm, Booz Allen, or Bain & Company, the third consultant in the running. "I asked each one of them to come up with a proposal," says Lane. "McKinsey understood what I needed better." He adds, "I didn't want a strategy. I wanted facts." Lane was finding it difficult to help the sales team understand why Sybase was growing at 60 percent and Oracle's sales were practically flat. The rather demoralized sales force, having lost two leaders in the past couple of years, didn't know why it was falling behind. Salespeople are accustomed to dealing with the world through specific parameters, like their quota, the expected rate of increase, their commission, and so forth. Lane didn't need sweeping generalizations from consultants that suggested new strategic directions but rather nitty-gritty information that came from the customers themselves. "I had to be able to say to the sales team, 'Here's what your customers are saying and why they're not buying from you,'" Lane recalls. He had joined Oracle in June, and "by the end of August, I wanted an understanding of how we dealt with customers, a real, fact-based understanding."

The McKinsey study confirmed what Lane had already heard from his informal survey of clients at Booz Allen when the Oracle offer surfaced. Of the ten or fifteen clients with which he spoke before joining Oracle, "not a single one had a good thing to say about the company." Among the kinder comments were "unprofessional . . . arrogant . . . difficult to work with . . . full of themselves . . . den of thieves." McKinsey, in a far broader survey, had similar findings. People did business with Oracle because they liked the technology, not because they liked the company or its representatives. And even the technology had slipped in the last few years, falling behind Sybase's offering. The hard-driving salespeople were interested in making their quotas, not in making their customers happy. Many customers had been left high and dry without product or with product that didn't function properly. "What the customers painted a picture of was Oracle as a dysfunctional family of gifted children," says Lane. He used the devastating findings of the McKinsey report to kick off changes in sales business practices as well as to announce some terminations. Another Oracle executive, Marc Benioff, remembers Lane's characterizing Oracle's corporate crisis as exhibiting "the Dallas Cowboys syndrome." Even though Lane was a Dallas fan, he believed that the Cowboys were headed for a fall because of their arrogance and unwillingness to change. Oracle had to make changes to avoid falling further.

In September, his fourth month on the job, "I made my first set of decisions," says Lane, which included terminating several executives. "I'd let them know I was assessing them and how I was doing it. I talked to their peers and their customers. Immediately, the [jockeying] games began. But there were some obvious ones who had to go." Among them was Conway, who had held a number of important executive positions at Oracle in sales, marketing, and operations. "Craig was a smart guy very close to Larry," says Lane. The relationship was so close that Ellison had designated Conway and Fields, who had already been ousted, as the two senior sales executives in the United States before Lane came. But Lane was getting negative feedback from Conway's coworkers. Craig Ramsey, a former sales executive whom Larry had brought back from sabbatical to help in the turnaround, told Lane bluntly, "I can't work with Conway." In fact, Lane says, "No one on the sales force liked Conway." He turned out to be the "easiest one to fire," even though "he might have been the smartest guy on the management team." Problem was, Conway was a control freak who alienated people. Lane notes, "At some point, you decide that no matter how good a person is, he's got to go. He doesn't fit in. That's how I felt about Craig Conway." Conway's version is that it was obvious to him that Oracle U.S.A. "was going to be Ray's show," so when Lane asked him to leave the company, he responded, "I think I should too."[1] Lane gave Conway a severance package and says their relationship remains cordial. After Conway took over PeopleSoft, he and Lane exchanged E-mails a few times on prospective hires.

Two other sales executives agree that Conway, who was very detail-oriented and tended to micromanage people, kept clashing with the freewheeling Oracle sales staff. Benioff worked for Conway when the latter was running telesales. One day, says Benioff, he showed up around 9:20 A.M. "Conway came running up the stairs telling me, 'Not 9:01, not 9:02, but 9 A.M. That's when I want you in every day.'" Ramsey adds that Conway treated people in a very demeaning way. In one phone conversation, "he accused me of lying to him and not doing what he told me. I told him that if he ever talked to me that way again, we don't even need to say goodbye. I'm gone." Conway, says Ramsey, "was very bright but totally demotivating for salespeople. If he said tie your shoelace, you'd have to do it the way he wanted." Consequently, the top salespeople would all jockey to find another boss than Conway, leaving him with new recruits and less-than-stellar performers in many cases. Terminating Conway had an unexpected benefit for Lane. "People had discounted me as a force at Oracle," he says, because he came from the consulting world, which was generally held in low regard by salespeople used to doing what they pleased. "When I fired Conway, that ended." (At PeopleSoft, Conway's toughness and attention to detail proved to be just the jolt in the arm that company needed. But his testy relationship with Ellison worsened when the Oracle CEO tried to buy PeopleSoft. See Chapter 11.)

CHECKS AND BALANCES

Lane picked a team of about two dozen executives in sales, marketing, and distribution to act as a task force and come up with recommendations on restructuring. "I wanted them to look at the way we operate, how we sell, how we related to customers, and how we provide customer service." Lane's predecessor, Mike Fields, had been trying to fix some of the problems. It was up to Lane to finish the job. "I went through a soup-to-nuts review of our processes," says Lane. For three to four months, his task force studied the company and came up with about thirty recommendations on how sales, product presentation, and customer service should be restructured. One of the early steps was to recentralize sales under Lane and a small team of executives who reported to him, restoring accountability to what had been a lone-gunman type of organization.

One key discussion revolved around whether Oracle should continue to offer site licenses, which allowed customers to get upgrades in perpetuity for however many people within their company used the software. "It was an 'all you can eat' contract," Lane says. He decided to switch to user-based pricing, which meant that if the number of people using the software went up within a company, that customer had to buy additional licenses. The switch did two important things, he says. "It guaranteed more long-term revenue from the customer, and consequently, there was more incentive to service that customer." Similarly, Lane eliminated so-called box pricing, in which Oracle would sell its product based on the number of "boxes"—that is, computers—where it would reside, with no limit on the numbers of users who accessed those computers.

Mike Hagan, who had worked extensively on Oracle's contracts, became the de facto business practices manager under

Fields and then Lane. "I was a conduit between legal and the sales force," he says. "We were trying to teach the sales force how to do business where the revenue was recognizable by the SEC [Securities and Exchange Commission]." He agrees with Lane that the site licenses had to be revised. With such a license, "you could take ownership of the software at any time in the future and you didn't have to pay support until you started using it." Because customers were getting products without having to pay for support until they actually started using the software, which could be years away, "we were giving away free rights," says Hagan. Under the revision, "if you're buying the software now, you pay support now. People weren't going to pay a service contract for something they weren't using. It was self-regulating." Lane also stopped Oracle's practice of "stuffing the channel"—that is, recognizing as revenue technology that was sold to a business partner that would then resell to end users over a period of several years. Partners were smaller companies, often referred to as value-added resellers, who specialized in certain areas such as government and acted as middlemen between Oracle and its customers. A business partner can add customization to make the product attractive to a specific sector, such as grant-writing software for government buyers, and take on the often arduous task of servicing that software for small and midsize customers. These partners, which exist for every major software vendor, are vital both for software vendors, who don't want to be bothered with small customers, and for customers, who might not have much clout with Oracle itself but would with a smaller business partner.

THE BUCK STARTS HERE

Oracle had always paid big bucks to its salespeople, accelerating the commissions sharply for those who exceeded their quotas. Hagan explains that a salesperson who made 100 percent of quota would get the base salary—say, $75,000. But for hitting a number 20 percent or 40 percent above that, the compensation would double or triple, to $150,000 or $225,000. "As you started to hit these accelerators, you really moved up," he says. The compensation practices at Oracle were based on a big hunter–like theory. "You bring back a squirrel, you get paid for a squirrel. You bring back a moose, you get paid for a moose. The bigger hit you bring back, the more you get paid."

Where the problem came was in setting the quotas, which were based on either geographic or vertical territories assigned to the sales force. When Lane came on board, nearly all the salespeople had the same quota, regardless of what companies happened to fall into their territory. "Whether you had General Motors or a bunch of little companies, you had the same $4 million quota," Lane says. That led to extreme gamesmanship among the sales force over who got the territories with large accounts. "The games started the year before you got your quota," says Lane. "You'd try to negotiate for the right territory," either one with big continuing customers or someplace Oracle hadn't been. "Then you go sell everything in the price book on one or two deals at a big discount and move on to another territory." That meant a salesperson could do a couple of deals with clients "willing to buy everything in the price book for a 90 percent discount. So they've sold $20 million and end up making a million." But the next salesperson who takes over the territory is screwed, because the big customers will never buy again.

Lane changed the system to variable quotas, based on what could be expected from a particular territory. "If you've got GM, you get a $10 million or $20 million quota. If you've got a smaller customer, you get a lower quota." After he was done with his restructuring, quotas still averaged $4 million, but the range was from $2.5 million up to $20 million. He also raised the total compensation and, above 100 percent of quota, put in place a scaled leverage model. "If you sold 10 percent [over quota], you might make 10 percent. If you sold 20 percent, you might make 30 percent over your base compensation," he says, still good numbers but not quite as sharply accelerated as previously. "The key is to set the quotas correctly," he says. "That takes out a lot of the gamesmanship." Lane estimates that a good compensation plan lets salespeople make 50 to 60 percent in base salary, the rest in commissions and bonuses.

Lane not only overhauled sales compensation, he revised distribution. Among the tenets: each product that Oracle sold—database, applications, tools, consulting, and support—had to have its own distribution strategy, and the leaders had to be accountable for growth of that product relative to its market. Second, the way to gain market share was to leverage Oracle's market-leading database by enlisting more companies to support it. Among these were software companies that sold applications running on the Oracle database, including Siebel Systems, PeopleSoft, SAP, and a host of smaller firms. (Because it also had an applications business, Oracle both competed and cooperated with many of these companies.) Oracle also wanted to establish better relationships with consulting firms and system integrators like EDS that put together hardware and software packages for their customers. And Oracle wanted hardware vendors, such as Sun Microsystems, to track how much of their sales of servers or workstations were sold as a package deal with Oracle software. Third, the compensation and selling structure would be realigned around account managers and territorial managers. Large accounts would be handled by account managers in direct sales, and geographical territories would be handled by multiple channels, including indirect sales done through business partners or system integrators.

CUSTOMER VALUES

The practical aspects of reorganizing Oracle represented one important step for Lane. Another, more subtle step was communicating to the salespeople that the underlying values had changed. It was time, as he puts it, "to stop beating up on customers." Benioff remembers a corporate managers meeting at which Lane talked about the old versus new Oracle. The old

Oracle was lack of trust and loyalty among coworkers. Instead of working for the good of the organization and its customers, each employee was strictly concerned with his or her own best interest. In the case of salespeople, that meant bringing in as much license revenue to earn the highest commission possible. Lane characterized the old Oracle as a company of "revenue junkies," with the sales force focused on closing the deal rather than servicing the customer. "We oversold, underdelivered, and did it in an environment without ethical boundaries," Benioff acknowledges. The values of the organization revolved solely around market share and revenue rather than making customers happy.

The new Oracle would encourage long-term relationships with customers, as exemplified in the overhauled pricing structure that emphasized not just license but also maintenance revenue. "Ray believed that both parties should win in a deal, and the customer relationship should continue even after the deal is made," Benioff says. So he emphasized cooperation and teamwork. "There is no *I* in *team*" became a common saying among senior managers who reported to Lane. The new Oracle endorsed such ideas as quality, trust, relationships, stability, and support. Leading-edge technology remained an important priority, but Lane also emphasized people and integrity. Raman Batra, a technology manager for Oracle customer Legerity Incorporated, remembers E-mailing Lane about a problem and getting an extended response. "Ray kept the thread going himself until we solved it," says Batra. "He didn't turn it over to a subordinate." Karen Brownfield, former president of the Oracle Applications User Group, says that Lane brought credibility to Oracle customers beyond information technology specialists. "Chief financial officers and accountants thought of Larry as a brash upstart," she recalls. "Ray Lane understood that the application customer was going to be the core of the business for future growth. . . . Ray had the posture to stand up to Larry, to push his idea of accountability to the customer throughout the organization."

The notion of customer accountability was enhanced in

October 1993, when Lane, now president of the entire company, established customer service as a single organization. He brought in Randy Baker, who'd had experience at Tandem and IBM, to run it. Previously, customers had to depend on the geographic sales office where they were located for support, which meant that a problem might have been solved in France but no one else knew about it. "The U.S. had its own support organization, and each of the various countries [where Oracle operated] did its own support," says Lane, "so we had something like forty support organizations." By consolidating customer service under one accountable executive, he sought to give customers a more dependable source of support, one that didn't depend on license revenue as an incentive. Under Oracle's previous pricing scheme, support would be priced around 15 percent of license revenue, "but if you were selling at deep discounts, the service would be at a deep discount, too," says Lane. That meant salespeople did not have much incentive to sell good support, because maintenance revenue was low. In addition, large customers, which bought in big volumes and got the biggest discounts, got a corresponding break on customer support fees. "Small customers ended up paying a disproportionate share," says Lane. He told Baker to price customer support on a stand-alone basis. "Sales hated that because support became a major obstacle to selling licenses," he says. "They'd negotiate a price, and then Randy would come in to negotiate a support agreement." Lane believes that Baker, by providing solid customer support for the first time, helped to rescue Oracle's struggling applications business and perhaps the company itself. "Randy did two things," Lane says. "He made sure the service organization kept our customers in the game, and he did it profitably."

Baker's reward was to be purged. In early 2000, he was demoted and then fired by Oracle, shortly before Lane himself left. In May of that year, Baker filed a wrongful-termination suit against Oracle, which was resolved in 2002 with neither side disclosing the terms. (On the advice of his attorneys, he declined to be interviewed for this book.) His lawsuit, filed in San Francisco County Superior Court, sought $18.5 million in lost compensation, primarily stock options, and damages for age discrimination and wrongful termination. It alleged that Ellison made "derogatory comments" to Baker about his age and the age of Oracle managers in general. In addition, Baker had his health insurance canceled and was told that his unvested stock options, worth about $16 million, would be "null and void," according to the lawsuit.[2] Ellison believed that Baker was overpaid for running customer service, Lane recalls. Baker's base compensation was $650,000, but one year he made $900,000 with bonuses. "I gave him the opportunity to create real services, to sell a real product, and rewarded him," says Lane. "Larry flipped out because he had lost sight of what the head of worldwide services is doing. Larry thought he's supposed to answer the phone and respond to complaints. But Randy had half a dozen services that he was selling."

FASHIONING A GIANT

Until Lane arrived, Oracle Consulting had been a rather sleepy operation, with a couple of hundred people who would help clients do database "tuning" and reformulate business processes to accommodate the database. Oracle had several, often overlapping, lines of business, which made the company's organization a confusing one. There were direct sales of its database and applications, handled by the internal sales force; indirect sales of the same products through business partners and system integrators; customer service, which handled maintenance on product contracts; and consulting, which helped customers build business processes around Oracle products. The consulting business and the internal sales force often competed with the indirect sales partners, and Lane never was successful in eliminating these kinds of conflicts. Of course, they exist at any company that decides to do more than just sell products directly. Microsoft, for one, is also notorious for competing with its business partners.

Lane tried to clarify the operations by naming direct

reports to run each one. At the same time as he tapped Randy Baker to run customer service, Lane put Robert Shaw, who had joined Oracle from Booz Allen's San Francisco office, in charge of consulting. Says Lane, "Oracle was the first pure software company to have a major consulting organization. I let Robert grow it as fast as he wanted to." It was a controversial move for Oracle to expand so dramatically in consulting. SAP, the German company that is the market leader in enterprise applications, had built partnerships with Andersen Consulting (now Accenture) to work with companies in restructuring after they bought SAP applications. In other words, Accenture would advise SAP customers on how best to deploy the software and what changes to make in their business to accommodate it. That avoided a conflict-of-interest problem that would dog Oracle, which provided its own consulting. The major consulting firms and system integrators such as EDS don't sell software themselves. Instead, they partner with the software vendors on installation and implementation of products that require complex restructuring, as enterprise applications generally do. The consultants and integrators thus can steer business toward selected software vendors but are reluctant to do so with a vendor that competes with them, like Oracle. "We still thought it was the right move to set this up ourselves as long as the [consulting] market was growing as fast as it was," says Lane. But he admits that in building up consulting, "we created a channel conflict with our partners."

Shaw says that before he and Lane came aboard, Oracle had not considered how to make money from consulting. It was an afterthought, thrown at customers who needed outside help in setting up applications. "In those days, if you worked at a [customer] project more than three or four days, there was something wrong with you," Shaw says. The two hundred people in Oracle Consulting "were a loose confederation with no particular direction." In Shaw's job interview, Ellison asked if consulting could be a billion-dollar business, and Shaw assured him it could. "I was hired to come in and take over the consulting organization, fix and grow it, make it profitable," he says. "Up until then, it had been a necessary liability to get the products to work." By the time he left, six years later, Oracle Consulting was more than seventeen thousand people, bringing in $2.5 billion in revenue and contributing 20 percent to Oracle's net.

How did he do it? "First, you had to build a set of service lines in lockstep with what the market wanted rather than people installing projects," says Shaw. What customers needed wasn't so much expertise in Oracle technology as someone who understood how to restructure, say, financial or manufacturing processes. "We brought in financial managers who understand the total cost of business," he says. Shaw also set up "boot camps" to quickly train "thousands of people in the way we do things." The advantage for customers was that, instead of trying to figure out whether they had to call the vendor or the system integrator/consultant, "there was a single point of accountability," says Shaw. "There was no finger-pointing; we couldn't say someone else is responsible," since Oracle was selling both the technology and the consulting that went with it. "The customers liked it—since it said Oracle on our paycheck, we had to deliver," he adds. "We had ways to access the development teams to solve problems." However, he acknowledges, "we all knew this wasn't a channel-friendly approach." Oracle continually had to weigh the potential loss of business from partners like system integrators versus the benefits of having its own consulting business. Since profit margins on product sales are higher than on consulting, it wouldn't seem to make a lot of sense for Oracle to build such a major business in the latter. On the other hand, when product sales began to sag in a soft economy, consulting was another leg for the company to stand on. It was a continual balancing act that sometimes got off-kilter in one line of business or another.

Another conflict came with Oracle's own sales force, which had cultivated relationships with the consulting firms and system integrators to bring in business. Shaw and Lane recognized that the sales force had to be rewarded for selling consulting as well as product licenses. Eventually, says Shaw, in dollar value, salespeople wound up with a larger quota for consulting than for license revenue: something like three dollars to five dollars in consulting fees for every dollar in license sales. Thanks to multiyear contracts, "it became an annuity for the salesperson." This was another step in transforming Oracle's old "run and shoot" model of selling products and dropping the customer cold. "The sales force incentive systems had to start recognizing that we had moved out of pure technology into solutions," says Shaw. "In consulting, you couldn't recognize the revenue until you performed the work." While salespeople were at first resistant to the change, fearful that it would slow closing on deals, eventually they recognized the value of selling consulting along with a product license. "SAP couldn't deliver our message—we were a one-stop shop with rapid implementation by our own consulting team," says Shaw. "No one could match that."

Barry Ariko, whom Lane tapped in 1994 to run sales in the Americas, believes consulting was a good idea carried too far. "Oracle went from selling product to solving problems," he says, which was a much-needed move. But as he sees it, Shaw became infected with Oracle machismo and "wanted to build the biggest, baddest consulting firm around." That generated animosity with the sales force. "Oracle created such an aggressive consulting business, it wound up really hurting our relationship with other consulting companies who might have brought us business," says Ariko. Consulting was not balanced with sales from an overall business perspective, he maintains. "Someone had to stand back and say, 'On this deal, I'm willing to give up some consulting revenue or licensing revenue to get the deal.'" It was Lane who wound up making those decisions, but "you can't be running to the president on every deal," says Ariko. Consequently, conflict went on for years about how much internal consulting should grow versus product licensing. "Selling software is a more lucrative business," he says. "You don't want five times as much consulting revenue as product revenue." While the consulting business helped turn Oracle around, its growth had to be checked, Ariko says, to avoid a possible death spiral. If other consultants "are afraid to bring you in, there's less demand for your underlying technology. If your technology sales diminish, then the foundation of your consulting business starts going away. You can go off a cliff."

Today, in Lane's absence, Oracle continues to have the same internal conflicts, exacerbated because there's no strong operations manager at the top. Ellison, typically, is fixated on an overriding idea: that customers should buy the complete package from Oracle and be so thrilled with the technology that they don't change it—in other words, they don't customize, a very common practice among software users. "Larry has mentioned that over and over again: Do not customize," says customer Batra. "But you always have situations where your business model is unique. There's always 10 percent which is an exception. We had to customize." In contrast to its competitors, Oracle likes to sell customers a package deal: database, applications, support, and consulting, all under its own imprint. No one else does it quite that way. IBM, for example, sells a database and consulting but relies on partners to sell applications. SAP and PeopleSoft have no database of their own, so they'll resell Oracle or a competitor underneath their applications. And they usually partner, SAP with Accenture and PeopleSoft with Ernst & Young, on consulting. The consultants and system integrators don't sell software, but they advise customers on how to get disparate products to work together. Oracle's one-stop shopping works well when customers trust one company to provide everything from the database to consulting but creates difficulties for any customer that wants to mix and match. So Oracle's history of dissing customers (see Chapter 9) hurts it when the message is, count on us for everything.

ALLIANCES, ALLIANCES

Oracle had other channel partners besides the system integrators and consulting firms. These were software companies that created specialized applications on top of the Oracle database, ranging in size from SAP to very tiny companies that did just one or two narrow applications for a specialized field. These partners, also known as value-added resellers (VARs), could steer millions of dollars' worth of business to Oracle, but as usual, the latter couldn't quite decide how to treat them. For one thing, some of the application VARs, such as SAP and PeopleSoft, competed with Oracle in its other major line of business. For another, it was more lucrative for the sales force to sell products directly rather than take indirect deals through the VARs, so Oracle would both encourage and discourage its partners, depending on the mood of the salespeople. Lane created a specific organization, called Worldwide Alliances, to foster relationships with VARs and enlisted Polly Sumner, who'd had experience in both direct and indirect sales, to run it. "This was the first time we were serious about VARs," she says. "But there was still an inherent competition," because many of the VARs also created software for other companies' databases. "In many cases, it was the customer who made the buy decision, influenced by the VAR. VARs were totally in control of these sales." (It was a VAR that handled the controversial $95 million deal between the state of California and Oracle, as detailed in Chapter 12.)

Even with the Alliances program, Oracle had a strained relationship with its channel partners. Ned Miller was an Oracle VAR for nine years, from late 1991 to 2000, as vice president and cofounder of DLT Solutions in Herndon, Virginia, which sold to government entities. "If Oracle couldn't find a way to get the business from a customer, they would look to the channel [that is, the VARs] to try to fill in the gaps," Miller remembers. As a VAR, DLT had to be very conscious of when Oracle was closing a quarter and do its best to bring in all the deals for the period. This often meant that the VAR became a temporary "bank" enabling the customer to buy Oracle products. In the late 1990s, DLT was working on a deal with the Washington Metro Area Transit Authority. Oracle wanted the $1.6 million deal to close by the end of May, its fiscal year, although the Transit Authority wasn't quite ready. DLT stepped in and provided the interim financing: $1.6 million plus $220,000 for maintenance. "We got screwed on the $220,000 for maintenance," says Miller, since the Transit Authority wasn't going to pay for support on a product it hadn't yet taken delivery on, and Oracle wouldn't make up the difference. "There's an example of how pleasant it is doing Oracle a favor," he notes. "But if we hadn't gone along, we would have lost business with Oracle." He compares being an Oracle channel partner to being on cocaine: once you're hooked, you've got to stay in because you can't rebuild the business from scratch.

Sumner says she tried to assuage some of the abuses by requiring an actual company order before booking a sale from a VAR. "We were very proactive about making sure we had rigorous business practices where [the VAR] had to show us proof the company ordered the product," she says. Lane adds that at one point, he encouraged the sales reps to cooperate with VARs by changing the commission structure. "For a while, I paid 1.5 times the commission if you sold it through an alliance partner," he says. Typically, the Oracle salespeople found a way to game the system. "I had to stop the program because even if they sold it themselves, they went through an alliance partner to boost their commission," Lane remembers. Nonetheless, he was committed to the Alliances effort. He estimates that in the mid- to late 1990s, about 25 percent of Oracle's business in the United States, 50 percent in the United Kingdom, and 90 percent in Japan were sold through alliances. As a result of his efforts, "alliance structures are now embedded in each [sales] organization."

INTERNATIONAL COHERENCE

When Lane became president of worldwide operations, he faced another challenge: what to do with the mini-Oracles that existed within the forty or so countries where Oracle did business. Geoff Squire, who departed in 1993, had built up international. Under his direction, each country became a small kingdom with its own consulting, sales, customer service, even financial operation (although the latter had already been consolidated under Jeff Henley). Lane wanted to install the business practices he was using in the United States overseas, but that required turning Oracle into a truly global organization.

In March 1994, Lane convened what was supposed to be a two-day meeting of his direct reports in Maastricht, the Netherlands, including U.S. and European sales managers. "I announced we were there to figure out a new business model for Oracle to operate as a global business," he says. The gauntlet thrown, the meeting turned into a marathon that lasted four days, with sessions extending far into the nights. "Nobody slept. We finally broke up on Sunday morning, and people went back to their rooms and collapsed," says Lane. "We had moments where we were throwing things at each other—little toy balls." The outcome was that consulting, support, and alliances all became global businesses, run, respectively, by Shaw, Baker, and Sumner. The country managers and regional leaders remained responsible only for direct sales. "This was implemented over the next fiscal year, and I wound up terminating most of the country managers and regional leaders," Lane says. "They refused to operate that way." These executives were so used to running their own show, they couldn't go back to taking orders from someone else. Meanwhile, Lane and Ellison selected Pier Carlo Falotti, who had previously run database competitor ASK/Ingres, to head Oracle Europe. (Falotti, ousted from Oracle in 2000, is involved in dueling lawsuits with the company over stock options he claims he was due. Like Baker, he declined to be interviewed on the advice of attorneys.)

One person who left amid the international restructuring was Ad Nederlof, a country manager for the Netherlands who became a regional leader for the Nordic countries. He admits he disagreed vehemently with Lane's changes. "My region was doing extremely well, the fastest growth in Europe," he says. "I had a great team. All of a sudden, it was all put aside."

Within his area, Nederlof was responsible for everything from support to training. "Ray took it all away except license sales. I had to go to three other managers to do a special deal." Before that, Nederlof had been free to structure deals just about any way he could. " 'Act now and apologize later' was our motto," he says. "I would cut a deal with IKEA and worry about the permission afterward." Lane's new structure was much more complex, with defined lines of business reporting to U.S.-based global managers, and the country manager/ regional leader overlying that. "There were all these points of friction," Nederlof complains. In an impassioned phone call with Lane, he argued that an overarching sales model wouldn't work in Europe. When Lane stood firm, Nederlof quit. He still admires Lane for what he accomplished in terms of improving customer relations and humanizing Oracle. "No one leaves Oracle without conflict," Nederlof says. "I disagreed with Ray, and I lost my position."

IDEAS IN DEVELOPMENT

Lane's oversight of Oracle's sales operations allowed Ellison to focus on his passion: product development. No doubt the CEO was relieved that Lane and Henley were dealing with the stuff he didn't care much about. Ellison's bias toward development became more apparent in the early 1990s, because he felt the sales force had let him down. "In hard times, you have to protect R&D," says Peter Relan, a vice president within Oracle development during the mid-1990s. "You lay off sales and marketing people but not engineers." Ellison always felt as if he was running development, and Lane never had a real counterpart on the product side, except possibly for Gary Bloom. Generally, development at Oracle has been structured as a series of vertical groups, for applications, database, tools, and so forth, each headed by a senior vice president reporting to Ellison, but there was never anyone horizontally over all of development except the CEO himself. Lane says that Ellison's interest in running Oracle waxes and wans, and he's often content to leave the entire company in other people's hands. For example, Ellison was gone for several months during the America's Cup sailing races, which took place off New Zealand in late 2002 and early 2003. This has not been a negative when there was a strong second-in-command to provide visible leadership, such as Lane, but leaves a void when that is no longer the case. Even when he's present, Ellison pays more attention to matters like product development and marketing, which intrigue him, and little to operations and finance, which don't.

The group SVPs and others involved in product development would meet weekly in the product development management committee (PDMC), which became *the* forum for Ellison. "The PDMC started off with Bob Miner, Larry, and a bunch of other people whom Larry liked," recalls Nimish Mehta, a longtime Oracle developer who was a member of the committee through most of the 1990s. At first, the focus was on specific products and how to improve them. "Miner was a very good influence," says Mehta. "He was sensible and not given to extremes." Miner was also laid-back and informal, propping his feet on the desk during the discussions and allowing other people the same privilege. As Miner's role diminished, Ellison subsumed the committee as the testing ground for his grandiose ideas, some of which were brilliant, like moving applications to the Internet (see Chapter 8), and some of which were merely wild. In contrast to the executive committee, which was oriented to financial and operational matters, "the PDMC was where Larry was comfortable," says Mehta. "Without a doubt, he enjoyed it more [than the EC]." Product-related issues, such as adding features or doing upgrades, might be on the agenda, but Ellison could shove everything aside if he wanted. "Larry got more and more autocratic with the PDMC," says Mehta. "Other people were in the room, but they were all incidental. Only what Larry thought was important. The whole discussion would center around him and his ideas." Adds Relan—who, though not a formal member of the PDMC, made regular presentations—

"The PDMC was like Larry's court. The EC was serious business: revenue, are we going to make our numbers, are we going to close this $100 million contract? The PDMC had much more of a 'house of Larry' flavor. He dominated that meeting. If he wanted to spend half an hour talking about the villainy of Bill Gates, he would."

Ellison would often stroll into the PDMC meeting, which seldom started at its prescribed time of 2:00 P.M., every Monday, and launch forth upon his latest flight of fancy. At one meeting, Mehta remembers, Ellison came in and announced, "Cisco is one of the most overvalued companies on earth. In three to five years, Cisco will be worth nothing." This was Cisco Systems, the networking king, which at one time was the world's most valuable company in terms of market cap. Ellison's argument was that networks with routers were going the way of wired telecommunications. Just as developing countries such as China and India embraced cellular rather than wired telephone, wireless networks were the future for data transmission as well. "The whole world will go wireless," Ellison proclaimed. At another meeting, in about 1997, Ellison digressed into an area of personal interest: pharmaceuticals. The whole notion of testing drugs on the same populations makes no sense, Ellison maintained. "To try to give one drug to all humans is crazy." He told Mehta, "You, Nimish, born in India, are genetically different than I am. There should be personalized drugs for each of us." Here, Ellison was prescient. With the mapping of the human genome, pharmaceutical researchers today are talking seriously about designing drugs to fit different genetic profiles. Ellison's ideas always have a certain rationality at their core, even when he's pushing them to the extreme edge. Says Mehta, "Larry would start a lot of discussions by making an outrageous claim." Then he would wait for the response. "You can argue whether any of this [Ellison's predictions] will ever happen, but it makes you think," says Mehta. "The PDMC was the first place he'd lob these ideas and wait for pushback." Ellison always forces people to think through ideas to their ultimate possibilities. This can be exhausting, but it's also exhilarating and challenging. In all my interviews with Oracle employees and managers, not one ever complained about being bored.

Still, down-to-earth product issues did get attention at the PDMC. Oracle's reputation has always been based on its technical achievements, such as being the first to sell a relational database. Customers put up with a lot of grief because they believed that, ultimately, they would be able to make Oracle's technology work to their benefit. But in the early 1990s, customers had lost that belief. No matter how much restructuring Lane was doing on the operations side, if the development side didn't fix the problems with Oracle's database, the company would sink. It had had two disastrous product releases in a row, Oracle 5 and Oracle 6, both of which corrupted customers' own data. There was a standing joke that, as with the Roach Motel, data went in (the Oracle database) and did not come out. In the early 1990s, the PDMC discussion revolved around how to rebound with the next release, Oracle 7. "Larry would be right in the middle of the discussion, driving it," says Mehta. "He was very technically savvy and quite capable of making decisions on the database side." Ellison's contribution was key because he would decide how to make the requisite trade-offs between product quality, features, and release date. Says Mehta, "It's hard to have all three"—that is, a high-quality product with few bugs and the latest features— and make the deadline. "Larry would trade off quality in favor of features and time," he adds. Oracle customers might have to put up with patching bugs, but they would get the latest technology.

A WORKING PARTNERSHIP

The symbiosis of Lane and Ellison's different approaches to governing Oracle is evident in their successful partnership in the early to mid-1990s. Ellison was the product visionary and driver, leading the development team in getting out a much-needed competitive offering. Meanwhile, Lane was fixing the machinery for selling that offering. Neither could have done it without the other. For all the restructuring and new controls and processes that Lane was installing on the operations side of Oracle, he acknowledges they would have been useless without a "sellable product." The other half of the Oracle rebound was due to the release of Oracle 7, which started shipping in December 1992. "Oracle 7 allowed the new sales force to compete against Sybase," says Lane. "Oracle 7 was a big piece of the turnaround, but so was the reorganization of the sales force. I was fortunate that I had Oracle 7 coming on-line."

Ellison himself lauded Lane's hard work in making a series of tough decisions that transformed Oracle into a more dependable, mature company. In an extraordinary letter sent to Lane on July 6, 1994 (see "A Touching Letter," below, for more of the text), Ellison wrote, ". . . you have put the eagerness back into the eyes of a team turned miserable by cynicism and exhaustion. . . . Oracle is on a path toward real greatness . . . due in no small part to your efforts." Too bad that Lane and Ellison's era of good feelings would all too soon come to an end, and so would Oracle's path toward real greatness.

A TOUCHING LETTER

Following are excerpts from the text of a letter that Larry Ellison sent to Ray Lane on July 6, 1994, after he had been on the job for about two years:

Two years ago you set to your task head down and sleeves up, with an awesome single-mindedness of purpose, unencumbered by the historical 'wisdom' that we did not yet fully realize we had outgrown. . . . Your outsider's perspective made it possible for you to . . . assert that problems which had for years enmired our progress were solvable. For you and your teams, I know the work was back-breaking, organization convulsing, creatively challenging, and often toll-taking emotionally. To my eyes, however, the return of Oracle U.S.A. to health was sure, swift, and amazing. I feel that you have put the eagerness back into the eyes of a team turned miserable by cynicism and exhaustion. . . .

Your success this past year in undertaking the mammoth task of globalizing our many and diverse companies around the world while at the same time marshaling these groups toward—and reaching—the heart-palpitating $2 billion mark in the face of depressed economies and organizational challenges was as marvelous as it was needed.

Oracle is on a path toward real greatness. As all of us toil in our different jobs along that path, toward that goal, I will look to you, Ray, not only for your experience and success in making things happen, but for your skill in making the right things happen. . . .

7

BECOMING A HOUSEHOLD NAME

["THE PC IS A RIDICULOUS DEVICE."]

Until the mid-1990s, Larry Ellison did his grandstanding upon a rather small stage. He was well known within the technology industry for having built a software powerhouse, but to the general public, database software was an arcane field, of interest mostly to technologists. As a result, Ellison never enjoyed the fame accorded to Microsoft's Bill Gates or Apple's Steve Jobs or other chief executives whose companies sold to consumers. Microsoft and Apple made products that people used daily in their homes and offices. Oracle's database, by contrast, was invisible to its users, vetted by the corporate information technology whizzes, noticed only when something went wrong. As Oracle moved into enterprise applications, its relationship with users broadened, but still, these high-powered apps are relegated to corporate strongholds. No one at home would ever sit down and call up Oracle Financials to balance a checkbook.

As a consequence, Ellison was not a household name. Ray Lane, when first approached by a headhunter, didn't know much about Oracle's chief executive, nor did most people. What largely changed this was one sweeping statement by Ellison at a technology conference in Paris. On September 4, 1995, Ellison got up onstage and began ruminating about a low-cost computer device that would be priced around five hundred dollars, connect to a centralized network, and allow you to access the Internet and other needed applications without a desktop PC. It would be a "network computer," not a PC, the difference being that NCs would depend on the network for their functionality. The PC, with its host of resident software such as a program manager (think Windows) and productivity applications, was dubbed a "fat client," while the "thin-client" NC would only need to access the network to work. In remarks after his speech, Ellison refined his idea further, telling reporters that "the PC is a ridiculous device," too expensive and complicated, that would give way to cheaper, simpler devices, finally bringing computing to the masses. "What the world really wants is to plug into a wall to get electronic power and plug in to get data," Ellison said. Ray Lane, who was also in Paris addressing a European user group meeting with a number of reporters present, was startled when "cell phones started going off and people started running out of the room" in the middle of his talk. He learned that, across town, "Larry had just done a mind dump with his idea" of the network computer.

Ellison's ad-libbed speech accomplished a couple of things. It galvanized the anti-Microsoft coalition with a new idea that would allow them to bypass Microsoft's monopoly hold on the desktop computing world by rendering the PC obsolete. And it caught the media and public fancy in a way that a database never could. Here was a brand-new paradigm shift, from elitist to accessible and affordable. By this time, everyone was feeling frustrated by the PC, the increasing complexity of its software, the quick obsolescence, the endless upgrades, the price tag that seemed stuck around two thousand dollars, limiting it to the relatively affluent. Sociologists debated the new "technology divide" between rich and poor. Poor kids didn't have computers at home, so they were in danger of getting left even further behind in an era that rewarded technological skills above all else. Ellison's network computer—although it didn't even exist yet—could expand the horizons of technology to ghettos and grandmas, factory workers and waitresses,

Third World countries and First World schools in poor districts . . . The network computer became what *Wired* magazine would call a "meme," an idea that caught fire and spread inexorably, and Ellison was its torchbearer.

CONCEIVING THE NC

It's not clear when Ellison's fertile brain first came up with the notion of an NC. More than a year before the Paris meeting, in August 1994, he'd broached the idea—though not the name—to Silicon Valley executives and President Bill Clinton as part of a promotional rollout of Net Day, which was a Valley-conceived project to equip all the nation's schools with computers. Clinton had traveled to San Francisco for the rollout to convey his administration's support for technology. Among the others present were Sun Microsystems' Scott McNealy and Apple Computer's then CEO Michael Spindler. As Ellison told my former *Upside* magazine colleague Richard Brandt, he urged Clinton to undertake a project similar to John Kennedy's push to get a man on the moon. "I proposed that the president challenge the computer industry to build a machine that would sell for no more than $500," says Ellison.[1] But the proposal didn't catch fire, either with Clinton or with the executives at the meeting, not even with McNealy, who hates Microsoft almost as much as Ellison does. Both CEOs are convinced that Microsoft has sought to expand its monopoly on the desktop into other technology arenas, including the corporate enterprise on which Sun and Oracle depend for their livelihood. They and others within Silicon Valley see Microsoft as an evil menace that, by forcing everyone to adhere to its way of doing things, strangles innovation and unfairly prevents competitors from prospering. Microsoft is the formidable enemy that everyone loves to hate, in part because it has wielded its monopoly power with a heavy hand and in part because it is the most successful company in the world.

Marc Benioff says Ellison refined the NC concept when he and a group of Oracle executives were traveling in China in late 1994. Benioff was working on a low-level version of Oracle's database for work-group consumption and wanted to build a browser into it. He'd toyed with the idea of using Apple's Macintosh operating system for that purpose. "We were in a hotel room in Beijing," Benioff says, "and Larry looked at the whole plan. I had called the Mac an 'Internet terminal.'" The following day, Ellison called another Oracle executive, Farzad Dibachi, to talk over the possibility of building a new device that would browse the Internet and run HTML, the Web-based markup language. "It would be a new kind of access device for the network," says Benioff. For his part, Dibachi notes that he and Ellison had already discussed an information appliance in the context of Oracle's interactive-TV initiative (see the next section). "Most of it was Larry's idea," he says. "He came up with the name *network computer*," weaving together ideas from a number of Oracle products.

Just before the trip to Paris, Dibachi says, "Larry and I were in my office going over his presentation. He was trying to decide whether or not he was going to mention the NC." Obviously, he decided to do it, Dibachi adds. "I didn't go with him to Paris, but he called and was very excited because it was all over the news." Not only that, the Oracle executive was getting invitations to speak on CNN and other major networks. And for once, he had put Bill Gates on the defensive. "It was very pivotal," recalls Dibachi. "Before then, Oracle was not a household name. Now it was." Becoming better known had two obvious benefits: it boosted Oracle's status and name recognition in the corporate world (free advertising, in effect), and more people wanted to own the stock, driving up its value. In further press conferences with reporters, Ellison continued to finesse the NC. "Every meeting with the press, he'd come up with something new," says Lane, all coalescing around the central notion that servers (where Oracle's database resides) become more important than clients (where Microsoft Windows resides). "I don't think he had a real understanding of how this would work," Lane says, "but it was a compelling economic vision that struck at the heart of the infidel, Microsoft."

FROM MEDIA SERVER TO THE NC

The roots of the NC can really be traced to another technology that never quite coalesced at Oracle or anywhere else. In the mid-1990s, interactive TV was the darling of both the technology and the media industries, with its glamorous promise of video on demand. Sitting at home, consumers could order up any movie they wanted anytime, utilizing a set-top box. Gigantic servers would deliver the movies as streaming video, which was where Oracle thought it had a play. Time Warner kicked the whole thing off with its announcement in 1993 of the Full Service Network, which was to undergo a trial run in Orlando, Florida. Everyone from Microsoft to Sun to Silicon Graphics to Oracle piled on. Oracle came up with a product called the Media Server—in essence, a database that can easily store and retrieve thousands of videos. Benioff remembers that Ellison was caught up with the vision of interactive TV for the masses, as epitomized in the Time Warner Orlando trial. Here Ellison showed his adeptness at combining two different threads of technology. He had bought a company called nCube, which did parallel processing—that is, rather than one massive server running a single piece of software like a database, the task was divided into components running on multiple computers that could handle lots of different software. "Larry was in love with this concept of parallel processing, dating back to the mid-1980s," Lane says. With interactive TV, "he found one application that could use parallel processing, and that was video streaming." Oracle Media Server was software that provided video for consumers to download.

Oracle planned a grandiose event in Hollywood to introduce the Media Server, enlisting famed newscaster Walter Cronkite to appear onstage with Ellison. Former Oracle marketing director Kate Mitchell remembers rehearsing the presentation until early morning on January 17, 1994, the day the event was scheduled. Everyone had gone back to the hotel, exhausted, only to be awakened a few hours later by the Northridge earthquake. "Stuff from the minibars was flying around the room," recalls Mitchell. The Media Server launch was postponed until February, when it took place with great fanfare. Jerry Held, whom Ellison had recently enticed away from Tandem Computers to run the interactive-TV initiative, calls that presentation a "defining moment" for Oracle, a forerunner to the NC phenomenon. "Up until that time, Oracle was a database company with zero brand recognition," says Held. "The man on the street thought it was Oral-B." The Media Server began what the NC and later the Internet would finish: Oracle's, and Ellison's, trip to the mainstream. Says Mitchell, "We were trying to position Oracle as more than a database in the back room." Now moving heavily into selling applications, where end users influenced the purchase, Oracle needed to be known to people outside the tight IT world.

Meanwhile, to Held, who came in as senior vice president of interactive TV and multimedia, fell the unenviable task of actually making this vision a reality. "This was a classic Larry play," says Held. "When he sees a problem, if he can imagine the solution, it becomes trivial to complete it. The solution should be done in a couple of days." Ellison, sums up Held, "is time dyslexic. He sees things earlier than anyone and over-promises on delivering." Held believes that Ellison is a greater visionary than Gates but a much poorer implementer. When Held arrived at Oracle, he found that he had 120 days to come up with a product. Oracle had three contracts, all in the $20 million range, to deliver media servers to US West, Bell Atlantic, and British Telecom, although it had failed to land the Time Warner contract. "I had the kernel of a sales team, that was all," Held recalls. With Ellison's backing, he built up a development team of about one hundred people, working around the clock. "We were doing an impossible feat," says Held. "Of everyone working on it—Silicon Graphics, Digital

Equipment, IBM—we were the only ones who ended up delivering cost-effective interactive TV." He says the Oracle Media Server, running on nCube parallel processors and connected to a set-top box with Apple's Macintosh operating system, was able to deliver home banking, shopping, and movies on demand to five thousand homes in Virginia and England.

But there was a catch. "We were using this weird new communications technology called DSL to hook the whole thing together," says Held. In 1994, DSL was still experimental, and "it was going to cost a huge amount of money to roll all this out, including DSL." The estimate was that each phone company would have to make an investment in the range of $10 billion. It wasn't evident that consumers would be willing to pay enough for video on demand to justify that kind of investment. The high cost of entry, coupled with an alternative to private networks called the Internet, soon shoved the proprietary video-on-demand trials onto the dustheap of history. "What we had running in these homes—full-motion video—was what the Internet will be in 2005 or 2008," Held proclaims. "We were about ten or twelve years ahead of our time." He doesn't regret the experience. "It was the most fun I've ever had. Hollywood and Silicon Valley coming to conferences, trying to talk to each other, trying to find common words. The concepts of E-commerce were tried out. It was an exciting time that would trigger what was going to happen in the Internet." At the end of 1995, Oracle folded the Media Server back into the database. However, many of the ideas surrounding the Media Server morphed into the NC, which was a browser-based version of the set-top box. Not only that, the Media Server bought Oracle marketing and brand recognition that money couldn't buy. "The product never made a lot of money, but it was the genesis of all these other things," says Held. "Larry was called a technology visionary."

As the interactive-TV project and Media Server wound down, Dibachi left Oracle. "What we did was go down to the ten-yard line in doing an on-line network like AOL or MSN," he says. Even though the project petered out before crossing the goal line, "it was very important in moving Oracle to the next level," Dibachi adds. "It allowed us to have products interesting to the masses. I got calls from seventy-year-old grandmothers saying you guys are doing great work." In 1992, when Oracle surveyed *Wall Street Journal* readers, only 3 percent could identify the company, with assistance. By 1995, thanks to Media Server and the NC, along with Oracle's rising share price, the recognition level was up to 86 percent in a similar survey, Dibachi recalls. And the internal effort set up to do Media Server, funded by $50 million of Oracle's development budget, also tackled the NC. "It was a means of creating new ideas that wasn't bound by the watchful eye of Jeff [Henley] or Ray [Lane]."

THE GAP: PERCEPTION VERSUS REALITY

Having dangled the idea of the NC in Paris, Ellison continued to milk it for publicity for himself and Oracle. I remember his presentation at an *Upside* conference where he took a pencil out of his pocket and proclaimed that the NC is the pencil of the future. He linked the NC to computer literacy in the schools, drawing on his own background in Chicago to talk about the need to bring low-cost devices to less-privileged children. Amid all the press coverage, it occurred to people within Oracle—like Lane and Dave Roux, who'd recently joined the company to head corporate development—that they might have to actually produce this five hundred dollar machine. "The sales force was taking orders for this NC," Lane recalls. Ellison had picked the price point out of his head, and it was an ambitious number at a time when a PC retailed for two thousand dollars. Says Roux, "It was designed to be a breathtaking number that would really rock the industry." But the reality was, to build an NC required changing all the standard underpinnings of the PC, including the processor and the architecture. This presented a stunning challenge for a company that had never done hardware.

Lane recalls setting up meetings with Intel executives, among them then CEO Andy Grove, in an effort to cooperate on several projects, including having the chip maker produce a low-cost processor for the NC. "Intel could have prospered in an NC world," says Lane. But the collaboration never got off the ground, in part because Ellison kept showing up late for the meetings, and that annoyed Grove, "who was very particular about specifics," Lane recalls. "The first time Larry was late, he called and said his son broke his arm riding a horse," says Lane. Grove was sympathetic, but the Oracle executives looked at one another and rolled their eyes, because they had all heard the story before. "The second time Larry tried to use that excuse, Andy didn't buy it," Lane adds. A bigger problem was Ellison's vagueness about the NC. "Andy wanted real details about how it was going to work, and Larry had no details," says Lane. Then, too, Intel had a close relationship with Microsoft, which engineered its operating system, Windows, to work on Intel's chips, leading to the nickname "Wintel alliance." Finally, stymied by the lack of progress at Oracle and the other factors, "Andy just gave up," Lane says. Oracle then initiated a collaboration with Digital Equipment Corporation for a chip, but, Lane suspects, that was blocked by Microsoft, which was also a partner with DEC.

The clamor for the NC continued. "People kept asking to see this machine," says Roux. "Having said it was possible, we had to show it." Oracle set up a small skunk works project to build a working NC. "Over the next year, it went from being an idea in a speech to a prototype to a pet project to a small division," Roux says. But there were soon internal clashes over the resources and attention flowing to the NC group, which got 99 percent of the publicity but was contributing nothing to the bottom line. Oracle's traditional line of business consisted of selling very expensive software to a relatively small number of large customers. The NC meant selling a high-volume, low-margin device to millions of people. "It was a consumer business with consumer pricing and channels, extremely different from the core Oracle business," says Roux. Lane adds that while the Oracle executive committee gave cautious support to the NC, "it was a vision that had no business grounding. We didn't know how we'd make money except that more stuff would go into the server to support this thing." But interested NC customers were besieging Oracle salespeople, who naturally wanted to sell the machine that was getting so much attention. "We had a difficult financial year because we lost our focus," says Lane. "We had to think through, what does the database have to do with this?"

In May 1996, Oracle staged another one of its slick promotional events to announce an NC alliance that would move computing into the direction of a telephone model—with cheap, easy-access units that would reach 90 percent plus of U.S. households, in contrast to the 30 percent penetration of the PC at the time. Oracle was joined by four other companies that had widely divergent motives for pushing the NC: IBM, Sun Microsystems, Apple Computer, and Netscape. All, however, were wary of the Wintel domination of the PC and were eager to offer an alternative. Sun figured its recently developed programming language called Java, then a technology in search of a market, could become the operating system for the new device. At the same time, Oracle disclosed that it was spinning off its NC division into a subsidiary, Network Computer Incorporated (NCI). "Larry made the call that if this were to succeed, it would have to separate from Oracle," says Roux.

For a number of reasons, the NC never met expectations. For one thing, the five partners were competitors at many other levels and never cooperated fully. IBM had the most successful effort to sell the NC into the corporate market, but plummeting PC prices—dipping below one thousand dollars per machine—soon made it uneconomical. "NCI was making good technical progress but terrible sales progress," says Roux. "The issue is, people didn't just run the browser. They wanted to do other things." And a PC could do a lot of other things for almost the same price as the NC. Nonetheless, the idea had enormous staying power, and Ellison was wedded to it. NCI became Liberate Technologies, which has returned to the project's original roots: making software for interactive TV. And Ellison set up his own private NC company and recruited, of all people, a journalist to run it: Gina Smith, who as a syndicated columnist had been an avid NC supporter. (See "The Thing That Won't Die," page 152.)

FLIRTING WITH APPLE

At least twice during the mid-1990s, Oracle and/or Ellison seriously considered buying Apple Computer, which was floundering against the powerful and increasingly dominant Wintel world. The company that had made the personal computer "cool" in the 1980s now seemed doomed to irrelevancy. And Ellison considers Steve Jobs one of his closest friends (the two CEOs do have a lot in common, including both narcissism and vision). Jobs had been ousted from Apple, and Oracle's acquisition would give him a way to return. Apple and Oracle were both firmly in the anti-Microsoft camp. There were also some business synergies. As indicated, Oracle used the Macintosh operating system to run its interactive-TV set-top box. Finally, Apple's share price had been hammered because of its problems, making an acquisition attractive. Ellison even consulted junk bond king Michael Milken on how to accomplish such a high-stakes, hostile takeover. In early 1995, "Larry was talking about buying Apple in conjunction with the set-top box," says Lane. "Apple had a great kernel OS with a small footprint"—that is, it had a low memory requirement that allowed it to run on small devices like a set-top box or network computer. But Lane says the speculation got blown out of proportion by the press. "We considered it seriously internally, but it didn't go much further than that." The sticking point became spinning off the hardware from the software. Oracle wasn't prepared to take over Apple's retail computer business. So Ellison met with officials of Philips Electronics and Matsushita and came up with a scheme under which Oracle would take the software business of Apple, Philips the computer business, and Matsushita the portable products. But Philips backed out of the deal "because they didn't see the value in it," says Lane. "And we couldn't afford

to buy Apple without a partner to take over the hardware."
Later in 1995, Oracle considered licensing Apple's Newton
technology as the NC operating system, but that never materi-
alized either.

Then, in March 1997, rumors of another Apple takeover
attempt surfaced after Ellison met with the *San Jose Mercury
News* for what was intended to be a routine press briefing.
Roux remembers the meeting well. One of Oracle's public
relations people "decided we needed to do a better job talking
to our regular constituency and instituted a quarterly press
briefing." The first one was scheduled with Silicon Valley's
home newspaper in San Jose. Given Ellison's notorious reputation for not showing up at these things, the public relations
staff always had a backup. In this case, it was Roux. Since
Ellison had not yet appeared for the noontime meeting, Roux
launched into a summation of Oracle's expectations for the
quarter and priorities for the year. "Thirty or forty minutes
later, Larry comes rolling in, plops himself down, and says,
'What would you like to talk about?'" He was sitting on one
end of the table, with the PR person on the other side, and
Roux in between. Roux could see that Ellison had the briefing
sheet containing all the "talking points" he was supposed to
make. Instead, the CEO went off on one of his patented musings. "I'm sure Dave has done a wonderful job telling you
about the business," said Ellison. "You know what I've been
really thinking about . . ." Here, Roux recalls, the reporters all
straightened up in their chairs and whipped out their pens. "If
I tell you this, my PR person is going to go nuts," said Ellison
mischievously. "Let's just forget this briefing. I'm going to tell
you about why I'm going to buy Apple." Roux looked over
and saw the PR person put her head down on the table. "I just
sort of laughed to myself," says Roux. It was such classic Ellison. "He would spend the evening before thinking about it,
decide it was a cool idea, but he wouldn't talk to anybody
about it. He was just bored and wanted something new." Ellison rambled on about buying Apple for twenty or thirty minutes, says Roux. Then one of the reporters jumped in: "This is
quite newsworthy. I'd like to go tell someone." After the brief-

ing, Larry confided to Roux, "Maybe I better call Steve [Jobs] and tell him about this." That was the end of the quarterly press briefings, Roux adds.

This second proposal differed from the first in that Ellison was now prepared to raise the money himself. "This was Larry personally buying Apple, not Oracle buying Apple," says Roux. "Larry's view on Apple is that Steve is one of America's great treasures, and Apple is to technology as Yosemite is to national parks, one of the natural wonders of the technology world." Ellison felt that Apple "had been desecrated after Steve left," Roux says. "He couldn't understand how an organization of such talent could be allowed to wither away." As the story of the takeover attempt widened, Ellison said that he was considering raising $1 billion to take about a 60 percent stake in Apple; the other 40 percent would remain in public shareholders' hands. Meanwhile, an Oracle spokeswoman had to do some frantic spadework. "It's Larry Ellison as a private citizen," not a formal offer by Oracle, she told the *Washington Post*.[2] Apple's then CEO Gil Amelio dismissed Ellison's plan as "nonsense." Ellison, admitting that his idea was a trial balloon, set up an electronic mailbox to gauge interest among Apple employees and shareholders.[3] Evidently, there wasn't enough, for in April, Ellison announced he was suspending his plans, deciding "at least for the time being" not to pursue any transaction involving Apple.[4]

NAVIGATING WITH NETSCAPE

In August 1995, the initial public offering of Netscape Communications, which more than doubled in value on its first day of trading, signaled the start of the Internet era in very high-profile, hard-to-miss fashion. Of course, the elements that would create the Internet, including the Department of Defense's funding of a predecessor called Arpanet, had been gelling for years, but Netscape was the public personification of all the hopes for this paradigm. The PC had liberated computing power from the mainframe to the individual desktop;

the Internet would allow all those individual desktops to communicate with and augment one another. Netscape, which had been the first to commercialize an Internet browser, became a prime piece of the puzzle in anyone's conception of the future. Even though it was dwarfed by Oracle, Sun, IBM, and Apple, Netscape was included in the NC alliance because you couldn't have an NC without a browser. That was the whole point of the NC.

Netscape's ownership of a key piece of technology drew Oracle's interest. According to Lane, Netscape approached Oracle about a possible merger a little less than a year after the Internet company went public. Netscape was fearful that Microsoft's development of its own browser, Internet Explorer, would undermine Netscape's primary product, Navigator. In June 1996, Netscape CEO Jim Barksdale, along with venture capital investor John Doerr and investment banker Frank Quattrone, met with Ellison, Lane, Jeff Henley, Dave Roux, and Oracle's counsel at Lane's unfinished house in the wealthy Silicon Valley enclave of Atherton. "We put in a couple of workman's horses and a plywood table to hold the meeting," says Lane, because the house was not furnished. "We didn't want anybody to know, so we kept it very private." Netscape was trading around $52 a share, which gave the still-tiny company a market cap near $5 billion, Lane recalls. "We offered $50 a share, and Barksdale wanted $53." The pricing negotiations were not the only stumbling block. Kingmaker John Doerr thought that Barksdale should run the combined company, an idea that "didn't go over well with Larry," Lane says dryly. At the end of the day, Oracle decided against the deal. "It was too much money for what essentially would have been a great countermove against Microsoft," says Lane.

From then on, Oracle, the feisty behemoth, and Netscape, the feisty upstart, had a rocky relationship marked by Ellison's off-the-cuff remarks questioning the smaller company's staying power and Netscape's reluctance to be smothered by a larger partner. By early October 1996, Ellison and Barksdale were trading jabs in the press. Ellison declared that "Netscape has no chance of surviving," while Barksdale retorted that Ellison was talking down the stock "because he wants to acquire the company."[5] A month later, Oracle and Netscape, which both had greater reasons to fear Microsoft than to snipe at each other, patched things up and signed a joint marketing agreement. Oracle would bundle Netscape's browser, Navigator, with the network computers being produced by NCI. And Netscape, which was moving into corporate network software, would offer the Oracle database as part of its package. In mid-1997, Oracle bought Netscape spin-off Navio Communications, which was developing software for Internet appliances, and merged it into NCI. It was almost as if Netscape and Oracle were exchanging market strategies. Netscape, which had introduced software to manage business messaging and collaboration, was seeking to move into the corporate world that was Oracle's traditional core market. Meanwhile, with NCI, Oracle wanted to move into the consumer market for Internet access. Neither strategy, incidentally, would prove viable. Netscape never got enough of a foothold in the corporate market to survive as an independent company (so Ellison's rather mean-spirited prophecy proved accurate), while Oracle failed to make the NC a real business.

In 1998, Netscape, its market cap having sunk below $2 billion, held discussions with a number of possible suitors, including America Online and three of the erstwhile NC partners: Sun Microsystems, IBM, and Oracle. Matt Mosman, then Oracle's senior vice president of corporate development, says that Oracle now wanted not Navigator but Netscape's business software, called SuiteSpot, to go after a new market called application servers. In contrast to the client-based browser, SuiteSpot was centralized software, residing on a server, that managed corporate applications. Thus, it would have fit neatly between the Oracle database and Oracle's growing applications business. "Application server has been a tough market for Oracle," says Mosman. "They're really getting their butt kicked." (For more, see Chapter 11.) He thinks Netscape's SuiteSpot could have filled the gap and got Oracle into the market much sooner rather than having to wait and build the product internally. "Netscape had a pretty good application server," says Mosman, but "we couldn't construct a deal that made any sense." While he was working the spreadsheets to come up with a reasonable value for an acquisition of all or part of Netscape, "we never got them in the same time zone." At the close of 1998, it was America Online that structured a complex $4.28 billion stock swap for Netscape, enlisting Sun as a partner to take over the corporate software business.

THE THING THAT WON'T DIE

NCI never introduced a hardware product. Instead, it was repositioned in mid-1998 to make software for Internet appliances and eventually renamed Liberate. In reassessing NCI's focus, "I told Larry that we didn't need a new device. We needed to recognize that the NC already existed, but it was called something else," says Roux, "like game machines, TV sets, cell phones, PDAs." Instead of going forth to build a new device, "we need to colonize existing devices that meet this criteria." Roux ran the company briefly and then suggested bringing in a permanent executive. A search turned up Mitchell Kertzman, who had, ironically, just finished a stint at the head of Oracle's database competitor Sybase. Kertzman knew and respected Roux, "and he convinced me that [Liberate] was increasingly independent, and the goal was to make it fully independent of Oracle." Kertzman met once with Ellison, "who told me the mission of the company is not fulfillment of his agenda. He said on issues where we differ, you're the CEO and you make the decision." Ellison kept his word. "We only differed once, and my point of view prevailed," says Kertzman. That was on whether to rename NCI simply "Liberate" or "Liberate.com." Kertzman thought the *.com* suffix was too trendy and wouldn't last. "History has proven I was right."

In 1999, Liberate went public in a less-than-spectacular debut for those times. "We priced at $16, went up to $20, then drifted back below the offering price," says Kertzman. At one time during the Internet bubble, Liberate sold for $245, he says, but by 2002 was back below its offering price. Oracle, which once owned 70 percent, had just under 30 percent of the company and no longer had a representative on the board. Kertzman says that Oracle "has literally no say" anymore in running Liberate. The company's mission, as he phrases it, "is to become the leading platform on which other people will develop applications for multichannel video, like cable, TV, and telephone." In a sense, it's the flip side of the Oracle Media Server. As of 2002, Liberate was running in about two million set-top boxes, but looming on the horizon was Microsoft. "Microsoft is still way behind," says Kertzman, but "there's a saying in the software industry: 'Never underestimate Microsoft's ability to eventually figure things out.'"

Apart from Liberate, Ellison has not let go of the original notion of the NC. In 1999, he formed a small company in San Francisco called The New Internet Computer Company (NICC, for short) and named Gina Smith as the CEO. Smith, who'd been covering the technology industry for fourteen years as a journalist, thought Ellison wanted to give her an exclusive on reviving the NC when he first called her for a meeting. Among the computer press, she was a contrarian who had stoutly defended the NC. "He offered me this job, and I told him the only thing I'd ever run was a magazine." But Ellison told her, "You understand the concept." He wrote out a check for $2 million to start the company. "Larry wanted somebody who really believed in this and didn't have preconceptions that you needed to spend millions of dollars," she says. "The idea was to do it as a virtual corporation, outsource everything, and have fewer than thirty people." Smith carried out that vision. A Taiwanese manufacturer makes the computers, which NICC's small staff sells direct to schools, travel agencies, call centers, and other small businesses aiming to keep their cost of technology low. Ellison, who owns 85 percent of the company, buys about twenty thousand of the devices a year and donates them to schools, representing over half of NICC's sales. Says Smith, "Larry's goal is to leave a legacy. He's got money, power, and influence. He wants to be known as the guy who brought computers to the desk of every kid, every country that can't afford them." In March 2002, Smith left voluntarily, replaced by CFO Peter Clark, who says he will continue running NICC as a lean-and-mean "virtual company." To increase sales, he plans to partner with companies such as AT&T and EarthLink that want to bundle their Internet access with the needed hardware. In 2002, NICC raised $2 million in additional funding, and "we're cash-flow positive and profitable," says Clark, "able to control our own destiny."

Although neither Liberate nor NICC can be counted as anything more than modest successes, Ellison's view of a low-cost alternative to the PC has had enormous ramifications for the industry. First of all, it helped to establish him as a public figure recognizable for more than just personal pecadilloes and establish Oracle as more than a database company. Second, it caused a sea change in how PCs were used and defined. Since the mid-1990s, PC prices have dropped precipitately, in part due to the decrease in the cost of components but also in reaction to the potential competition from an NC. Obsessed with beating Microsoft on the desktop, Ellison and the other partners at first saw the NC primarily as an alternative to the PC, a view that was narrow and flawed. But the NC was the precursor to a developing vision that swept up Oracle, Microsoft, Sun, IBM, and so forth along with all the coming dot-coms. The Internet would tie together devices of all kinds: not only PCs but cell phones, gaming machines, smart cards, and a host of things as yet uninvented. In a totally unintended way, aided by the confluence of serendipitous events, Ellison did indeed change the world. The ubiquitous network has permanently displaced the PC as the center of the digital revolution.

8

TURNING THE ORACLE BATTLESHIP

[EMBRACING THE INTERNET]

Oracle's move to the Internet reinvigorated the company's flagging applications business, which had always taken a backseat to the database, and helped cement Larry Ellison's stature as a visionary. In the mid-1990s, established companies were warily eyeing the emergence of the Internet into popular consciousness. *What should we do about it? Should we change how we do business?* As usual, it was start-ups like Netscape, with its new technology called a Web browser, that seized the day, while older companies lagged, because moving to the Internet meant enormous change—and pain—for themselves and their customers. Among those hanging back were Oracle rivals IBM, Microsoft, and SAP, along with nearly every other major technology company. Larry Ellison's genius, and sometimes downfall, has always been that he continues to think like an entrepreneur heading up a feisty little start-up, even as Oracle grew into a $10 billion behemoth. Before most of his contemporaries, including Bill Gates, Ellison was trumpeting the Internet as the force for a new way of doing business. It didn't matter to him that remaking Oracle's applications (the database wasn't as affected by the Internet) posed tremendous technical challenges for the company nor that skeptical customers would have to be dragged along. He saw the future, the future was the Internet, and immediately pointed Oracle in that direction, while his executives frantically tried to work out all the details in such a massive repositioning.

Ellison's reasoning was elegant, based upon a now-accepted notion that the Internet was radically altering the "edge" of technology—the place where end users on their PCs interface with servers and databases and other "center" technologies that make up a network. Ellison figured that by making this center technology powerful and sophisticated, so that it performed most of the complex calculations, the edge could be made more user-friendly, more simple. He also realized there was a place for the Oracle database as an important piece of this center, acting as a server for browser-based applications. "Larry reasoned that if the center of the network standardizes, that's going to force standardization of the periphery [or edge]," says Dave Roux, formerly head of corporate development at Oracle. Then Ellison considered the properties of already-mature networks, like water or electricity or public sanitation. "You started with a septic tank, then you moved to a public sewer system," says Roux. "As the center of the network gets very complex, the edge is simple." Ellison had thought out these notions of centralized networks and edge interfaces in 1996, long before they were embraced by gurus and journalists.

Marc Benioff remembers that Ellison sent out an E-mail around the middle of 1996 stating flatly, "No more Windows development." Instead of creating products that relied on the Microsoft interface, "everything has to be in HTML," the hypertext markup language that became the basis for the rich linkages of the World Wide Web, accessed by a browser like Netscape Navigator. Out of his thinking related to the network computer, "Larry realized he had to get all of Oracle's products to work with a browser. He had to turn the Oracle battleship to HTML," says Benioff. Along with HTML, Oracle embraced the Java programming language developed by its hardware partner and fellow Microsoft hater Sun Microsystems. That positioned Oracle for the Internet era. Even though the NC failed as a product, "as a strategy, it succeeded for Oracle," says Benioff. "It got us refocused as an Internet company."

Even more than the database, the applications business was affected by the Internet. Oracle was a sometimes reluctant player in the high-level corporate applications arena known as enterprise resource planning (or ERP, for short). Starting with a financials module that managed general ledger and accounting functions, ERP expanded into human resources, such as payroll and benefits; manufacturing and supply chain; and finally, sales force automation and customer relationship management (CRM). At first, these complex applications were configured as client-server, meaning that users would access them by means of a "client," typically a PC, connected to a centralized server. At this time, "fat clients," whose operating systems required a lot of computing power and user expertise, were common. (Microsoft's Windows operating system is a prime example of a "fat client.") The browser (and Ellison's notion of the NC) ushered in the era of the "thin client," the simplified edge referred to previously. Running a browser takes very little computing power or knowledge on the part of a user; all the work is done at the center of the network—the server. Moving from client-server to the Internet model required changes at both levels. Using a browser—a "thin client"—meant that most of the heavy lifting had to be done at the server level. Little, if any, code ran at the client level, the domain of Java and HTML. An application server now sat between the database, where information resided, and the clients, to dish up ERP programs to multiple clients running browsers. As corporations developed intranets, their customers and supply partners also had access to some of these ERP functions. It made for a much more interconnected, but also more complicated, world, with need for heightened security and better firewalls to protect sensitive information.

Ellison had never been too interested in Oracle's applications business, which he considered rather mundane compared to the cool technologies of databases, development tools, NCs, and media servers. But his intermittent attention revived when he conceived the masterstroke of redeploying Oracle's applications from the client-server to the Internet model. Suddenly, applications could be cool, too, not just programs managing boring stuff like accounting and payroll, but gateways to the entire restructuring of business practices. In an ironic twist, this renewal of Ellison's focus signaled the beginning of a long slide for Ray Lane, although the latter had no inkling of this at first. By reinvolving himself with aspects of the company that had been pretty much Lane's province up until now, such as customer relations and sales, Ellison was encroaching upon the unwritten pact that had worked so well between him and Lane, allowing each to carve out a territory. Going forward, they would increasingly step on each other's toes. For Oracle, consequently, Ellison's renewed interest had pluses and minuses. He forced Oracle to redeploy to the Internet much more quickly than it would have under a more conservative chief executive, thereby temporarily at least seizing leadership of the applications market. On the other hand, his alienation of Lane destabilized the balancing act within Oracle. Lane had been the voice of moderation, helping to restore Oracle's tarnished customer relations. Ellison did what was needed in moving Oracle to the Internet, but his failure, as always, lay in the execution. Having thought a thing—move applications to the Internet—to him, it was done. As he increasingly divested himself of strong operations managers like Lane, there was no one to go back and fill in all those messy details.

MOVING INTO APPLICATIONS

Unlike the database, the foundation of Oracle's business and the initial reason for its existence, the applications business was developed almost by accident. In the mid-1980s, when Oracle was still operating in extremely decentralized fashion, over in England Geoff Squire decided to fill out his conception of an integrated product line by creating an accounting application. Not only could he use it within his own organization—

Squire was never an admirer of Oracle U.S.A.'s aggressive methods for booking sales—but he could sell it to international customers. Meanwhile, in the United States, Ellison had brought in Jeff Walker, who had founded a financial applications company called Walker Interactive, to come up with an accounting application for domestic customers. Walker, who would also double as the chief financial officer, built the application to meet his own needs. Dismissing Oracle's toolset, which was primarily geared to database development, Walker incorporated some outside software code into his accounting application. This did not increase his popularity within Oracle. Cofounder and head of development Bob Miner, for one, was outraged that Walker would not "eat his own dog food." Longtime Oracle developer Nimish Mehta remembers that Walker took the unusual step of setting up his organization outside the walls of Oracle. "You had to sign an NDA [nondisclosure agreement] to walk into Jeff's organization, even if you were from Oracle," he says. This was naturally resented by Oracle insiders.

As a result of Squire and Walker's separate efforts, Oracle wound up with two different toolsets and two different accounting applications—one in the United States and one overseas. "The relationship between the tools and apps groups was very bad," says Mehta. Since customers had to use Oracle tools to customize the applications, they felt shortchanged if Oracle wasn't using its own technology internally. "Customers would say, 'If it's not good enough for you, why is it good enough for me?'" Mehta recalls. Having two accounting products, both of which were new and buggy, also caused enormous headaches for customer support. Financial customers were not geeks in the way that database users were, willing to tinker with something until it worked. The application buyers were accountants and payroll clerks who just wanted their ledgers to balance. "Applications were a nightmare," recalls John Luongo, who was running international sales from U.S. headquarters in the late 1980s. "There were tons of bugs, and we were selling to a different type of customer, not IT [information technology] but an accountant. It was a significantly different business, and it took a long time for Oracle to make the adjustment." However, Squire did a better job of supporting customers on his product than the United States did on Walker's product. "If you didn't support the customer, your reputation got burned in Europe," says Luongo. "We spent more energy in Europe holding customers' hands. You couldn't get away with what you did in the U.S."

The stage was set. Walker had a product that was better technically but incorporated non-Oracle code. Squire had an Oracle-standard product and better customer support. For at least two years, there was an internal battle between the two over whose accounting system was going to win out, Luongo recalls. "Neither product was top-down driven," he says. In typical Oracle intrapreneurial fashion, "Squire wrote his own, so did Walker." Ellison finally stepped in and told both men to rewrite their products to conform to Oracle specifications. Squire did it with Oracle tools, but Walker cheated, still feeling that Oracle tools were inadequate for sophisticated applications. "Jeff [Walker] ignored Larry, so the U.S. product was ten times better because it didn't have the restraints of the Oracle toolset," says Luongo. "Larry eventually picked Walker's product in 1989." Squire was pissed off because he felt he had followed the rules and lost out as a result. He believes he was forced to concede to Walker's product because it was built for the U.S. market, which always trumped international. "Our product was switched into a vertical niche and later got spun off to a third party," he sighs.

To do Ellison justice, here's one situation in which his policy of allowing two executives to charge ahead with similar, competing projects worked in some ways to Oracle's advantage. Sure, this created logistical nightmares for customers and salespeople, but in the end, the better product won out. Perhaps a chief executive who was more sensitive to the feelings of subordinates or to an organizational chart would not have let this happen, but for Ellison, technology ruled. Again, however, he faltered on the execution—paying little attention to applications because they were boring products used by accountants ("bean counters," in his lexicon) and other nontechies. So Oracle's applications, whether the client-server or Internet versions, always had a lot of technical problems that gave customers fits. And Lane, whose influence was draining off into internal politics, couldn't exert enough authority to fix the situation.

POLITICIZING APPLICATIONS

Even with only one product, the applications business continued to generate political conflict inside Oracle. In the first half of the 1990s, there were three different executives running applications development: Jeff Walker, who had doubled as CFO and then left in the wake of the financial crisis; George Koch, hired by Walker and forced out by Ellison; and finally, Ron Wohl, one of Ellison's handpicked bright young men who had joined Oracle after a stint with the Boston Consulting Group. In a chilling foretaste of things to come, Lane remembers how Ellison disposed of Koch. "In 1993, Larry started letting the executive staff know that George Koch was out of favor," he says, by talking him down behind his back. In addition, Koch didn't get invited to executive committee sessions. He desperately sought a personal meeting with Ellison, but the CEO refused. Says Lane, "It's a suffering process you have to go through. It took at least a year" before Koch was terminated. In conversations with other people, "Larry criticizes the way you're managing something or moving your organization. He hates confrontation, so he'll never do this directly to your face," Lane says. Ellison's insecurity no doubt stems from his childhood—given away by a mother he never knew to distant relatives, with an adoptive father who verbally abused him. But that trait wreaks havoc in his relationships with subordinates. He's not good at constructive criticism nor at tolerating weakness. He also possesses a keen instinct for when someone has outlived his or her usefulness at Oracle, but he can never dispose of that person gracefully. Rather, his insecurity causes him to snipe at the person, bouncing negative opinions off of coworkers until the very repetition seals his belief that someone needs to be axed. Such was the case with Koch, and with many others before him and since, including, eventually, Lane himself.

In 1994, Koch was finally ousted, and Ellison named Wohl to replace him. Says Lane, "Larry never really embraced the applications business," which left it in the hands of whoever was running the engineering side of applications. While Wohl was handling product development, "no one was in charge of applications strategy overall," says Lane. "There was no one comparable to the CEO of SAP or PeopleSoft," Oracle's primary competitors in applications. Ellison was still focused on the database and defeating Sybase and Informix, while Wohl was generating conflict with the Oracle sales staff because he couldn't deliver workable applications products on time. "Ron is a bright guy, but in no way did he have any experience in applications," says Lane. He thinks appointing Wohl to that position was Ellison's "single biggest personnel mistake." Ellison owed Wohl because, functioning as chief of staff during the 1990–1991 crisis period, he had been critical to negotiating the Nippon Steel deal that had saved Oracle. Still, "Larry put him in the wrong job [with applications], expecting him to compete with SAP," Lane sums up.

Other executives agreed. "At some point, you needed products that did what they said they were going to do and were delivered within a reasonable timetable," says Robert Shaw, the former head of Oracle's consulting business. "There was an unwillingness on Ron's part to even admit there was a product plan. He didn't want to be held accountable." Not only that, Shaw adds, but basic components would be missing from the applications. The accounts payable system, for example, wouldn't print out checks for a time nor close out accounts. "Major promises were made when stuff wasn't even close to being ready," he says. "Ron couldn't communicate a plan and deliver anything that made me seriously trust him." Even Nimish Mehta, a fellow developer and thus a peer of Wohl's, concedes that Wohl has shortcomings. Wohl's chief attribute is that he's good at working with Ellison. "Larry has a very defined view of his position in the company. The only way you can be successful long-term is if you just execute on what he says," says Mehta. "Ron fits that bill completely. He doesn't generate ideas on his own. He executes. The problem is, he hasn't done that very well."

GOING TO THE WALL OVER WOHL

Controversy between Wohl and the rest of the executive team continued to smolder, flaming so high that it enveloped Oracle's board of directors. Joe Costello, a respected CEO brought in as an outside board member during the 1991 crisis to provide a much-needed counterbalance to Ellison, thought that Oracle wasn't pushing hard enough on the applications business. While the database product was a good legacy business, "apps seemed like it could be much bigger and broader and way more important," Costello says. In the early to mid-1990s, there was no strong player. Oracle could have been the market leader but never quite capitalized on the opportunity. "What happened was a failure of leadership on the part of the people [Ellison] had running applications," Costello maintains. "There was never anyone strong enough or with enough marketing pizzazz to make it happen, starting with Jeff Walker." He also pins blame on Ellison. "Larry doesn't get apps," says Costello. "For apps, you have to know the customer, you need people deep in the space who understand the customer's mentality." Oracle didn't have that.

The board tried to get a handle on the applications business by asking for the results to be broken out separately from Oracle's other product lines. "It took us half a year just to get Larry to start calling out the different businesses separately, for us, the board," says Costello. "We wanted to see how the database looks as a stand-alone business, along with the tools business and apps business." Finally, Ellison started delivering those breakouts, "and it didn't look very good for apps. We were smaller, and we weren't growing as fast as everyone else." (In fact, according to Lane, when he left in 2000, applications had never been a profitable line of business for

Oracle.) The board demanded to see the man in charge, Ron Wohl. "We said we want a presentation on apps. We need to see this guy," says Costello. Wohl came in and made a presentation that was, in Costello's words, "stunningly bad." If Wohl had been "a junior marketing guy, it might have been OK." The presentation was "plain vanilla," lacking in intensity and energy, with no clear strategy for where Oracle fit in the marketplace and who its customer should be. "There was this deafening silence after he finished," Costello recalls. He adds that Ray Lane and Jeff Henley, who were also in the meeting, seemed dumbfounded as well by Wohl's ineptness, while Ellison was uncharacteristically quiet. "I thought it was so obvious that everyone would say, 'Come on, Larry, let's do something different,'" Costello says. When nobody did, Costello jumped in, pointing out that Wohl was completely overmatched by his SAP counterparts. "You put those guys in a room with Ron Wohl, and you'll be lucky to find two connected molecules left of Wohl." He urged the board, "We've got to do something about this. We need someone who's gonna kick ass, take no prisoners." But Ellison remained stubbornly loyal to Wohl (who in early 2002 was promoted to oversee all applications products, both ERP and CRM). "Larry just didn't want to change," says Costello. "It was totally irrational. This is the same Larry who will off people in public for the sheer hell of it."

From then on, says Costello, "I knew I was dead meat." In a 1995 board meeting, he and Ellison blew up at each other again over the applications business. Says Costello, who is outspoken and tolerates no foolishness, "Larry was irritating me by not listening." He remembered back in 1991 when "Larry was in deep shit and dead-ass scared." Then he was forced to listen because "we were in danger of losing the company. Larry knew he was in trouble and did end up having people help him." But as Oracle climbed out of the trough, "Larry wasn't listening again." In this particular board meeting, Costello tried to advise him that Oracle should be making needed changes now, not waiting until it hit a wall. "The time to do it is when you're riding high and have the resources to do it." But Ellison shrugged him off. Costello was peeved. "You're part of the problem," he told Ellison, who exploded. "Are you questioning whether I should be the CEO?" he demanded. Costello responded, "I didn't say it, but maybe it's not a bad thought." Ellison looked daggers at him, screaming, "You little fucker," and other profanities, Costello recalls. He warned Ellison, "Don't get so damn egotistical about success. You're not meeting potential. You'll sow the seeds of your problems again."

The shouting match was followed by another bitter argument triggered when Costello's own company, Cadence Design Systems, selected SAP rather than Oracle for its applications. "We went through an extended review," says Costello. "I made our team look at it three different times." He even tried to coach Oracle in how to make the presentation. But in the end, the Cadence team voted unanimously for SAP. "I couldn't override them," says Costello. "They were the ones who have to use it. Oracle lost fair and square. They didn't have the right product for us." Ellison was outraged and demanded Costello's resignation. Says Costello, "He even intimated he wanted Don Lucas's resignation"—the same Don Lucas who had rescued Ellison with a personal loan back in the early days of Oracle. In the small world that is Silicon Valley, Lucas was chairman of Cadence's board. Costello describes Ellison's attitude as hysterical. "How can my board member choose SAP?" he demanded. "Larry was playing brinkmanship, trying to get at me," says Costello. "He threatened to ruin me and ruin my reputation. He was flaming me." Costello says he didn't take it seriously. "I knew it was Larry posturing. He wanted me off the board, and this was his cue." Costello complied, resigning from Oracle's board in late summer 1995, because "I just wasn't going to argue anymore with Larry."

Lucas managed to get Ellison to back down, and he continued serving on both companies' boards, but Lane, who had replaced Ellison on Cadence's board a year before, did leave that post. "Joe [Costello] disagreed strongly with the decision to put Wohl in charge of applications development," Lane says. "Then Cadence chose SAP for its ERP. It was the last straw." Lane says Costello supported Cadence's decision in Oracle board meetings, telling Ellison that "I don't believe Oracle's applications are as good." It was obvious, says Lane, that the relationship was shredded beyond repair, but he was sorry to see Costello leave the board. "Joe was a very valuable board member, and his resignation should have sent a signal to everyone: the board serves at Larry's will."

Why does a chief executive who seems to delight in ousting people champion someone like Ron Wohl? The answer says a lot about Ellison. Basically, he rewards loyalty above all else and drives out people who dare to disagree with him. Ellison only wants to hear his own voice or someone echoing his own voice. "Larry's very simple: if you're loyal to him, he'll stick by you, no matter how badly you do," says Peter Relan, a former Oracle developer and vice president. Wohl "will do exactly what Larry says, whether it's good, bad, or ugly." By hiding within Ellison's shadow, Wohl was able to deflect criticism. When Lane or Shaw or anyone else complained about Wohl, they were treading on dangerous ground. For Wohl = Ellison, and thus, the critics were complaining about Ellison's own leadership, or lack thereof.

Not that Wohl is a fool, for Ellison would not put up with that. In his appearances at Oracle's trade conferences, the still-youngish-looking Wohl, who is slight, with dark hair and eyes, comes off as competent and savvy. (Upon the advice of Oracle's public relations staff, Wohl declined to be interviewed for this book.) He is by all accounts a promising manager who was promoted beyond his depth and got squeezed into the middle of the ferocious infighting between Ellison and Lane. Mehta remembers a discussion at the product development management committee about the developers' request for upgraded workstations. Ellison was resistant because of the cost. He told the committee he'd gone into Fry's Electronics, the Silicon Valley computer store, to ask about the price of a PC made to order. Ad-libbing, Wohl quickly told him that disks in the Fry's PC have an rpm rating far below what the Oracle developers would need. "He [Wohl] hadn't prepared for it," says Mehta, "but he knew all this arcane information. Ron has an inordinate memory for detail." As a result, Wohl fills a needed gap for Ellison. "Larry is a master of strategy and completely lacking on detail," says Mehta. "Ron is the master of minutiae and is completely obedient to Larry."

ELLISON TAKES CHARGE

So Wohl stayed as head of applications development and Oracle continued to lose ground to its competitors, particularly in Europe, where SAP had an undeniable edge. For about four years, from 1993 to 1997, says Lane, "we competed poorly against SAP." Even though Oracle's applications business was growing, "the industry was growing even faster." One big problem was that SAP, based in Germany, had features to handle European business processes, such as currency transactions, while Oracle's generic product did not. "We would promise to develop all of the European features," says Lane, "but we had no developers who understood the needs in Europe." Lane says the senior sales staff "had a couple of 'come to Jesus' meetings with Ron," urging him to do what needed to be done to boost growth, like fix the bugs in the applications and add features for Europe. "What we really needed was new leadership, somebody who understood applications," says Lane. "Our applications did not deliver what the marketplace wanted."

He credits Robert Shaw for the limited success that Oracle managed to achieve in Europe. That success depended on Oracle's partnering with other companies—in this case, early adopters—to come up with the needed functionality. In a masterful presentation to Ellison and Lane in 1996, Shaw persuaded them to partner with two European energy companies, Apogee and British Petroleum, in developing an ERP system to serve that niche. First, Shaw put up a map on the wall listing all the features that SAP had; then he overlaid it with a map showing what Oracle could deliver with its partners. "Larry got very enthusiastic, said we can beat SAP, and approved the plan," says Lane, leading to about forty wins against SAP in the energy sector. "We were very successful from a selling standpoint, but it was complicating delivery, and Wohl was very reluctant to support it."

In the United States, Oracle teamed up with customers in vertical niches, such as consumer packaged goods, to get needed features in its applications. It also partnered for a time with vendors like Manugistics and i2 for a supply chain module. "We knew we couldn't compete with SAP in areas like consumer goods and energy," Lane acknowledges. "Finally, we came up with a strategy to supplement our applications with partners. The only reason we did this was because Wohl wasn't putting in the features that we needed to compete." But partners demand release dates and features in line with their own agendas. "They would hold us hostage," says Lane. "It became very complex and costly to maintain the partnerships." For those reasons, Ellison felt that Oracle should build its own products rather than depend on partners, and his view ultimately prevailed.

During this mid-1990s period, Lane brought in Jim Bensman, who had been president of SAP America from 1989 to 1992, as a consultant to make recommendations on what to do with Oracle's applications. Bensman says he and two other ex–SAP officials did extensive research lasting the better part of a year, with about a half-million-dollar price tag. One of the first suggestions Bensman made was for Oracle to move into the midlevel market, where SAP was not competitive. "We recommended leaving SAP alone at the top and do[ing] a blocking strategy to keep SAP from moving down-market," says Bensman. As always, this generated fierce conflict at Oracle. The sales force got more revenue from database than applications, and SAP was driving database sales because its applications more often than not ran on Oracle. (SAP, like Oracle's other applications competitors, does not sell its own database.) But the applications development team fumed that the Oracle sales force was undermining its own application products to sell more databases loaded with SAP.

Bensman finally suggested that Oracle either acquire a competitor to bolster its applications or spin off the business altogether, an idea that made developers like Wohl and Mehta livid. In a rancorous meeting of the entire management team, Ellison and Wohl squelched the ideas, Bensman recalls, although Ellison did agree to reorganizing the applications business inside Oracle to give more responsibility to consulting head Robert Shaw. Ellison always sided with the developers, Bensman recalls. "From his point of view, the developers came up with a product and sales sold it. 'Don't come back and tell me you can't sell it,' he would say. If customers wouldn't buy it, they were stupid." Like Lane and Costello, Bensman believes that Oracle fumbled away its opportunity to dominate the applications market, in part because Ellison wouldn't listen to anything that might undermine development. Says Bensman, "I've never seen a chief executive tilt so blindly toward one guy [Wohl]. I've never seen it before or since."

GROWING TENSION

For several years, Wohl and the sales staff butted heads. Lane felt caught between the two. "I had a mandate from Robert [Shaw], who threatened to resign unless Ron was out," Lane recalls. For his part, Shaw says bluntly that "Larry had a semi-incompetent running [applications] development. Ron would do anything for Larry, but he doesn't have the balls to stand up to him. He knows where his bread gets buttered." What it takes in applications is a topflight manager who can make sure that everything—applications, tools, and database—works together, Shaw says. Wohl lacked the communication and leadership skills to elicit that kind of teamwork.

Another top executive, Barry Ariko, who was overseeing sales in the Americas, also recalls the "tremendous friction" between development and operations at Oracle. "There were a lot of half-truths about when a product would be ready. You could never quite get a straight answer," he says. "You thought you knew the date, and then you'd find out it wasn't the date, and there was no new date. It was hard for me because I never knew when things were supposed to be ready." He remembers that the sales executives challenged Ellison and Wohl repeatedly about the lack of specific delivery dates. In one of those executive meetings, says Ariko, Ellison took out his bankbook, looked over it, and told the rest of them, "I think I'll do it my way. I have all this money. I must be doing something right." Shaw was even more unhappy because his consulting staff had to pick up the pieces. "The pressure was on the consultants to make apps work," says Ariko. "It was a frustration to sales, but consulting was a bigger problem." He supported Lane's campaign to oust Wohl. "If you're not making schedules, what's the point of running applications development?" says Ariko. "Ron can't meet schedules. He's not very customer-focused."

However, a longtime Oracle customer, Mark Farnham, formerly with Burlington Coat and now head of a consulting firm, says that the dynamic tension between Wohl and Lane "ended up being good for the customer in some ways." He believes that Wohl "was doing the right thing in not committing to deadlines on applications." Applications were so complicated that making a change in one area could destabilize another feature. Consequently, while the salespeople always wanted extra features and an on-time product, so they could generate more revenue, apps users "would rather have it six months late and right," Farnham maintains, even if that meant holding off on some of the features and missing a deadline.

Despite the pressure from Shaw and Ariko, Lane was reluctant to give Ellison an ultimatum about Wohl, knowing the CEO's notorious dislike of confrontation. Finally, in early 1997, he approached Ellison and said other executives would be leaving the company unless he appointed an applications czar who could guide the overall business. He suggested Robert Shaw. But Ellison was alarmed by this seeming power grab, feeling that Shaw was Lane's guy and that would mean that Lane would oversee not only operations but development, too. Lane protests, "I never thought that Robert would report to me. I was thinking he would report to Larry. I don't know how to run products." Ellison saw it differently. He wanted development to remain under him, with no horizontal executive responsible for the entire business. In a rather strained telephone conversation with Lane, Ellison agreed that Wohl was not the best choice to run applications and proposed himself as a replacement: "Why shouldn't I be Mr. Applications?" Lane responded, "This isn't a game." Ellison persisted: "I will run applications." Lane pointed out that as the CEO, Ellison had other duties. Ellison said he would give applications the majority of his time. "You're going to spend 60 to 70 percent of your time on applications?" Lane asked incredulously. "I will," Ellison promised. "I paid almost no attention to the application business for ten years," the CEO acknowledged in a speech at Oracle Analysts' Day in June 2001. "I was very happy with overseeing the database, sailing, and flying. Then I realized I had never seen our applications. It struck me odd that I'm the CEO and I'd never seen them."

Ellison may have been exaggerating slightly, but here he put the finger on one of his chief weaknesses: the way his attention to Oracle's business ebbs and flows, depending on his own inclination. He loves the database side of the business, for that is where exploitation of cutting-edge technology allowed Oracle to flourish in the first place. And the database is sold to people who think like Ellison: they enjoy technology for its own sake. Couple this attitude with his growing enthusiasm for expensive hobbies made possible by his now-immense wealth—sailing his own multimillion-dollar yachts, flying his own plane—and you can believe he never really looked at Oracle's applications. After all, Ellison deliberately did not involve himself in most of the tasks for which applications were designed, like balancing the books or establishing customer care. Those were too petty for him. He's great at seeing the big picture but too farsighted to glimpse anything close up.

TO THE INTERNET

With Ellison's vow to fix the problems with applications, Lane convinced Shaw and Ariko to stay on, although both tenures would be brief. When Ellison started to check into applications, he soon found that they still contained the nonstandard code that Walker had inserted. "Larry spent about three or four months looking at applications," says Lane. Then he came back to the executive committee, raging that the applications lacked competitive features. "And they have code that's not Oracle," he complained. It has never been Ellison's way to take the tedious road. "Rather than say we'll fix the bugs, one by one," says Lane, Ellison decided to scrap everything. "Let's start over, develop our applications on our technology, and use a browser-based operating system on a thin client." Presto! Oracle applications would move to the Internet. "Larry took the idea and ran with it, stomping in front of the press about driving applications to the Internet. He was very excited about it," says Lane. "He was doing what he does best: coming out with a new strategic positioning." As Ellison says, "I always feel good when everyone says I am nuts. It's a sign we've done something new and different." He would much rather conceive the new than fix the old.

While Lane says he supported the Internet strategy, as did the executive committee, the divide with Ellison came over what to do with the existing applications—which operated on a client-server architecture—while the Internet version was being developed. In a typical paradox that besets all software companies trying to make a paradigm shift, customers still clamored for fixes to the old version. First of all, no one wants to be first to move to a new architecture because, inevitably, there are multiple problems that have to be fixed. First-mover, or beta, customers are the testing ground for new applications. But for companies, the question becomes, how many resources do you commit to supporting the old, but still used, product when you're trying to move on to the new? Ellison, naturally, wanted to dump customer support for the client-server product right away, but Lane and other members of the executive committee were more cautious. "There were many meetings with the executive staff where Larry heard us say we've got to fix the client-server applications because we're losing business," says Lane. "Actually, I wanted both [client-server and Internet] products," he adds, but it was obvious the Internet release wouldn't be available for at least a year. "Our sales force still had to sell product, and all we had was release 10.6, which was client-server." In the absence of a new product, "I wanted to fix the existing version. I was trying to improve the competitiveness of our applications, but Larry believed that I didn't agree with the new strategy."

Ellison's version is that he dragged Oracle's executive staff and customers kicking and screaming into the Internet era. "Larry says he ignored all of us and went ahead with the E-business suite," says Lane. "That his own executive staff fought him and wanted to fix the present system." Lane insists his strategy was to support existing applications until the Internet suite came out, which, as it turned out, would take almost three years. "In the fall of 1997, Larry was presenting our applications as fully Internet-capable," says Lane, but release 11i of Oracle's applications, the first real Internet version, was promised for delivery in November 1999 and actually came out in late spring of 2000. "It took nearly three years to get a valid Internet application out," says Lane. "Larry gets all the credit for coming up with Internet applications," he acknowledges, but there was considerable pain for customers (see the next chapter)—and for the executive staff—before that vision was realized.

Says Ariko, "If you believed it was going to take as long as it did to get the applications product on the Internet, you couldn't abandon your existing customers. What does it say if you say we're not going to support this old stuff anymore?" He adds, "I still believe long-term credibility is based on your ability to deliver a consistent message to customers." The executive staff was caught in a political trap in pressing for a time frame for delivery of Internet applications. "When you argue against something at Oracle, it sounds like you don't support it," says Ariko. At any other company, "the right answer would be, 'Yes, we want to push customers to do this [move to the Internet], but we'll support you through a couple of releases.'" Within the tortuous politics of Oracle, it was all or nothing. You were with Ellison or against him.

Indeed, the conflict over Wohl, exacerbated by Lane's insistence on supporting client-server customers, was the turning point in the relationship between Ellison and his second-in-command. Previously, Ellison had been content to run engineering and leave almost everything else to Lane, save for occasional forays into marketing. Now that would change. "Larry interpreted all this as evidence that I was running a palace coup," says Lane. First, he'd wanted to give applications responsibility to Shaw; then he'd pressed to fix the client-server product rather than concentrate solely on developing an Internet product. Ellison was convinced that Lane was after the top job, although he said nothing directly.

Not only was Lane at odds with the chief executive, but he would soon lose two of his staunchest allies. Shaw, fed up with the infighting and the lack of accountability for delivering workable applications, departed in early 1998. "I'm the one who had to deal with the customers," he says. "It got very frustrating." In addition, Shaw felt that he now had the skills to run his own company. At Oracle, "I'd made a lot of money, but I was never going to run the place," he adds. "Before I got out of the business, I wanted to go run something." Later that same year, Lane says he was forced to fire Ariko, after the Oracle president came back from a vacation and found that salespeople were leaving in droves because they'd lost confidence in the sales leadership. "I had to fire Barry and the other two who were managing the Americas—all three of them on the same day in 1998," Lane says. The soft-spoken Ariko acknowledges he never quite fit in with Oracle's culture. "I was swimming with the sharks," he says. He tried to focus the aggressive behavior outwardly, against the competition, rather than inwardly. "I did not want to make myself into one of those back-stabbing people," he adds. "You can get a whole lot done without screaming at someone." Ariko was ready to leave Oracle in late 1997 to join networking software vendor Novell. "I told Ray that everybody's second-guessing me at Oracle. I want to run my own business, be measured on results." At that point, he got promoted to executive vice president and joined the executive committee, "but it became very clear that nothing was changing. I got the title, more money, more options," but not the autonomy that he really craved. "My only grudge is that they should have just let me leave rather than promising things that never happened."

BEGINNING OF THE END

From this point on, the relationship between Ellison and Lane would fray until it snapped in mid-2000. In the history of Oracle, Ellison had not had a strong number-two executive like Lane. Bob Miner probably came the closest, but as cofounder and friend, he had a different relationship with the CEO. And he was never a threat to take over the top job, as Lane clearly was. Compounding that, little camaraderie developed between Ellison and Lane outside the office. They never got to be friends; indeed, they didn't even feel comfortable together. Although Silicon Valley chief executives sport big egos, most have the grace to recognize their limits and to build up strong teams around them. Ellison did this, with Lane and Henley and others, when he was forced to, but his narcissism couldn't tolerate the rising challenge from an executive like Lane, who was getting too much of the limelight. Lane was praised by customers and quoted in the press, which invoked his name whenever Oracle's turnaround was cited. No wonder that Ellison, whose self-esteem had been battered by his childhood experiences, became estranged from his putative second-in-command. Lane had become the authority figure at Oracle, telling Ellison what he should and shouldn't do even in the CEO's cherished realm of development. It was too much for Ellison. And Lane made mistakes, too. His failure to see that Ellison was threatened by his proposed elevation of his own guy, Robert Shaw, to oversee development proved to be a fatal blind spot. After that, Lane was on his way out.

Starting in 1997–1998, Ellison, who had spent a lot of time away from Oracle indulging in his passion for sailing and other hobbies, reasserted his control and began chipping away at Lane's responsibilities. The loss of Robert Shaw deprived Lane of his chief backer among the senior executives. "Ray and I were the only two executive committee members who would stand up and argue with Larry about decisions, like the quality of the products and the direction," says Shaw. Gary Bloom, who at first worked in tandem with Lane, found himself pitted against the president as Ellison shifted responsibilities from Lane to Bloom. "There was a window where Ray filled a big leadership void while Larry was off doing his [sailboat] racing," says Bloom. "Ray stood up as the visible leader of the company both internally and externally. He actually started believing he was running the company, which collided with Larry's belief, and then Larry reengaged with the company."

George Kadifa, another of Lane's handpicked executives, says he saw the end coming more than a year before Lane was ousted. In mid-1999, Ellison started second-guessing Lane's decisions, even on areas that had been exclusively in the president's province, such as the sales quotas, the territorial divisions, and the vertical strategy. "Larry started getting involved in all those issues," says Kadifa. Ellison even announced that he was "back in control" at the user group conference that year in San Diego. "Everyone thought Larry would get back on the boat and by July he would leave us alone," says Kadifa. It was not to be. Ellison began complaining about the things that Lane was doing wrong. "He can be very violent in the executive meetings. It got to a point where it was extremely unpleasant [between the two of them]," Kadifa adds. Lane's empire continued to be chipped away. Bloom got marketing, alliances, field development, support, and on-line business. All that was left was sales and the president's title, which, of course, disappeared in the phone conversation detailed in Chapter 1.

"There's a saying in Oracle: the moth that flies too close to the flame gets burned," says Lane. Subconsciously, he knew a parting was near, but consciously, he tried to ignore it. Today he regrets never becoming an insider with Ellison. "It would have been great to have a more personal relationship, where it wasn't just about business." A closer relationship "would have given me a better awareness that my attack on Ron Wohl was threatening to Larry." Perhaps it would have helped Ellison to see Lane's value as more than just monetary. When Lane was wooed in 1996 to become CEO of networking software maker Novell, "Larry didn't have to respond by showering me with options. We could have just sat down and discussed what I wanted at Oracle." Instead, Ellison, in an attempt to keep his second-in-command, offered Lane 2 million options and then got the board to boost it to 2.5 million. "He obviously felt very vulnerable after that," says Lane. Then again, given Ellison's track record with executives who dared to stand up to him, Lane's departure was probably inevitable. Ellison doesn't like to mention Lane's name anymore in public forums. At Oracle's OpenWorld conference in December 2001, he referred obliquely to the dispute: "I tried a strong number two, and it didn't work out. I'll never do it again. Once someone perceives himself as number two, he gets blinded by the limelight and becomes less effective. It's very heady stuff. I don't think it was healthy for Oracle to have that kind of management structure."

However, the conflict over Wohl, which was the trigger point for Lane's fall, also had positive effects. It resulted in Ellison's taking a hard look at applications and repositioning Oracle for the Internet era. For a time, this vaulted Oracle to the center of the Internet revolution, where, in the late 1990s, it profited by selling its technology and Ellison's vision to the booming dot-com world. Moving applications to the Internet also meant that established companies, including Oracle, had to restructure internal business processes. The database and the NC were more conceptual; applications required material changes in the way companies operated. Sums up Lane: "With applications, Larry saw that real businesses can use the

Internet. He morphed the vision: The Media Server became the NC. The NC became the browser-based client. The browser-based client became the basis for Internet applications." In retrospect, it's obvious that the Internet move was the correct one and provided a much-needed shot in the arm to Oracle's moribund applications business. Lane and his allies were too cautious in embracing Ellison's new vision, no doubt because they had been burned so often before, as with the Media Server and NC. Through all of this, however, Ellison was relying on his formidable sense of where technology was headed to steer Oracle in the right direction. Still, there was a lot of suffering to come, particularly for Oracle's customers, before Ellison's vision became a reality.

9

MEMO TO ORACLE

["STOP BLAMING CUSTOMERS."]

From a developer's perspective, customers are a necessary evil. You want to code the brilliant new product of the future, but your customers want you to fix yesterday's product, the one they're using now. Customers seldom ask for a paradigm shift; they just want what they already have to work better. Customers focus on incremental improvements, while technology companies like to lead the way to the Next Big Thing. So it's not surprising that there is little love lost between Larry Ellison, the ultimate technology visionary who's interested mostly in the future, and Oracle's customers, who could never quite catch up with where Larry is. "Customer satisfaction was never a priority in the early years at Oracle," says former sales executive Craig Ramsey. "As a salesperson, you closed a $2 million deal and you moved on," leaving the customer to figure out how to make this multimillion-dollar purchase work. As Anneke Seley, who worked in both sales and customer support, notes, "The salespeople we hired were motivated to make money, not to please customers." That attitude came directly from Ellison, who was impatient with customers' slowness to adopt new technology. Old-time customers say that it wasn't until Ray Lane joined the company in 1992 that they had a true champion.

Many companies have built business processes around

treating customers as partners and building a customer-centered enterprise. Oracle, as always, has been the contrarian. In the 1980s, it was the newly invented relational database that created headaches for customers. The idea underlying a relational database was that it could create connections among apparently disparate information and thus answer unpredictable queries, such as whether a snowfall in Minneapolis affected sales in Miami. The old hierarchical database couldn't do this; it could only output information by topic. So customers were clamoring for Oracle's database, and the company, as has become its pattern, released the product before it was ready. Even Ellison acknowledged that version 2, the first commercialized product, was a "piece of shit." Version 3 was slightly better, but then later releases, especially version 6, were also riddled with problems. It wasn't until version 7, released the same time that Ray Lane came, in 1992, that Oracle had a stable, mature database product.

Fortunately for Oracle, database buyers were generally information technology experts who were willing to tinker until they got a functioning product. Not only that, in the 1980s, database technology was still so new and alternative suppliers so few that customers had a certain tolerance for bugs. They realized that the relational database was an extraordinarily complex piece of software that would not operate perfectly upon installation. As Ellison quipped at one trade show, "Our products can be terrible, but as long as they're better than everyone else, we'll win." Indeed, the inside joke in the entire software industry was that you had to wait until the third version of any product before it functioned in a reasonably dependable matter. Microsoft's Windows was another example of this.

The real crunch for Oracle came when it began to release enterprise applications, starting with Financials, introduced in the late 1980s. At this point, the customer base shifted from the IT expert, who had bought the database, to an end user—like a CFO or a benefits administrator—who wanted the product to work out of the box. But at Oracle, those kinds of customers weren't cool, and neither were the people who created products for them. "An applications company is very different than creating technology [like a database]," says Polly Sumner, a longtime Oracle sales executive. "The applications group uses the technology, they don't invent technology. They are second-class citizens." Even though applications are mission-critical to the company that buys them, "to our developers, they're boring stuff like Accounts Payable and General Ledger," she says. All of this reflects Ellison's own prejudice— in favor of developers and technology and against "bean counters" and other mundane occupations that don't interest him. He likes to create technology, not perfect it, and so he admires engineers, not end users. In his eyes, when something goes wrong with Oracle products, it's because the customer did something stupid.

As a result of these attitudes, Oracle's application users are often frustrated, unhappy, and vocal about it. So Oracle's reputation among customers, not to mention organizations like Forrester Group, AMR Research, and Gartner Group that advise users, ranges from terrible to, at best, mediocre. "The issue I have with Oracle is that they just don't treat their customers very well," says Patricia Seybold, author of *Customers.com* and CEO of The Patricia Seybold Group, a management consulting firm specializing in customer relationships. "I come from a place that says if I'm going to invest in a company, I want to look at the quality of the customer experience. Then I evaluate whether this company will gain or lose customer loyalty and referrals based on how well they treat their customers. Oracle still has a black eye compared to all its competitors, even Microsoft." In a February 2001 release, AMR noted, "Oracle's application history has been checkered at best. The company has a legacy of shipping software to early adopters and relying on them to shed the blood, sweat, and tears necessary to debug the system and make it reliable." In March 2001, Forrester chimed in, commenting that Ellison's keynote address at Oracle's customer user conference "was notable for its finger-pointing at customers— blaming their customizations for [the latest application suite's] instability."

Lane, who as a former consultant brought a much more customer-focused approach to Oracle, was able to improve the situation for a time by setting up new internal processes and incentive plans that depended on satisfying the customer. A half year after joining Oracle, he set up a customer advisory board, which consisted of chief information officers from about a dozen of Oracle's major customers, including Time Warner, Coca-Cola, and R. R. Donnelley. "Ray's concept was that this body of people who were practicing CIOs would be a good sounding board for all the elements of his marketing program, service, and support capabilities," recalls John Reece, the former CIO of Time Warner who served on the board for three and a half years. "We were all executives in relatively sophisticated environments who used Oracle as an integral part of our main business solutions." The group met semiannually with senior Oracle executives, including Lane, Randy Baker, and Robert Shaw. Lane even scheduled one meeting, in the fall of 1993, with Ellison at Oracle's headquarters. "You could see that Larry was not accustomed to this," says Reece. "He walked in very tenuously [late as always], sat down, and they brought him a sandwich with the bread crusts neatly trimmed off." Then the customers started telling him why Oracle needed to be more responsive to their needs. Ellison's response was to give Lane more control over customer-related issues. For a while, "things got better," Reece says.

But the persistent conflict with applications development head Ron Wohl over delivery dates and product quality eroded Lane's ability to be a champion for the customer. Then came the increasing friction between Lane and Ellison, which further undermined the former's political strength inside Oracle. After Lane was forced out in 2000, Oracle's customer relations abruptly worsened, to the point where the company engaged in an embarrassing public spat with its own applications user group. One problem was Oracle's failure to deliver a working version of its E-business suite, 11i, even while it was determined to abandon support of previous versions. "The worst piece of application software I've ever had to install has been Oracle," recounts Joe Imbimbo, an Oracle applications database administrator who has worked for several companies. "It was excruciating trying to figure out how to set it up without instructions." Lane sums up, "Oracle's approach is to ignore the customer. Senior management doesn't see the customer as important, which pisses off the user group."

"ESCALATING" PROBLEMS

Oracle customers have ample reasons to be pissed, but in general, they're also intensely loyal to the technology. This is partially due to the switching costs of moving from one database to another or one set of ERP (enterprise resource planning) applications to another, which are horrendous, to put it mildly. But a key part of the loyalty is due to the fact that Oracle does have leading-edge technology. To summarize the customer experience with Oracle: the company is a pain in the ass to do business with, shoves out products before they're ready for prime time, but, usually after a lot of moaning by the customer, eventually gets things right. Now, to be fair, a lot of other high-tech companies, such as Microsoft, do the same thing, but none is quite so brazen about it as Oracle. Larry Ellison is, as far as I know, unique in publicly blaming customers for problems with his company's software. I've heard him berate customers for having the temerity to impose their own business processes on Oracle software when, really, Oracle knows best. "We give you one database, all the [application] pieces fit, no customization," he says, but customization is the way users make the software conform to their own ways of doing business.

Customers that have problems with applications often go through a series of "escalations" with Oracle Support, upping the ante each time they call. For instance, if the bug is so bad that it threatens to shut down your whole operation, you can declare an emergency. But such tactics have to be used judiciously, or like the boy who cried wolf, you find yourself getting less rather than more help. When you first call Oracle for help, "basically, the people you get are fairly inexperienced, working off a checklist," says Cliff Billingsley, the controller for Metropolitan Transit Authority of Houston, which has been using Oracle's database and client-server applications since 1992. "They try to match your problem with one somebody else has had and give you a canned solution. If you have a significant problem, you have to escalate one or two levels to a TAR [technical assistance request]."

Customer Joe Imbimbo agrees with Billingsley. At Bombardier, which makes Learjets and other business aircraft, he helped convert the Oracle applications from a client-server to a browser-based system (10.7SC to 10.7NCA), a forerunner of the Internet suite. (In client-server systems, users, or clients, all tap into a central server to access the database or applications via proprietary commands. The Internet architecture replaces those commands with a browser, like Navigator or Explorer, to access company information and applications by means of an intranet. Internet architecture is far more flexible and multidirectional, allowing sharing of information with customers and partners.) The installation instructions for the latter took a year to come out after the software was released. Meanwhile, Imbimbo had to call other customers and industry analysts to find out what to do to make the applications work. As for the database, "that technology is excellent," he acknowledges. "I never had any downtime with the database." Like many customers, he finds most of the problems with applications. "Oracle is constantly tinkering with them," he says, creating unexpected changes that can cascade into other areas.

With Compaq Computer (which has since become part of Hewlett-Packard), a star customer for Oracle, the escalation worked the other way. Paul Box, director of corporate procurement, selected a version of 11i that Oracle dubs its "I-procurement suite," covering basic applications as well as a special self-service module. Since it's a reference customer for Oracle, meaning the vendor directs potential clients to it for comments, Compaq is accustomed to very good service. "We

enjoy a unique relationship," says Box, because Oracle and
Compaq jointly market technology that they work on
together. "If I ever felt we weren't getting the attention we
deserved, I'd tell them we'll have to stop these reference calls
from other customers," says Box. Nonetheless, he has been
annoyed when Oracle decided it wanted Compaq to utilize the
applications in certain ways just because it would look good
for Oracle. "Oracle can be very, very supportive as well as
very, very abrasive," says Box. "Occasionally, I felt like Oracle
acted as if they know my business better than I do." For
example, Box decided that implementing a particular module
wouldn't benefit Compaq, and Oracle went over his head and
talked to his bosses. "They escalated our lack of deployment
to get senior management to do what Oracle wants. They
weren't working in our interest but in their own."

WHAT'S THAT AGAIN?

Another issue raised by several customers concerns Oracle's
complicated product and pricing lists. To put this in perspective, almost no technology vendor really sells based on its
publicly disclosed pricing. There are always discounts related
to the volume of the sale or the size/prestige of the customer or
the nearness to the end of a quarter, when salespeople are
feverish to make their numbers. Companies like Oracle that
offer core technology, such as the database, plus applications
will often sacrifice pricing on one or the other to make the
sale. Oracle can virtually give the database away to sell a big
suite of applications or vice versa. Not only can the initial
pricing be confusing, but the way Oracle handles its upgrades
varies. Supposedly, if you buy one version of the applications,
you get the next version free (except, of course, for maintenance fees)—this is standard industry practice. But Oracle
puts limits on the number of people who can use the software
or on the number of processors on which it can run, which
sometimes forces customers to buy a new product license for

an upgrade. Although it's not unusual for software companies to do this, Oracle games the system more than most, by changing the rules or renaming products.

"This is the biggest complaint I have about Oracle," says Billingsley, of the Metropolitan Transit Authority of Houston. "Every time you go to add another product, they want to change the overall arrangement." MTA was originally licensed concurrently for all the products it bought, based on numbers of users. At first, these users were counted by how many would be active at peak times. "They wanted us to change that to pay for every named user," says Billingsley. As he added products, "they wanted to license different ways on different products." For example, with Payroll/HR, "they asked us to pay for all employees." Another tactic: early adopters pay extra for peripheral products that are later incorporated into the base product. "With our initial license, it took us six months to select Oracle but almost a year to write the contract," he says, because the licensing terms were so complex.

Beth Jinkerson, director of the information systems department for Oak Ridge Associated Universities, a public-sector group affiliated with the federal Department of Energy, says Oracle's contract terms can sometimes work to the customer's advantage. Oak Ridge bought from Oracle in the early 1990s, before Lane banished site licenses, and got a really good deal. "So long as we keep renewing our contract [on the initial products], it cannot be changed," she says, much as Oracle has pressured her to do so. However, whenever Oak Ridge buys a new product, it becomes subject to the new terms. "You would not believe how many hours it takes to figure out what you want and buy something new," she says. "Oracle renames their products and pricing structure so often, it's anybody's guess what you're trying to buy. They say we can charge by the number of processors in your computer or the number of users, or we can do a site license." Recently, Oak Ridge wanted to buy a module then called HR Self Service, although it's had several different names. As she negotiated the deal with Oracle, "they kept saying, 'Wouldn't you like to redo the contract?'" Jinkerson's answer is always "No way."

ORACLE EVERYWHERE

There are two kinds of software applications vendors: best of breed and integrated. "Best of breed" vendors such as Siebel Systems sell software that does one thing very well—in Siebel's case, customer relationship management (CRM). But Siebel's CRM suite must be hooked to other applications, such as financials, to function properly, giving consultants and system integrators guaranteed employment in helping companies get all their diverse applications to work together. By contrast, an integrated software vendor such as Oracle stresses buying the entire suite of enterprise applications, ranging from financials to HR to manufacturing to CRM, from a single source, theoretically avoiding the headaches of dealing with different packages. "Integrated" suites provide all the capabilities in one package. Oracle's approach is bolstered by the fact that, unlike the other enterprise application vendors, it sells the all-important database that runs beneath these suites. In fact, many analysts compare Ellison's pronouncements on the subject to the apocryphal quote attributed to Henry Ford: "You can have any color car you want so long as it's black."

As Ellison jokes, "Think about buying separate products with separate databases and trying to attach all of these together to run your business. The customer is responsible for making this work. System integration—the gift that keeps on giving." Oracle's model is different, he says. "We don't think our customers are capable of modifying our software." Rather, Oracle offers a complete solution. "We're not best of breed in everything, but we have enough core technology to run GE" (see the section on page 193 entitled "Moving to 11i" for another side to this). Ellison notes that even though he's a former programmer himself, "I don't know how to fit these pieces [of an ERP suite] together. The only way you can make these pieces fit together is engineer them from the ground up." In other words, trust Oracle's development team to do the job properly and don't mess with what it gives you.

This approach resonates well with small to midtier companies that prefer to deal with only one vendor for their database and applications. Where it does not play so well is with large companies that have an array of software products and aren't likely to dump these in favor of an all-Oracle solution. Rather, their preference is generally to go for best of breed and let the vendors and their internal IT departments deal with integration issues. Ford Motor Company is one of Oracle's star customers, yet "if anybody thinks Ford is running entirely on Oracle, they're naive," says Brian Kelley, Ford's vice president of global consumer services. Ford is in the midst of a three-year project modernizing its business processes and purchasing procurement largely on Oracle's E-business suite, 11i, but parts of the suite, including the Supply Chain module, aren't robust enough for the automaker. "We recognize the challenge of integration, but we're not ready to compromise best of breed by going for a product that isn't up to what we need," Kelley adds. "If [Oracle's] product meets with our requirements, we see an advantage in integration. But we have not at this point felt that other areas of their product were strong enough to consider."

By contrast, smaller companies are willing to sacrifice some robustness in exchange for simplicity. "We're not GE," says Lisa Harris, senior vice president and chief information officer of Gevity HR, a human resources outsourcing company in Bradenton, Florida, that uses the Oracle database and the 11i suite across the board. It also bought Oracle Portal, a new product that allows companies to set up personalized Internet portals for employees and customers. "If you can get 90 percent of what you need out of the box, what is that 10 percent going to give you if you're a small or medium-sized company?" she asks. "You can get caught up on that best-of-breed thing. It's much easier to be in a single-vendor relationship than multiple." Gevity selected Oracle because of its integration message. "We didn't want to be in the finger-pointing mode when we had a problem," Harris says. "Integration is really a wonderful story if you can get it to work." Harris says that even if Oracle lacks functionality in a certain release, "they keep bringing out new modules, so eventually you get what you want." On the flip side, "when it comes to upgrades, you have to upgrade the whole suite, not just a portion. So every two or three years, you have a major upgrade that is scary and difficult." Not only that, Harris adds, with a single vendor, "you are at their mercy. You really have to work the relationship, know when to escalate [problems] and when not to. You have to act like you're married."

HAND IN HAND WITH ORACLE

Consultants who help customers with Oracle installations are a hardy breed. Most of them told me that if they had to do it over again, they probably wouldn't choose Oracle as their area of expertise because it's so difficult to work with the company. With the possible exception of software firm Computer Associates, which is notorious for dictating terms to customers and partners, Oracle gives off the most negative "vibes" with its erstwhile partners of any company in the technology industry. One large system integrator/consultant, EDS, refused to talk to me about Oracle because, according to a spokeswoman, there was nothing its representatives could say that would be positive. Nonetheless, as an individual consultant, once you've developed Oracle expertise, you're sucked in. The switching cost of trying to develop that same expertise and a new relationship with a competitor, like SAP or PeopleSoft, is almost insurmountable. Rick Bishop, an Oracle consultant for more than a decade, first with Andersen Consulting (since renamed Accenture) and now with Deloitte & Touche, sums up his "love-hate" relationship with Oracle: "We love them because they are the eight hundred-pound gorilla. They have outstanding market share and very aggressive, very effective sales and marketing. As a result, there are a large number of opportunities for us to provide consulting services. What we hate about Oracle is that all of that aggressiveness causes them to walk pretty close to the integrity line. A fundamental of our practice is that we work in the best interest of our client. Oracle works in the best interest of Oracle."

Bishop, who deals primarily with Oracle applications, says the company's aim is to maximize its own license or consulting revenue, "even if that puts the client's long-term success at risk." As a consultant, that leaves him in the tricky position of "trying to counsel the client on what their realistic expectations should be but also work constructively with Oracle to help them close a deal. There's a gap between Oracle's message and what our real-life experience has been." He cites as an example a $600 million manufacturer that selected Oracle as its ERP vendor in 1999. Oracle Consulting Services (OCS) was the lead consultant, with Andersen providing support. During the software-testing phase of implementation, the customer encountered problems on the commission piece of the sales force automation module. Oracle's software did not allow the client to calculate different commission rates for different volumes or to split commissions. "During the software demos six months previously, Oracle had claimed this capability was a standard part of their functionality," Bishop recalls. For a month, the client "tried to hold Oracle's feet to the fire" to make that alleged functionality a reality. But the patches that Oracle sent never fixed the problem. Finally, the client returned the module to Oracle for a refund and picked another vendor to do that piece. To get the refund, "they had to escalate all the way to Ray Lane, who authorized it," says Bishop.

When I asked another Oracle consultant, Faun DeHenry, chief executive of FMT Systems in Oakland, California, to cite some examples of customers who'd had problems, she laughed. "I wish I could give you examples of customers who didn't have problems." DeHenry concentrates on helping clients reengineer their business processes when they adopt Oracle ERP applications. "Oracle has a nasty habit of releasing products before they're ready," she says, forcing customers "to do the beta testing they should have done." Then, instead of being helpful, "they're hostile when you come back to them with questions." To be fair, all ERP software typically requires considerable tinkering, on both the technical and business process aspects, to fit it to any customer's needs. DeHenry acknowledges that but notes that when she works with customers of other vendors, including SAP, PeopleSoft, and Siebel Systems, "I don't hear the kind of unbridled anger that I hear when they're dealing with Oracle."

Oracle's recommendation is to install its applications without customization—in other words, without changing any of the methods that the software uses to do things, like write checks or process orders. "They're telling you that they know how to run your business better than you do," says DeHenry. "They want you to accept their vision of what is best practice. Larry [Ellison] says, 'If we didn't build it this way, you don't need it.'" (Other ERP vendors have fairly similar attitudes, she notes.) She worked with one company that had purchased a CRM module from Oracle to manage field service operations. Oracle had designed its system so that everybody could see all the service requests, "but this company did not want that. They don't want their service branches to see how the requests are being doled out." The company had to call on FMT to handle the customization because Oracle insisted its module didn't need to be changed. In another case, DeHenry handled training for the city of Oakland when it bought Oracle's financial and HR applications in 1999. "Oakland had massive problems implementing the technology," she says, due to mistakes by both sides. At the end, the city had poured nearly $20 million into the project. She says it was difficult getting anyone from the local government to make decisions, while frustrated Oracle consultants didn't want to deal with it. DeHenry had to bridge the gap. "I'm the one who said, 'I'm not going to walk out of here without providing a solution.'"

Sanjeev Gulati, vice president of Polaris Software, an India-based company that specializes in applications from Oracle, SAP, Siebel, and Baan, says the company got started as an Oracle consultancy in 1990 with the database. In 1997, Polaris added its applications practice and expanded to the other vendors because it didn't want to be dependent solely on Oracle. Now a $100 million company with offices in the United States and elsewhere, Polaris still handles Oracle applications to serve clients that have chosen that technology. "One of the reasons we added SAP is because of all the difficulties of working with Oracle," he says, "but we cannot simply dump Oracle apps. We'd love to if we could, but we can't tell our clients we're quitting just because Oracle is a pain to deal with." The pattern is that consultants first try to deal with technical problems arising from an installation. "Once you've exhausted all your options, you conclude that the software has a bug in it, so you escalate to Oracle, which is supposed to get back to you within a certain period of time. That's where the pain starts. Most of the time, it takes forever for them to get back to you." More than those of any other vendor, "Oracle's products are released before they're stable," says Gulati, which means a lot of expensive time goes into figuring out where the problems arise. "The losers are the clients who have to pay for that time and the consultants who get criticized because they don't know the software is full of bugs."

On top of everything else, Oracle often competes directly with its would-be partners for deals related to Oracle software licenses, with all the obvious conflicts of interest. Bishop cites an example involving a $100 million European manufacturer of products for the construction industry looking to expand into the United States It chose Oracle as its ERP vendor and then considered OCS versus Andersen (now Accenture) to handle the implementation. According to Bishop, OCS gave a lowball estimate of $300,000, compared to a range of $800,000 to $1 million by Andersen. (The software license fee was around $400,000.) Naturally, the client selected Oracle for both the software and the consulting. "After eighteen months, Oracle had been through at least three change orders, and the client ended up paying $1.8 million in consulting fees compared to the initial estimate of $300,000," Bishop says. Since Oracle has set up its consulting arm on a separate P&L, there's always going to be conflict, he maintains. "Larry delivers mixed messages. He says he wants to downsize OCS and be more partner-centric. But when you're holding your [consulting] managers accountable for P&L, will they follow what you say or how they're measured?" Bishop acknowledges that Oracle has made strides in working with its partners by giving the sales force more authority to determine when OCS will be brought in. "Oracle has put more programs in place to try to improve the business partner relationship," although the strength of the partnership is very much dependent "on the volume of business you can share with them. If you bring several deals to Oracle, they are more likely to work productively with you."

As usual, this is a reflection of Ellison's attitude: once Oracle has built a product, it's great technology, and customers should be flocking to it. Ellison sees only the end, not the means. The latter can be tedious, and he's not one to concern himself with all the work that has to be done to get to a stated goal. It's like the wagon train leader pointing to lights on a far-distant hill: that's our destination, he says, and then leaves the train members on their own to find it themselves.

MOVING TO 11i

A great flurry of complaints came as Oracle stiff-armed its customers (by threatening to withdraw support of earlier products) into moving from the client-server release, 10.7SC, to the integrated Internet suite, 11i. (There was an intervening browser-based version of some of the applications, release 11, but it was not fully integrated and was considered an interim step.) Although the original release date for 11i was November 1999, it was released in sections in late spring 2000. Even by 2002, the majority of Oracle's customers had not yet made the transition, mostly because of concerns that 11i was unstable. It didn't perform many of the functions it was supposed to; for instance, for a time, the Payroll module wouldn't print out checks. At the November 2001 meeting of the Oracle Applications User Group (OAUG), an independent organization of application customers, the buzz was that 11i just wasn't ready for full-bore use. When I E-mailed attendees to ask them about their experiences in moving to 11i, I got responses like, "We are just starting to address the 11i problem. . . . It seems to us to be a huge mess designed to bring Oracle more cash, via consulting services. If we designed and released a product as buggy as 11i, we would be out of business in less than six months." Another customer wrote, "The upgrade process has been a nightmare and frankly one of the biggest obstacles is Oracle Support, or more accurately lack thereof." A common irritant was that when Oracle put out a patch to fix a bug in one piece of the applications, it did not check to see whether that patch caused problems elsewhere, as was often the case. A number of users who asked not to be named said that they were holding off on 11i as long as possible.

Not everyone was dissatisfied with Oracle. One customer that did the upgrade early was Gevity HR, the staffing bureau that meets many other companies' human resources needs. "We process one hundred thousand paychecks a week," says chief information officer Lisa Harris. "It's a big task. It's especially big when you cannot be down for long or people don't get paid." Consequently, Gevity faced the monumental task of implementing about two dozen modules—pieces of software designed for different functionality such as payroll or order management—in 11i over the course of a weekend. Harris started planning for the switch in January 2001, hoping to go live by midyear. Actually, the company wound up making the switch in September, allowing three extra months for Oracle development to work on stabilizing 11i. Over a long weekend starting on Thursday, September 13, and complicated by tropical storm Gabriel, which hit Florida the next day, Gevity replaced its release 10.7 and 11 modules with 11i. "We closed our corporate offices because the tropical storm made it too dangerous to drive for employees," says Harris. The IT people simply lived at the office for three days. "We finished at 3 P.M. on Sunday, and Monday morning we were live." The first week saw a few problems, including payroll application and flow processing, which was very slow. On Wednesday, "we got a special patch from Oracle development, which worked twenty-four hours around the clock to help us do a quick fix. The following week, it was like we'd never done an upgrade."

Lane says that Oracle's engineers are capable of working hard to help a customer in trouble. On many occasions, he took calls from fed-up customers, contacted Ron Wohl, "and he would have an engineer drop everything to fix the problem." However, Lane maintains, this ad hoc method of addressing software bugs is inefficient, for customers and for Oracle. The resulting fixes don't always get posted to Oracle's on-line site, which explains why the OAUG does a huge business in enabling customers to exchange information about fixes and patches. Indeed, the main problem with 11i was the inordinate number of flaws—at least five thousand, as documented by the Forrester Group, which meant the software wouldn't install or run properly until a patch was applied. And the patches often created additional problems, which, in turn, had to be fixed.

The industry consulting groups, which advise large companies on their technology buys, weighed in on the fray over 11i. In March 2001, Forrester's Laurie Orlov wrote an uncharacteristically sharply worded report entitled "Memo to Oracle: Stop Blaming Customers." In it, she declared, "Oracle has stooped to a new low—blaming its unhappy 11i apps customers for doing too much customization." (Remember Ellison's comment that customers aren't capable of modifying Oracle software.) Orlov, noting that release 11i had undergone more than five thousand patches and that big deployments are "hitting the wall," suggested that Oracle provide "less blame and more customer support." Later that year, in August, Gartner Group analyst Betsy Burton put out a report, "Oracle under Fire," that stated, "Oracle is rightly under a degree of fire from some of its customers. Although many of Oracle's challenges are not insurmountable, we believe that recent actions and events will leave an indelible scar on customers' view of Oracle." Among the "chinks in [Oracle's] corporate armor," she cited slowdowns in database growth and actual declines in applications sales, the defection of senior executives such as Lane and Gary Bloom, the withdrawal of support from the OAUG, adoption of a "widely unpopular" new pricing model, and slow adoption of 11i due to stability issues. Burton also suggested that although the issues are "a natural part of being an aggressive, bleeding-edge competitor," they also cause enterprises to question their buying decisions on Oracle and open the door to competitors. Oracle posted an article on its Web site accusing Gartner of having a "documented bias toward Oracle in its coverage," and the two entities traded charges in the *Wall Street Journal*. Oracle accused Gartner of failing to give the company enough time to respond to the criticisms and of not making changes in response to input. Oracle also said a six-month review of Gartner reports showed that 23 percent were critical of Oracle while only 8 percent were critical of IBM. A Gartner spokeswoman retorted that the reports reflected what was happening in the marketplace. Gartner analysts "are in touch with Oracle customers. We certainly come under fire from vendors displeased with what we've written. They call it 'bias,' but I think you are talking about 'independence.'"[1]

It's no surprise that there were some glitches as Oracle moved its application suite from one paradigm to another. ERP applications are complicated even in normal releases, and a product transition as sweeping as 11i was bound to have bugs. However, the defiant stance that Oracle took—embodied in exchanges such as those cited above with Gartner, its user group, and the press—revealed again how much this seemingly mighty corporation resembles a small boy, elbows askew, shouting, "But I didn't do anything wrong." Larry Ellison was, as usual, the loudest defender, proclaiming on television after one earnings release that big customers like General Electric, Ford, Alcoa, and Hewlett-Packard were all running their businesses on 11i. Trouble was, as a detailed lead story in the *Wall Street Journal* made clear, these claims were hardly accurate. General Electric's power division was using 11i only at a small plant in Hungary. The other three companies had similar stories. "Indeed," said the *Journal*, "11i, which was supposed to represent Oracle's future, has been plagued with bugs and has made only modest inroads, despite company claims to the contrary."[2]

As detailed in the previous chapter, a vexing dilemma for Oracle customers is Ellison's tendency to assume, once he thinks of a new product, that it exists. Consultant DeHenry says customers were left completely adrift during the transition from client-server to the Internet product. "Larry didn't just change the underlying architecture from client-server to [Internet]," she says. "He changed processes as well. It was a whole new animal, from the interface to the server." This new animal was so changed that some modules, such as Order Management, "were just broken and didn't work," she says. "Every time they issued a patch, it was broken even more. It was incredibly frustrating for our clients." By contrast, she says, SAP kept its client-server functionality intact longer than Oracle and introduced a Web front end as an interim step, before moving to a fully Internet-capable architecture. (However, as we'll see in the next chapter, SAP paid for that patience in the widespread perception that Oracle was first to move to the Internet with ERP apps, while SAP lagged.) "Nobody can fault Larry for his vision. The issue is execution," DeHenry sums up.

Ellison has always emphasized delivering groundbreaking products first rather than getting everything right, in contrast to competitors ranging from IBM, which wanted to perfect its relational database before releasing it to customers, to application leader SAP. Ellison's strategy worked brilliantly in the days when the markets for databases and enterprise applications were growing rapidly and technology spending was high. Customers eager to get these technologies that were supposed to give them an edge would put up with the flaws to get there first. That's why Oracle was able to seize and hold the relational database market leadership for two decades even though IBM actually invented the technology. Big Blue spent too much time on execution in an era when customers would have cut it some slack. In the late 1990s, Oracle threatened to wrest leadership of enterprise applications from SAP based on first release of an Internet suite. But then the pendulum swung, and Ellison's disregard for execution began to hurt Oracle. Technology spending dried up, and customers were demanding software that worked right away. In an era of downsizing, they no longer wanted to pour resources into fixing someone else's product. *Execution* became more important than *getting there first,* and Oracle had a tough time adjusting because its entire quarter century of existence to that point had been predicated on the latter.

Consultant Bishop says his customers struggled with Oracle's CRM suite, the last piece of the applications to be released. "Oracle is always claiming software functionality before a product has stabilized," he says, necessitating an inordinate number of patches. Over the last six months of 2001, Oracle "dramatically improved functionality" with the CRM suite, to the point at which it finally approaches that of competitor and market leader Siebel Systems. Meantime, Oracle had been claiming CRM functionality for about two years. While Bishop agrees with DeHenry that Oracle has been extremely aggressive in pushing customers from client-server to the Internet, he adds that customers often need the push. "It takes dramatic action to convince customers to move," he says. "Oracle's industry-leading position is attained by these kind of actions, many of which piss existing customers off. They take heat in the media, but a year or two later, their installed base has migrated to a Web-based package and they're a lot further down the road than the competitors." However, the consultant also cautions his customers not to be the first to move: "Let Oracle work the bugs out and then go through the migration." By early 2002, Oracle reported that 1,178 customers were running live on 11i and another 4,000 had implementations under way, out of about 12,000 total customers. Based on a 2002 survey of Oracle customers, Morgan Stanley analyst Charles Phillips* predicted that 75 percent of application users would have started converting to 11i by the end of 2003. The fact that most

*In May 2003, Phillips joined Oracle as an executive vice president.

Oracle customers were now willing to migrate indicated they believed that the 11i suite was finally mature enough to tackle.

OAUG VERSUS ORACLE

The crowning blow for many Oracle customers was Ray Lane's departure in mid-2000, coming as it did with the release of the notoriously buggy 11i. "The timing of Ray leaving and the shoving of 11i out the door too soon was not a coincidence," suggests Mark Farnham, president of Rightsizing Incorporated, a consulting firm that advises clients on how to use Oracle applications. "Ray understood what was good business, including telling you the truth about bad news." Raman Batra, the Oracle IT manager for Legerity Incorporated, an Austin, Texas–based supplier of communication chips and circuits, calls Lane the "softer side of Oracle." With no executive to stand up for the customer, Oracle developers cast the burden of fixing 11i on users rather than the company. Lane had been considered the "customer-facing executive" in Oracle's senior management suite, and no one stepped up to fill that void. (When Phillips joined Oracle in 2003, that was one of his designated tasks.) Since then, Ellison has urged customers, particularly small and medium-sized companies, to the Internet to download standardized solutions to their problems with Oracle software rather than assign live personnel to help. Of course, this saves Oracle money, but it leaves customers fuming when they can't find the fixes they need. "You wonder how hard you have to shout before you are heard now by Oracle," says Batra.

It was probably no coincidence that, with Lane's departure, the disagreement between the user group he had championed, the OAUG, and Oracle became a chasm. OAUG was formed in 1990 by a group of early adopters of Oracle applications, including Burlington Coat and Bechtel Corporation. "Burlington Coat and a few other companies were live with Oracle apps," says Farnham, who was with Burlington at the time.

"There wasn't any customer council to talk about what was needed for existing customers." OAUG supported itself with membership dues and fees for conferences it sponsored—two a year, at which customers could network, exchange information about patches, and interact with Oracle developers. "Oracle supported us to the extent that they sent people [to the conferences] who mostly paid to attend," Farnham says. Oracle also got selling opportunities from the OAUG conferences, with live customers on hand to provide word-of-mouth recommendations. It seemed like a win-win for both sides.

But from the beginning, there was resistance within Oracle to having an independent user group. The older database user group was subsidized by Oracle and had a considerably more cooperative relationship. The interests of Oracle and OAUG diverged: the company wanted to showcase its products and make sales, while the user group wanted to find out how to get the stuff to work properly. Many of the OAUG sessions were devoted to gripes about Oracle's applications. "It's a shame," says Farnham, "that Oracle went on this kick that they've got to control the whole message" and consequently pulled its attendance from the OAUG conferences, starting in spring 2001. "To essentially rip away their presence at the conference and focus all their efforts on a straight sales pitch at their own conference I view as a huge business mistake," he adds. "Larry sided with marketing rather than customers."

Former OAUG president Karen Brownfield, who has been on the user group's board for eight years, says Oracle got about 25 percent of the agenda at the conferences to present technical papers and also participated in the product question-and-answer sessions. In addition, Oracle sponsored "Key Club," an accompanying marketing event for prospective customers. Despite all that, Ellison established his own show, Oracle AppsWorld. "Larry wanted a forum where he could better showcase his products, with no interference from OAUG," says Brownfield. "They told us, you're going to quit having your conference and work for us. We said to hell with that. Each side dug their heels in." OAUG surveyed its members, who said they preferred having their own conference, whereupon Oracle decided to withdraw entirely. Admits Brownfield, "Both sides declared war, and everybody lost." The debate spilled over into public forums. On its Web site, Oracle denied having any problems with OAUG or its members, but an OAUG spokesman told the *Wall Street Journal* on August 28, 2001, that that claim was "absurd," because the two organizations had been fighting for more than a year.

UNEASY COMPROMISE

In late 2001, Oracle and the OAUG made a less-than-convincing effort to bury the hatchet. At the OAUG's November conference, Oracle had no official presence but at the last moment dispatched Cliff Godwin, senior vice president of applications technology, to make a mostly technical, cheerleader presentation on upgrading to 11i. OAUG President Jeremy Young enthused, "We appreciate the goodwill of Oracle in sending him to speak." That afternoon, OAUG staged an awkward press conference, with Jim Finn, Oracle's vice president of worldwide operations, available via phone. Finn was terse and not very responsive to questions, while Young insisted OAUG would remain independent even as it "renewed the relationship" with Oracle. One press participant asked Finn, "Why did you disappoint your users by giving them a product that wasn't ready?" Finn answered, "I've got to be wrapping up," and hung up.

The compromise, according to Young, was that OAUG would reduce its number of North American conferences from two to one per year and have some presence at Oracle's AppsWorld conference. Meanwhile, Oracle also delayed the date for "desupport" of its previous applications version, 10.7, by six months to mid-2003, responding to an impassioned petition from OAUG. Withdrawing customer support for a previous product version is a common industry tactic to force customers to migrate to a newer version. It's a question of how much resources each software vendor wants to devote to products it's phasing out versus perfecting new products.

However, since Oracle's customers had postponed moving to 11i because of its initial flaws, they were outraged when the company announced a desupport date of year-end 2002 for 10.7. Fewer than half had even begun migrating to 11i at that point. Young concluded, "Oracle is trying to find ways to work with us. It's been a difficult process. We haven't won the lottery, but we're making progress." That kind of sums up Oracle's whole customer relations effort.

Oracle's damaged reputation with customers will hurt it more going forward, as it faces serious competition even in its database stronghold (see Chapter 11). On occasion, Ellison's preference for making the grand leap, rather than the incremental product fixes that users want, serves Oracle well. A company that confines itself to incremental improvements that perfect an existing product loses ground to flexible, less hidebound competitors that leapfrog its technology. It's a delicate balancing act to satisfy customers while at the same time defining the next paradigm. With Lane as the customer-facing executive and Ellison as the development-minded visionary, Oracle had that balance. Without Lane, it has lurched into arrogance and disdain for customers, a deadly combination—especially for Oracle itself.

WORD OF MOUTH

Here are the real-life experiences of two Oracle customers—one recent, another long-term—from the point of view of the people who actually had to get the applications up and running:

Hillsborough County Aviation Authority

The Aviation Authority, which runs Tampa (Florida) International Airport and three general aviation facilities, is a fairly new Oracle customer, having implemented the database and the financial applications module (the client-server version known as 10.7SC) in 1998. With the applications, "the number of patches [bug fixes] in the beginning was unbelievable," says Sharon Weaver, director of administration and IT for the authority. In fact, she also intended to implement Oracle's HR and Payroll modules, "but we kept hitting roadblock after roadblock." When Oracle told her it would cost an additional $250,000 to get Payroll up and running, "we ditched that and went with ADP." ADP is processing the authority's entire payroll for about the same amount annually "that it would have cost us for Oracle support," Weaver says. Meantime, the human resources department balked at Oracle HR, which they decided was too difficult to use, and stuck with an existing system. While Oracle was willing to help with the implementations, they insisted that the customer conform its processes to Oracle, not the other way around. "If we hadn't made a decision in three days, they were going to." Sums up Weaver, "They have a bad attitude: It's their way or the highway."

She contracted with Oracle Consulting Services (OCS) as well as Andersen Consulting in doing the implementation. While Andersen was on-site every day, Oracle Consulting came in on an as-needed basis. "Oracle is very expensive," says Weaver. "When I'm paying $375 an hour, I expect them to know their stuff." But sometimes Oracle was clueless. They sent a consultant to handle training on the Inventory module, and he told one questioner, "You don't have to worry about that because it's public-sector." Says Weaver, "We are public-sector. The blood just drained away from [the instructor's] face when we told him that, because he did not know public sector." She sent a few Oracle consultants like him packing before initiating a preinterview process to screen the people to make sure they had the required expertise. She also had to move the training from an Oracle to an internal site because the Oracle site was experiencing so many technical problems that it would be shut down for a day or two at a time. In yet another instance, Oracle sent the wrong database for training. "It took the trainer [himself an Oracle employee] a whole day on the phone to reach the right department to send the right database," Weaver recalls. When they sent it the second time, it was still the wrong one "and we had to postpone training."

However, she says, although the authority wound up only using Oracle Financials, the implementation was completed within budget and on time. "We were almost a beta site because we were one of the first to implement 10.7SC in an NT environment," she says. (Windows NT is Microsoft's corporate software platform, an alternative to Unix, where Oracle customarily runs.) "Oracle was sending us people who had never done this before." Another headache that Weaver cites is changes in Oracle personnel. Since 1998, "all the people we'd been dealing with are gone," she says. "There was a big housecleaning in April 2001, and we lost all of our local contacts."

In mid-2001, the authority got ready to implement the 11i Financials modules, not because anyone was that eager to do another Oracle install but because the company was supposedly going to stop supporting 10.7 at the end of the year (that deadline has since been extended to mid-2003). This time, the authority selected an outside consultant instead of OCS, which quoted a price about 50 percent higher than the alternative, Weaver says. Financials was completed within about three months, earlier than planned, she adds. But the authority backed off on implementing two other applications modules, Oracle Fixed Assets and Oracle Grants, because they lacked the accountability for funding that a public-sector entity needed. "Oracle says adding that is on their radar screen," but it'll be at least six to nine months, Weaver notes. "Every one of their public-sector clients is in the same boat. We were faced with all the cost of implementing these modules and still having to use a spreadsheet to track the funding." Despite everything, "if we had to make the software decision again, we would more than likely choose the same vendor," says Weaver, because of the strength of Oracle's technology and the great deal she got purchasing through a Florida state contract: $5 million for the whole project, which included all of Oracle Financials plus the database. Still, she says, it would be nice if Oracle were kinder to its customers and didn't issue "such buggy software."

Burlington Coat Factory Warehouse

Mark Farnham is a longtime user of Oracle technology, starting back in 1985 with Burlington Coat Factory Warehouse. (He is now president of Rightsizing Incorporated, a firm that consults on Oracle applications.) Burlington Coat is one of the companies Oracle likes to hold up as a showpiece customer, having bought both the database and a succession of applications. But Farnham's recollections show the give-and-take complexity of any relationship with Oracle. "The first product I used was an early version of Oracle [database] for the PC," he says. As a database architect and software engineer, he was accustomed to software that "didn't do everything it was supposed to do." That's OK with a database, he maintains. "When you're building tools and basic database utility and not selling the finished apps, you can develop work-arounds. If the software isn't perfectly in line with the specification, you can fix it. So the database not operating perfectly wasn't that big a deal. You could always find a way to program around it." Even though Oracle's database didn't match up with the feature list that the sales literature claimed, "you could massage it to fit your needs," he says.

The problem came when Oracle tried to take the same approach with applications. As applications started to ramp up, Oracle failed to boost its customer support to the needed level. "Applications requires a much higher ratio of customer service people than database, but they missed it by a lot," Farnham says. There was both a quantitative and qualitative disconnect. First, Oracle just didn't have enough customer support people for applications. Second, those people weren't knowledgeable enough. "With the database, it's how do I concoct a work-around?" that fixes a particular bug, which can be done on a technical level. With an application, such as

Financials, "it's how do I pay my checks on time?" That question is no longer technical but process-oriented. "Supporting applications is orders of magnitude more expensive than database," says Farnham, something Oracle failed to realize or adequately plan for.

In 1988, already live on Oracle database, Burlington Coat bought several Oracle financial modules, including Accounts Payable and General Ledger. "The first go-round, we had to make a number of customizations to get them to work," Farnham recalls. "It required a lot of manual intervention." But by 1989, Burlington Coat paid over a million invoices with Oracle Accounts Payable. Even though the retailer was using a very early release of the software, not yet certified for customers, "we decided we couldn't make it through the fall season on our existing mainframe-based system," necessitating the switch to Oracle. "The justification was, even if it failed and we had to use bullpens of accounting temps, we wouldn't have to buy a second mainframe, which would have cost $5–$10 million," he says. Oracle didn't have many applications customers in those days, "so they were very attentive to our needs," Farnham adds. "However, it was a two-way street." Burlington Coat, as is common with early software adopters, helped Oracle develop needed functionality for its kind of business.

In mid-1989, Burlington Coat started implementation of the next module, General Ledger. "We had to do a number of behind-the-scenes tuning sessions to make it run at the volumes we needed," he says. At the time, Oracle and Burlington Coat were roughly comparable in revenues, around $500 million, so Oracle assumed that its customer would be able to use the same software it was running internally. "What Oracle didn't understand was that just because it worked for them didn't mean it would work for us," says Farnham. "There was not a lot of attention paid to average transaction size." While Oracle sells expensive software packages to relatively few customers, Burlington sells coats to millions of people. "We were dealing with a vast number of transactions compared to

Oracle," says Farnham. And Burlington operated each of its stores on a stand-alone profit-and-loss basis. All this required a good deal of what Farnham called "tuning under the cover" to make Oracle General Ledger suitable. Much of that work found its way into subsequent releases of the product.

10

GOING FOR THE JUGULAR

["WE'RE KICKING ASK AND TAKING NAMES."]

If Oracle's customers felt abused at times, that was nothing compared to how the reeling competition must have been feeling. Larry Ellison delights in rousting competitors; he does it in Oracle's marketing campaigns, which he personally approves, and in his own appearances at trade shows and conferences. He never hesitates to disparage competitors by name, which delights the media looking for sound bytes but terrifies Oracle's public relations staff. In April 2003, he predicted that "at least 1,000 Silicon Valley companies need to go bankrupt," because most technology products are commodities and small firms can't compete efficiently.[1] In a follow-up article, he even singled out a few companies that could fail: "one-trick ponies" like Siebel Systems and BEA Systems.[2]

This attitude has been evident from the beginning of Oracle. Throughout the 1980s and early 1990s, it faced a number of other relational database companies—including Ingres, Ashton-Tate, Sybase, and Informix—and decisively smashed them all. The only one left today is Sybase, and it primarily sells in niches where Oracle doesn't. Oracle's competition now is different from these early vendors—IBM and Microsoft, both integrated companies for which database is only one of many products they sell. (Microsoft, in fact, licensed its database technology from Sybase.) Oracle's marketing campaigns are unusual in the technology industry in that they directly assail competitors. Oracle has always been serious about not just defeating the competition but, if possible, eliminating it entirely. Remember, "It is not sufficient that I succeed. Everyone else must fail." In the 1980s, Oracle initiated a series of "cut off the oxygen" campaigns against database competitors like Ashton-Tate and Ingres, handing out T-shirts that showed a patient in a hospital bed with an oxygen mask and somebody standing beside the bed turning the oxygen off. Oracle's approach also includes cutthroat sales methods like aggressive discounting of as much as 90 percent off list price, under the theory that it's better to win a customer than lose a sale.

When Ellison struts onstage at promotional events or press conferences, he cracks jokes about IBM, Microsoft, and the more numerous competitors on the applications side. This betrays both his insecurity and his small boy's pleasure in teasing the "adults." For example, at Oracle analysts' day in June 2001, he described how IBM, which is Oracle's biggest competitor today in the database arena, had claimed to run a certain performance benchmark twice as fast as a competitor. When Oracle duplicated the benchmark, the speed was one-half as fast, Ellison maintained. "I'm not saying they're buggering the books intentionally, but they did confuse one-half with two. When arithmetic is that challenging . . ." He also described IBM's DB2 database for Windows as having a "stupid-ass architecture one of the IBM teams screwed up." Later in the same rambling speech, he commented that Web-based applications providers Ariba, Commerce One, and E.piphany "aren't companies, they're features," and suggested they wouldn't last long.

While most competitors in the technology industry play nice, with advertising that stresses their own virtues, Oracle strips off the gloves and utilizes often-obscure and hard-to-prove "facts" to directly target the competition by name. It's justly famous (or infamous) for its memorable ad campaigns, one of which ran more than fifteen years ago but is still cited by Silicon Valley old-timers. The ad showed a fighter jet with the names of various Oracle competitors crossed off like "kills." Oracle was described as the last database company remaining. At the end of the ad was a disclaimer that said Oracle's use of the trademarks of its competitors in this ad "is the least of their problems." In the intervening years, Oracle hasn't mellowed, although it has turned more to technical markers of performance called *benchmarks*.

Much as a politician puts out damaging information about a rival, Oracle has publicized zingy tidbits about a competitor on the same day that competitor is going to release its own news, such as earnings. "We like to be really proud of the fact that we take out our competitors," says Oracle chief marketing officer Mark Jarvis.[3]* Often, he adds, "They commit suicide before we get there," singling out Baan, a competitor in the enterprise applications business, as one that did so. "It was a more ritual way to go," he jokes unapologetically.

PUSHING THE ENVELOPE

From early in its history, Oracle began creating marketing materials that reflected its razor-edged, take-no-prisoners approach. This was easier to do when it was an underdog, and the ads drew smiles rather than growls. Rick Bennett, a wild and crazy iconoclast from Utah, was a one-man ad agency for Oracle from 1984 to 1990 who crafted many of the ads that sealed the company's reputation. In fact, it was Bennett who convinced Ellison that advertising was worth spending money on. In their first meeting, at venture capitalist investor Don Lucas's office on Sand Hill Road, "Larry told me he didn't believe in advertising, it was a waste of money. He was meeting with me to see if I could change his mind." Bennett told Ellison to give him sixteen hundred dollars—one thousand dollars for a creative fee and six hundred dollars to run an ad in the trade journal *MIS Week*. "Larry took the bet." Bennett created an ad that essentially hijacked IBM's SQL language for databases and implied that it was now available on the PC, except you had to

---

*Jarvis resigned from Oracle in mid-2003.

call Oracle to get it. "Larry spent forty hours poring over every nuance and every word," he recalls. Bennett learned from this how to deal with Ellison: "The trick is to let Larry think all the ideas were his." The ad worked well, "the phone rang off the hook, and Larry had complete ownership of the success."

From there, Bennett went on to create a series of daring ads that established the virtually unknown database manufacturer as a force to be reckoned with, at least when it came to marketing. Here are some examples (all of which can be viewed on Bennett's Web site, www.rickbennett.com). In 1986, there was the Oracle jet plane with the names of its kills on the side. Then Bennett expanded on that with another ad that showed a sleek fighter jet shooting down an antique plane, which was identified as Ashton-Tate, a PC database manufacturer later sold to Borland. When you enter a market dominated by a rival, "you'd better make life too hot for them on their own turf," says Bennett. Oracle couldn't make a profit selling databases for the PCs, so it lowered the price and basically bombed Ashton-Tate out of existence. Says Pete Tierney, who came on board as Oracle's marketing director just as the ad was appearing in 1987, "That ad campaign finished [Ashton-Tate] off," a bit of an overstatement. There were other factors: Oracle's price slashing, for one, and Ashton-Tate's loss of a key copyright-infringement suit that it filed against competitors in another line of business, database management tools. Ashton-Tate was acquired by Borland in 1992, several years after the Oracle ad ran.

When Ingres announced in 1987 that it was ready to deliver a fully distributed database, a technology coup in those days, Bennett quickly produced an ad saying that Oracle would be delivering the same thing, thereby undercutting Ingres. Oracle's product was actually far from ready. Ellison told Bennett, "I'll be damned if I'm going to get outlied by a bunch of professors from Berkeley," referring to the origins of Ingres. After the campaign, Ingres was acquired by a competitor, ASK Computer Systems. Bennett's ad targeting that company featured big letters that take up half a page proclaiming: "WE KICK ASK." Other copy lines included "Kiss ASK good bye" and "Call 1-800-ORACLE1. We're kicking ASK and taking names." ASK/Ingres was later acquired by Computer Associates.

Bennett plunged the knife into Ingres even further. When the company was shopping for a buyer, he sneaked over to its headquarters; put up a sign in front, "For Sale by Owner— Call 1-800-4Ingres"; and took a photograph. He made a slide and gave it to Ellison, who displayed it at Oracle's annual sales award banquet in Hawaii. In the speech, Bennett recalls, Ellison told the top salespeople, "We're going to run them out of business and buy that building, which we're going to bulldoze. After that, we'll salt the earth. Then we'll go after their families." Bennett told Ellison he was a "bloodthirsty troglodyte," and Ellison smiled. Former Oracle marketing director Ken Cohen later informed Bennett, "Only you would attempt to ingratiate yourself with someone by calling them a bloodthirsty troglodyte, and only Larry would take it as a compliment."

Oracle was both a partner and a competitor with minicomputer manufacturer Digital Equipment Corporation. Oracle's first successful database product was created for a Digital minicomputer called the VAX. But Digital also had its own database, called Rdb. Recalls Bennett, "We heard that Digital was considering giving away their Rdb database with [sales of] the VAX. Since VAX revenues accounted for a significant portion of Oracle licenses, we had to make a frontal assault." In 1989, he crafted an ad that said, "Even if Rdb were free, you couldn't afford it," pointing out that Oracle was the leader in database technology and you wouldn't want a second-rate product, even at no cost. In 1994, Digital got out of the database business, selling Rdb, ironically, to Oracle. Digital itself was eventually taken over by Compaq Computer.

Tierney was recruited from Ingres in 1986 to become senior vice president of marketing, replacing Cohen, who went to rabbinical school. ("Oracle was so intense, we saw a lot of that kind of thing"—people leaving for religious or philanthropic endeavors, Tierney notes.) Tierney wound up squashing a lot of Bennett's over-the-top ideas. Bennett's Web site displays some of the vetoed ads, indicating that even Oracle was afraid to run them. Included in the "no-run" ads are several about IBM, such as "American manufacturing has IBM to thank for a chapter new in the history books, Chapter 11," and another ad that showed the IBM logo as a series of bars, with two hands grasping them, indicating jail time. The tag line: "What has IBM earned from American manufacturing? Some time off." Another ad asked the same question but gave a different answer: "Detention." The illustration showed the sentence "Cobol and RPG are outdated technologies" written over and over in chalk, referring to programming languages used, respectively, for IBM's mainframe and AS/400 hardware. Bennett, sums up Tierney, "was always pushing the envelope."

Bennett wasn't the only one. Oracle's next marketing maven, Kate Mitchell, who replaced Tierney, was on the job when Computer Associates bought ASK/Ingres in 1994. In response, "we mocked up an ad that I loved," she says. Derived from the movie *Four Weddings and a Funeral*, the ad had the other companies that Computer Associates had bought named on gravestones, with ASK/Ingres dressed as a bride and coming down the aisle. The tag line was "four funerals and a wedding." Alas, the ad never ran. It was vetoed by Ray Lane. "He told me, 'We don't need to go there,'" Mitchell recalls. In vain, she argued that the ad was clever, timely, and just poking fun. "That was my favorite ad that never made it."

SYBASE SELF-DESTRUCTS

While most of Oracle's database competitors came and went, typically disappearing through mergers with larger entities, the one that appeared to have staying power in the late 1980s and early 1990s was Sybase. Cofounded in 1984 by a refugee from Ingres, Bob Epstein, Sybase had a technical edge over Oracle: its database could process actual transactions such as a sale or purchase, not just queries for information. In the mid- to late 1980s, Oracle was still plagued by poor performance and glitches in its current database release, version 6. It wouldn't catch up with Sybase until version 7, released in 1992. This advantage made Sybase very attractive to industries that needed to do heavy-duty transactions, especially financial services, one of the leading-edge industry groups coveted by technology vendors. "Larry never respected Ingres," says Tierney. "The only one he feared was Sybase, which spooked him technically. [With transaction processing] they did an end run around Oracle that caught Larry by surprise." Adds former Sybase CEO Mitchell Kertzman, "Sybase for a while was kicking Oracle's ass."

One of the people most responsible for Sybase's success was Stewart Schuster, who worked for Ingres in marketing and business development capacities before joining Sybase to run marketing from 1986 to 1995. In positioning Sybase against the market leader, "we argued that we were technically superior," says Schuster, while Oracle's position was that it had the most portable database, running on more hardware platforms than Sybase, including the Unix operating system, which was emerging as the favorite on computers other than mainframes. "The race really heated up when the Unix boxes started coming out," he adds. The ultimate market leader in Unix workstations, Sun Microsystems, teamed up with Sybase to sell into the financial world. "Sun came into the market and made Sybase," Schuster acknowledges. "But Sybase changed the rules of the [relational database] game by offering transaction processing and high-volume performance."

Besides its technical edge, Sybase could also seize on Oracle's weakness with customers. "They beat up their customers, so their customers would bring in competitors to get a negotiating leverage over Oracle," Schuster says. Paired with Sun, Sybase won over the financial marketplace, where it retains a stronghold to this day. "Once we got Wall Street, we got stock exchanges overseas. Then we broke into the commercial banks," he says. From there, Sybase expanded into the defense industry, manufacturing, and telecommunications. "Up until Oracle version 7, we really were gaining market share tremendously," says Schuster. "Oracle version 6 didn't have the transaction-processing features we did. We could kill them on benchmarks." Borrowing a page from Oracle, he launched an ad campaign in 1991, running in *Computerworld.* Called The Sybase Forum, it announced that Sybase was going to talk about the subject of high-volume performance. "On one side of the ad, we ran the Sybase view with what our products could do on performance benchmarks," he says. On the other side of the ad was a headline reading "Oracle's view"; the rest of the area was blank. "We told Oracle they could explain what their products do," Schuster says. He even sent a FedEx package to his Oracle counterpart, Tierney, with an invitation to fill up the blank space. "They never responded," says Schuster. So in a series of ads, Sybase listed its capabilities and, on the other half, this disclaimer: "We're sorry to say Oracle doesn't have anything to say on this subject."

But as Oracle version 7 finally caught up with Sybase in transaction processing, Sybase got caught up in its own mistakes. First, in what proved to be a disastrous deal, it licensed its technology to Microsoft. Second, it released a database product, Sybase 10, with serious flaws. And finally, it did an ill-conceived merger with a tools company, Powersoft, that hurt both companies. In the late 1980s, when Sybase cut the deal with Microsoft, the former was still a tiny company with limited resources. "We were going after Unix systems and had no resources to do a PC product," Schuster says. At that point, "Microsoft came to us and said we'll do a deal with Ingres if you don't do it with us." Sybase gave Microsoft exclusive rights to its database technology on platforms that were derivatives of Microsoft architecture—that is, DOS and Windows. "We thought we were getting a great partner on a platform that wasn't important to us," says Schuster. But then Microsoft came out with Windows NT, positioned as the "Unix killer," and databases on PCs became big business. "We got into a huge argument with Microsoft," says Schuster, because Sybase wanted to offer an NT product but couldn't under terms of the contract. "We settled by giving up an older code line" to Microsoft, mistakenly believing that it would never catch up. "We thought we had a three-year jump, and we didn't," says Schuster. The upshot: Microsoft's SQL Server, derived from Sybase technology, is today the market leader in the Windows database market.

Meanwhile, Sybase's System 10, released in 1993–1994, was riddled with bugs and not very scalable. That is, it had problems when customers wanted to add additional computers running the database. "We were losing our technical edge, and we had a pissed-off installed base, like Oracle had in 1990–91," says Schuster. With a decent product in Oracle 7, Oracle's new management team began pouring resources into customer support. Sybase was still struggling to make System 10 work at all. Gartner Group wrote a series of damaging reports on System 10 that Oracle exploited in its advertising. "By 1995, we had hit the wall," says Schuster, and he bailed out. Looking back, he says, Oracle won the "database wars" by targeting the emerging Unix market and doing a credible product for mainframes. On the PC side, "Microsoft was gobbling up Windows NT for the masses." Sybase had to focus on internal problems and never got back into gear. Today, Oracle is ten times the size of Sybase.

Oracle marketing chief Kate Mitchell says she fought to keep the campaign against Sybase deliberately low-key, focusing on benchmarks rather than outright bashing. "I used to argue with Larry that we were much bigger than Sybase. If you're number one and you're targeting number two, that gives them more visibility. I thought we shouldn't be mentioning them at all." For a while, Sybase was the darling of the industry, the fastest-growing database vendor, able to recruit people from Oracle. "They were very confident, then they imploded," notes Mitchell.

"You have to screw up a lot of things to slide all the way back like that," admits John Chen, who came in as CEO in 1997 to turn Sybase around. As an outsider who wasn't responsible for the strategies that led to Sybase's demise, he can afford to be candid about the mistakes. First, "we allowed Microsoft to run away with SQL Server at the low end. We created an enemy we couldn't control," he says. With System 10, "the product didn't keep up," but compounding that, Sybase's market strategy was flawed. The market was moving away from internally customized applications, which required customers to buy their own development tools, to packaged applications. "People were shifting to packaged solutions, and we were out buying more tools," says Chen, in mergers with Gain (a company founded by Tom Siebel) and Powersoft. "Powersoft was the death knell," he says. "Sybase didn't have a culture that integrated other companies. It let them run on their own like silos." At a time when its core business was in trouble, Sybase didn't need the distraction of mergers with companies whose technology was peripheral to its main market. Oracle marketing chief Jarvis's comment about competitors' "committing suicide" comes to mind with Sybase. So does Ellison's epitaph, delivered at Oracle's OpenWorld in December 2001: "Sybase has been dead for a very long time. Let them rest in peace."

FINDING A NEW APPROACH

As the 1990s drew to a close, Oracle, having dispatched its primary competitors, could proclaim that it had won the "database wars." Lane recalls that from about 1995 to 1997, Ellison put the top executive bonuses at risk based on market-share change versus competitors. "He proposed that if we lose market share to Sybase, we'd cut our bonus by that ratio. If we grow at the same rate, we get our bonus. If we grow faster, we get more." This worked too well. After Oracle trampled Sybase, it turned its sights on Informix, a much smaller enemy. "We beat Informix so badly one year that it would have multiplied our bonuses by thirty-three times," says Lane. "The normal bonus was $2 million. We would have gotten $66 million each." In this case, the board of directors appropriately vetoed the bonus.

By 2002, Sybase was the only competitor left that still derived the majority of its revenues from database sales and maintenance, and it now focused on different markets, such as wireless databases, from Oracle. IBM had scooped up Informix and was becoming a significant competitor of Oracle's on high-end databases, while Microsoft was chomping away at the low end. But both IBM and Microsoft are diversified companies for which database is a minor part of revenues. Oracle had emerged at the opening of the twenty-first century as the supreme database vendor. However, like any fighting machine, it needed new enemies to keep its edge. So it trained its formidable marketing guns on the enterprise applications field, in which Oracle has a strong product offering but is hardly dominant. It has long trailed market leader SAP, vies with PeopleSoft for second place overall, and faces feisty competitors like Siebel Systems or i2 Technologies in newer niches such as CRM (customer relationship management) and supply chain management.

In the Internet era, Oracle developed a new marketing tool for disrupting these companies: press releases, posted on Oracle's Web site and sent to public relations newswires, that zero in on some alleged defect in a competitor's product or strategy. These releases were made public with diabolical timing, just when a competitor was about to do a conference call with analysts on its earnings or make an appearance at a major financial conference. Oracle's obvious intent: to get analysts and the press to focus on whatever negative issue it had raised, diverting attention away from the favorable impression a competitor would be aiming to make. Such tactics are common in political circles but not in the technology industry. In fact, many observers at first attributed Oracle's new tack to its hiring of former president Bill Clinton's White House press secretary Joe Lockhart at the end of 2000, since Lockhart was adroit at political mudslinging.

Jarvis says Lockhart was hired personally by Ellison and had nothing to do with the strategy. (In fact, Lockhart left six months after he was hired.) "I deal with the company's product PR," Jarvis says. "The things you're hearing are coming out of my organization. You can't blame Joe." He adds that while Oracle enlists outside communications agencies in its sorties, everything is worked out internally. "We definitely sit down with a calendar and work out which week we're going to pick on Siebel, which week we're going to pick on i2," he says, in his clipped British accent. "Some of these are based on whatever news is coming out, [but] don't think we have a plan six months in advance. We have a plan about six minutes in advance." Lane recalls that Ellison personally plucked Jarvis out of development and trained him in marketing. "Jarvis will do anything to undermine a competitor," Lane says. "When you're fighting a war, you need both your troops and your CIA. That way, you fight based on your strengths and the other guy's weaknesses."

SOFTENING UP PEOPLESOFT

In January 2001, PeopleSoft president and CEO Craig Conway was preparing for a rather pleasant earnings announcement: in the fourth quarter of 2000, the applications vendor had record revenue of $498 million, its best quarter in history, with net income of $44 million, compared with a loss in the year-ago period. The day before the release, Oracle put out a statement of its own: "As PeopleSoft prepares to announce earnings tomorrow, I encourage you to remain skeptical of the difference between CEO Craig Conway's claims and reality behind them." The release went on to question whether PeopleSoft's applications suite was fully integrated, suggesting that its purchases of other companies to supply portions of the suite have left it behind Oracle's integration. "PeopleSoft has only a handful of happy customers for PeopleSoft 8, and lags far behind Oracle, which provides e-business solutions to more than 1,000 customers worldwide. Just consider the revenue differential between the two companies—$1.4 billion for PeopleSoft versus $10.1 billion for Oracle." (Never mind that the majority of Oracle's revenues still comes from its market-leading database, which partners such as PeopleSoft in essence help sell.)

Conway, who's a former Oracle sales executive, termed the

release "a mutation of Oracle's tactics." He adds that the company has taken to "publishing something . . . which basically smears the competitors just before the moment of their announcement." The issue, he adds, "isn't whether [Oracle is] competitive or not. The issue is whether they cross the line. Periodically they cross the line between truth and non-truth."[4] With PeopleSoft, that was the case, he maintains. "The phraseology was very cleverly designed to be almost true," he says, noting that PeopleSoft doesn't claim to have a pure integrated suite but a pure Internet suite. He compared this fudging of words to the *Saturday Night Live* skit "where they talk about violins in America. Actually, it's violence in America." Likewise, "Oracle was saying you've got to be skeptical of an integrated suite. Actually, it was an Internet suite."

There weren't any unusual questions from analysts or press at the PeopleSoft earnings briefing, Conway adds. He believes that Oracle's tactics are ineffectual because they are now expected, "just another Oracle dirty trick." After the briefing, he got a call from fellow CEO and ex–Oracle alum Tom Siebel. "Tom called me . . . to tell me he couldn't believe this and [to] express horror over what had been put out by Oracle," says Conway. "Tom coined it 'Washington-style dirty tricks coming to Silicon Valley.' It's what you do to undermine political foes, [but] it's really unprecedented in the technology industry." Nonetheless, both agreed that everyone has become so skeptical of Oracle's claims that they really don't work. Says Conway, "I actually think Oracle makes a very solid database product. I enjoyed working there for eight years. I value the time I spent with Larry Ellison, but over the years, their reputation has been establishing itself. It's not something that Tom or myself or Hasso Plattner [of SAP] needs to speak to at all, because it speaks for itself." Conway reiterated an earlier statement summing up Oracle as a "sociopathic company." A sociopath is "incapable of separating untruth from fact. Over time, Oracle has stretched the truth so much, they're not quite aware whether they do it or not."

At any rate, he says, Oracle's comments "wound up backfiring" because they helped put PeopleSoft on the map. "Oracle had been paying so little attention to PeopleSoft," says Conway. "The analysts said, you must really be doing well if Oracle is starting to bash you." A few months earlier, in November 2000, Ellison had claimed in an earnings call of his own that he never runs into PeopleSoft as a competitor. "In our earnings call, I presented a list of twenty-two accounts, eighteen of them in direct competition with Oracle that we had won," says Conway. "Either Ellison is not aware of what is going on, or he's aware of it and chooses to ignore it." He points out that in the enterprise applications space, there are only three companies with full suites: SAP, PeopleSoft, and Oracle. "I guarantee you nobody buys anything without checking with the other two of them." (Ellison couldn't ignore PeopleSoft forever. See next chapter for analysis of his hostile bid for PeopleSoft in mid-2003.)

Jarvis accuses Conway of reacting emotionally to Oracle's techniques. "Any marketing organization worth its salt will make sure they look not only at what we're announcing but what the competition is announcing and make sure that we somehow get into that news," he says. "The thing you've got to remember about marketing is, it's all about getting your name in the right place at the right time. The people complaining haven't learned that trick yet." He adds that competitors are "smarting" because they're being outmarketed by Oracle. "That's their problem," Jarvis says. "I'm certainly not overly concerned about keeping them delighted with our marketing." Jarvis relates a key mantra that he presents to his PR and marketing people: "Our job is to be a helluva competitor and a competitor from hell. I think we're doing a good job."

"THE SIEBEL CHALLENGE"

On February 12, 2001, Oracle issued two short, pithy press releases, entitled "i2 Plays Me Too" and "The Siebel Challenge: Who's Your Best Customer." The i2 release said the supply chain management company "has woken up and smelled the Internet, but can they integrate their various products quickly enough to compete with Oracle? Through a string of acquisitions and partnerships—some successful, some not—i2 is trying to cobble together a 'suite' story. While i2 has been creating a huge integration project, Oracle has been building software." The other release suggested that if you asked the Siebel CRM system, "Who is your best customer?" you'd get several answers because pieces of the application, such as call center or Web store, might respond differently. "For Siebel, there is no simple answer," the release stated. "In an assembled solution, each application may have its own idea of the 'best customer,' and querying bolted-together applications can produce discordant answers. For Oracle . . . with all the customer data in one place, companies don't have to check data in multiple applications. There is one unified customer view and one simple answer." These releases were sent to newswires just moments before the chief executives of i2 and Siebel were to separately address analysts at a Goldman Sachs conference.

Siebel CEO Tom Siebel remembers talking to people at the conference about what Oracle had done to PeopleSoft a month earlier, and then, "twenty minutes before I was going to give the keynote speech, they put out something on us." However, like Conway, Siebel says he got no unexpected questions. "There was no effect," he says, although, he adds, "there is kind of a slimy feel to this." Siebel likened it to a "Kill Siebel" campaign that Oracle had launched a couple of years earlier, after which Siebel had an outside counsel write a strongly worded letter calling on Oracle to "cease and desist your unlawful campaign" against Siebel Systems.

That June 14, 1999, letter, addressed to Ellison, stated: "Over the last six months, Oracle has resorted to increasingly desperate measures in its attempt to position itself as a credible CRM solution provider. Siebel welcomes fair, honest competition, but your most recent tactics are nothing of the sort. It appears that Oracle's principal 'CRM strategy' has degenerated into a concerted attempt to inflict damage on Siebel Systems by issuing a series of false and disparaging public statements. . . . " The letter cited a number of claims that Ellison personally had made regarding inadequacies in Siebel products and refuted each one. The letter said that Ellison and other executives wanted Siebel "on a slab" and that Ray Lane had put Siebel on Oracle's "Most Wanted" list. It threatened to make a case against Oracle for false and misleading advertising, unfair competition, interference with business relations, and trade libel. It also said the Securities and Exchange Commission might be interested due to "your efforts to mislead the investing public, as well as your employees' blatant efforts to manipulate Oracle and Siebel stock prices. . . ."

That letter, Tom Siebel says, "stopped them in their tracks." Lane disagrees. "I do remember that coming in," he says. "Something like that would be laughable to Oracle. They'd think, *We're being effective*, and turn it over to the general counsel." After the 2001 incident, Siebel prepared an internal response. The senior vice president of marketing, Bruce Cleveland, wrote a nine-page memo to employees describing Oracle's charges and Siebel's rebuttal to each one. "So that you may be prepared to deal with any customer or prospect issues that arise from Oracle's latest competitive assault, we are providing you with a chronological view of the facts vis a vis Oracle and their CRM initiative," the memo stated. Lane acknowledges, "Oracle was rattling the sword," because it had failed to gain market share against Siebel in the CRM arena and a war of words was the only alternative. "When you pick a fight with someone who has a great product, how else do you fight it?" he asks.

WHO'S THE SAP?

It's curious that Oracle hasn't tried this sort of thing much with SAP, the largest enterprise applications vendor and the world's third-largest independent software company, behind only Microsoft and Oracle. One possible reason is that SAP, unlike Oracle's other major competitors in applications, is not headed by a former Oracle executive. "With Larry, everything is personal," says Lane. "He picks fights with ex–Oracle people like Conway and Siebel." Another reason is that SAP reacted rather swiftly and effectively when, at one point, Oracle claimed supremacy in applications software. A third reason could be that Oracle got its hand slapped in a case involving a terminated employee who sued, claiming she was fired in part for blowing the whistle on dirty tricks against SAP.

In mid-2000, Oracle subtitled a strong fourth-quarter earnings report with the headline "Oracle Passes SAP to Become the World's Largest Applications Software Company." This was based on figures showing that Oracle sold $447 million worth of software in its fiscal fourth quarter, ended May 31, more than the $352 million sold by SAP in its most recent quarter, the January–March period. Any software company typically does its best in the fourth quarter and its worst in the first quarter, so Oracle was comparing strength to weakness. A week later, SAP issued its response: "Oracle Fantasy Falls Short; SAP Still King of the Hill." SAP pointed out that Oracle was comparing apples with oranges, since the two quarters were not identical. "Recalculating license revenues proportionally from the last two quarters . . . would give Oracle total license revenues of about $290 million in the first three months of calendar 2000 . . . below the SAP revenue." Not only that, annualized license revenues showed SAP well ahead, $1.9 billion to $923 million for Oracle. "So, Oracle still has a long way to go to catch up with SAP," the SAP release concluded. Oracle's release also quoted Ellison as saying that the release of 11i had vaulted Oracle into the number-one position. "This is an interesting claim," SAP retorted, "considering that the product was only completed in May. . . . Oracle may be ahead in marketing rhetoric, but it is actually way behind SAP in delivering true Internet solutions."

Generally, says Herbert Heitmann, director of global communications for SAP, "we don't see value for our customers in doing public fights against Oracle." On this one occasion, after considerable internal debate, "we left the high road."

Heitmann says SAP couldn't allow Oracle to claim itself as the leader in applications software on the basis of misleading comparisons. "We have overlapping quarters [with Oracle] because we're on a calendar year," he says. "It's difficult to directly compare quarter to quarter. Oracle took its strongest quarter overlapping with our weakest quarter to claim it was passing SAP in revenue on applications. We put out a press release that said, compare apples to apples." SAP's PR agency also called Oracle's to complain. Since then, "we have not observed something similar," says Heitmann.

Later that same year, in August, a California court awarded $2.66 million to Sandy Baratta, the former vice president of global alliances at Oracle, for wrongful termination. Nearly $2 million of the award covered unvested stock options. Baratta, who was pregnant at the time, was fired in April 1999 as she was about to board a plane for a business meeting in France. The day before, she had told her superior, Gary Bloom, that she suspected that some of her coworkers were misappropriating information from SAP. In court, Baratta's lawyers alleged that an Oracle employee who worked with SAP at its headquarters in Walldorf, Germany, had gained access to trade secrets and used the information to help Oracle develop an interface between its CRM package and SAP's enterprise applications. The jury found that Oracle had retaliated against Baratta for complaining about Bloom's comments regarding pregnant executives. Oracle claimed that Baratta was dismissed because of an "inappropriate" attitude toward her coworkers.[5]

The company's appeal of the jury verdict was denied in February 2002. The case not only demonstrates Oracle's attitude toward what it considered disloyal conduct but also illuminates the conflicts that can arise when two companies are both partners and rivals, like Oracle and SAP. Oracle works closely with SAP to make sure that the latter's enterprise suite runs on the Oracle database; indeed, more than 70 percent of SAP's customers are on Oracle, according to Heitmann. But this cooperation gives Oracle access to information it may appropriate to bolster its own position in the applications market, as it allegedly did in the Baratta case. "There was some legal action by a former Oracle employee [Baratta] who got fired for complaining about some bad practices on the part of Oracle people working on our partner side," says Heitmann. "This was one instance, although we were not involved, that resulted in our building our own Chinese wall a bit higher. We want our people focused on database to have no touch point with [applications] salespeople."

GOING FOR THE JUGULAR

In the quarter century of Oracle's existence its competitors have changed, its markets have changed, its products have changed. Its mind-set hasn't. As voiced by Ellison, with his samurai's view of the world, Oracle doesn't just want to compete. It wants to destroy. If it were possible, Oracle would no doubt own 100 percent of the database market and the lion's share (or samurai's share) of enterprise applications. Consequently, its marketing campaigns were predicated not so much on selling its own technology as on disparaging rivals. But even Ellison recognized that in a down economy, with people rattled by security concerns, negativity doesn't go over well. So in late 2001 and 2002, Oracle refined its approach to refocus more on technology-to-technology comparisons, particularly with IBM on database performance.

Although Jarvis says his internal organization was the main strategist behind tactics like the timed press releases, if you check the Web site of a San Francisco public relations company called Applied Communications (www.appliedcom.com), you'll find a white paper entitled "On the Record: Stealing a Page from Politics." In that paper, published in late 2000, Applied CEO Alan Kelly describes how technology companies should copy political campaigns in branding their products and themselves. "Tech marketing has entered an era where the goal is competitive advantage and the process demands more of marketers than connecting or informing through relationships," Kelly wrote. "It's a two-way process of positioning and de-positioning, branding and de-branding, publicizing and de-publicizing. . . . It's about winning positions and rendering rivals insignificant." Until 2002, Applied Communications was Oracle's lead outside PR agency.

Although neither Oracle nor Applied was talking about it, the two apparently had a parting of the ways in early 2002, as Applied lost both the Oracle applications and database accounts. The speculation is that Ellison wasn't too pleased with the effectiveness, or lack of effectiveness, of this strategy. As Kelly himself writes in his white paper, " 'Going negative' in technology has higher risks, not only for the obvious fact that a tech company may be tarred with the same brush it sets out to paint with, but also because it might actually overwhelm the opposition. It might work too well" in making the opponent irrelevant and thus negligible. Sums up Kelly, "It's necessary to control rhetorical spaces, to spark and win debates, to render rivals mute but never to remove them."

Meanwhile, Oracle has shifted its advertising and marketing emphasis from its applications competitors to the company it now perceives as its biggest enemy: IBM (although Microsoft runs a close second, and Ellison has an unmatched personal rivalry with its chairman, Bill Gates; see the next two chapters). Along with Ellison's remarks in public forums, the campaign against Big Blue emphasizes performance benchmarks, with ads in prominent publications and on billboards along Highway 101 leading into San Francisco from Silicon Valley. For example, a 2001 ad in *eWeek* magazine featured the text "Oracle vs IBM Java Development." It showed three levels of a context menu under Oracle and five sheets of paper with 166 lines of code on them under IBM, implying that Oracle users can set up an on-line Java applet with three clicks, while using IBM is much more involved. In fact, both operations are difficult. In 2002, Oracle ran a series of prominent ads in the *Wall Street Journal* and other media with headlines like, "IBM Runs SAP SLOWER," and claims that Oracle's database clusters (a new type of database architecture) have fourteen international security certifications while IBM's DB2 has none. With IBM, Oracle faces a battle-tested survivor that it's in no danger of removing. Although it does not develop enterprise applications, IBM will work with a customer to supply everything that it needs from whatever vendor it chooses, a claim no one else can match. "We really only have one competitor; it's IBM," says Jarvis. "Siebel and i2 and PeopleSoft are little bit players. Sure we let ourselves growl at them occasionally, but we're competing with IBM."

11

UPHILL BATTLES

[
"IT'S NEVER A GOOD THING TO HAVE THAT
MANY PEOPLE IN AN INDUSTRY CHEERING
FOR YOUR DEMISE."
]

Oracle's intent in the 1980s and early 1990s was to annihilate the competition, and in many cases, it did, wielding its hard-charging sales force and aggressive marketing tactics to score decisive victories over early database foes. But today it faces competitors that will not be deterred by marketing muscle alone. In its cash-cow market, the database, Oracle remains the leader, barely, facing serious challenges from IBM and Microsoft. Figures from market researcher IDC showed Oracle controlled 39.4 percent of the overall relational database market in 2002, down from 42.5 percent in 2001. IBM was second at 33.6 percent, and Microsoft was a distant third at 11.1 percent. But another market researcher, Gartner Group, put IBM slightly ahead of Oracle in database market share in 2002, with 34.6 percent market share compared with 32 percent for Oracle, and 16 percent for Microsoft. Although Oracle disputed Gartner's figures, one can't dispute that Oracle is losing share to its competitors in the database market, its traditional stronghold. When the economic downturn put pressure on pricing, IBM and Microsoft, which sell databases along with other products (hardware in IBM's case, operating systems in Microsoft's), were in a better position than Oracle to lower their prices. "As far as [Oracle's] revenue, database is still 70 percent of their business and nearly all of their profits," notes Charles Phillips, an analyst who followed the company for Morgan Stanley. At the high end of the database market, IBM's DB2 is encroaching on Oracle both in mainframes and in its core platform, Unix servers. At the low end, Microsoft's SQL Server, which it bundles with the operating system Windows NT, is an increasing threat. "Oracle is getting nipped at from both sides," sums up David Nance, a former subcontractor for Oracle Consulting Services and now chief system architect for Kore Partners, an E-services firm whose customers primarily use the Oracle database. "Oracle has lost its positioning," he adds, because IBM can claim similar quality while Microsoft beats them both on cost.

The ERP (enterprise resource planning) applications business was supposed to give Oracle a strong second leg on which to stand. That's why the successful introduction of 11i, its E-business suite with a new Internet architecture, is critical. Given its database leadership, Oracle should have owned the ERP marketplace. After all, its primary competitors, SAP, PeopleSoft, and Siebel Systems, all run mostly on the Oracle database. But until recently, Oracle never considered applications much of a business. It was always a poor stepsister to the golden child of database. Then Larry Ellison made applications cool by pairing them with the Internet, and Oracle belatedly made a big push to make this line of business successful. "Oracle had the right product and the right message at a time when their competitors were having problems," says Jim Shepherd, a senior vice president of AMR Research who follows Oracle. But as SAP and PeopleSoft also readied Internet suites and Oracle fumbled the introduction of 11i, "part of the advantage that Oracle had is going away," Shepherd adds. The upshot: Oracle faces an uphill battle to become the market leader in applications, even if the hostile bid it launched for PeopleSoft in mid-2003 succeeded. At that time, Oracle was number two in the enterprise applications market, with 13 percent, edging out PeopleSoft at 10 percent. Both trailed longtime leader SAP, which had 35 percent of the market, according to AMR Research.

Looking for a third line of business to enhance its revenue stream, Oracle introduced a weak entry a few years ago into the application server marketplace. Application servers are important because they allow companies to develop and run all the new applications and business processes related to the Internet. Indeed, the application server is replacing the database as the key development platform for these efforts. IBM and BEA Systems are the leading application server software vendors, with Oracle far behind. Oracle bundles the application server with its database and doesn't even break out the revenue separately. "Oracle ignored that market for so long," says Betsy Burton, an analyst with Gartner Group. "Then they put forward a halfhearted solution and haven't been very clear about their goals." The application server, although a minor part of Oracle's business, is nonetheless a springboard into a new paradigm called Web services, in which nearly every competitor of Oracle's is trying to play. "Web services" aim to help customers become Internet-ready by offering them technology, such as Microsoft's much-ballyhooed, little-understood .NET (pronounced "dot-net"), upon which to build these services. Oracle has yet to articulate much of a strategy on Web services, allowing others to claim at least a marketing advantage.

BLUE NO LONGER

As it ceded the PC operating system to Microsoft and the microprocessor to Intel, IBM also enabled Oracle to slip in and take ownership of the relational database market. It was Big Blue's research that Ellison commercialized back in the late 1970s. IBM, although it has always sold databases for its mainframe computers, was glacially slow in entering the market for databases on Unix servers. "We didn't get moving until the 1990s," says Steve Mills, senior vice president and group executive of IBM Software. "Some of us were quite frustrated that IBM had abdicated its position." In 1988, IBM began to refocus on software, first with a division and now with the

Software Group, which Mills heads. Since 1995, "we've built a complete sales and development capability," he says, with thirty-five thousand people and $14 billion in revenue, which would put it second only to Microsoft if it were a stand-alone software company. You can tell by the amount of verbiage that Ellison directs at IBM that Big Blue is now a prime concern of Oracle's. IBM is not a player in the enterprise applications market, preferring to offer its hardware and software as platforms for other companies, but "in terms of the direction that Oracle has taken in database and services, IBM has to be the biggest competitor," says Ray Lane.

Oracle's strategy is to get customers to buy its database, application server, and enterprise applications as an integrated product offering. IBM will sell you either or both its database, DB2, and application server, WebSphere, and you can run whatever applications you want. IBM's advantage on DB2 is primarily that it can package in so many other things, including the hardware and its vaunted consulting services. After that, IBM promises to make whatever solution the customer wants (that is, the "best-of-breed" approach) work with its software and hardware. Oracle's response is that you don't have to spend so much on consulting if you buy integrated database/applications from a single vendor and that it's the only vendor that can offer that combination.

Mills believes that Oracle's weakest point is its attitude toward customers. "Oracle has a profoundly flawed overall approach, based on attacking competitors," he says. "The customer is not important. Promoting their image is what they're focused on." With Lane gone, the customer-focused view is gone, he adds. "The whole nature of the business model is not grounded in long-term satisfaction, it's grounded in the lock-in characteristics of their software." And that gives IBM an attack point. "All of the DB2 licenses we've sold since 1993 have been sold into the Oracle installed base," Mills says. "We have put a huge dent in Oracle's business over the last nine years. We've installed over one million DB2 servers in fifty thousand businesses around the world." Why do customers buy DB2? "Nobody buys my product because they love IBM," he says candidly. "They buy it because I compete against Oracle and I do a better job of supporting and delivering value. My culture is based on customer satisfaction, and their culture is based on beating competitors."

Gartner analyst Burton agrees that IBM's consulting culture tends to treat customers better than Oracle's culture, which stresses making sales. "Oracle's credibility with its customers has been damaged," she says, because of this history of aggressive sales and marketing. "When Oracle was viewed as one of the few choices out there, people put up with it. What's happened today is that many of Oracle's customers have started to look at alternatives. Oracle's business practices have caused the door to open to its competitors. It's not a technology issue. It's a business practice/customer interaction issue." Canopus Research President Will Zachmann adds: "Oracle is the company that everybody loves to hate. A lot of people would be happy to use something else if they were able to."

IBM also sees an advantage in Oracle's conflicted relationship with vendors like SAP, PeopleSoft, and Siebel Systems, having decided early on that enterprise applications weren't its forte. "We dabbled in the area without realizing all that much success," says Mills. (In the 1970s, Big Blue had a few manufacturing applications but decided not to pursue the field. Several members of the team working on it, including Hasso Plattner, left IBM to found SAP in 1972.) "Our skills are focused on middleware," which is software that integrates differing application suites, Mills adds. By deciding to go into apps, "Oracle did wonderful things for our business by competing against their own partners. If Oracle had not done that, we'd have a much more difficult time with these app providers, who wouldn't see as compelling a reason to do business with us." As the Baratta whistle-blowing lawsuit detailed in the last chapter showed, "you have to know where to draw the line here on these 'coopetition' relationships," Mills adds. Even though he acknowledges that IBM missed the last computing paradigm, client-server, thus providing the opportunity for Oracle to become as big as it is, "dissatisfaction with

Oracle [among customers and partners] gives us a chance to recoup substantial market share."

Oracle's recent marketing against IBM is based on technical rather than strategic factors: it promotes the latest version of its database, 9i, as capable of running on "clusters"—that is, on a number of low-cost PC servers rather than a single high-priced mainframe or Unix server. Clustering, says Ellison, creates three major advantages. First, multiple machines are fault-tolerant, or less likely to fail. If one goes down, the others pick up the slack. "It's unbreakable," he sums up. Hence, the Oracle ad campaigns about making Microsoft E-mail "unbreakable" by running it on 9i. (A video introducing Ellison at Oracle's 2001 OpenWorld conference showed a huge demolition ball coming down on one of his cars, a Mercedes, and not making a dent. "What's the secret?" the voice-over inquired. "Maybe the 9i database" inside the car.) The second advantage of clusters is what Ellison calls "performance on demand." He adds, "To go faster, you simply buy another machine. There's no limit to performance or scalability." Finally, there's a savings on hardware costs. "It's more economical to have four or eight midsize inexpensive machines than a single high-powered computer." Ellison says clustering has been the "Holy Grail" at Oracle for years. When Oracle first attempted it with Oracle 6 back in the late 1980s, "it almost bankrupted the company," he says. But Oracle persisted in its goal: "We wanted to be able to use a group of computers to manage a single database. It took us more than a dozen years to do that with [9i]." Mills says IBM can handle clusters as well but doesn't dictate to customers what they should have. "Clustering as a technology is fine," he says, "but we do environments for a wide variety of uses." Clusters have an advantage in complex, computation-heavy environments such as financial services but not so much in commercial settings, he adds.

Another Oracle claim of superiority is that 9i is based on a so-called shared-cache architecture, which means that anyone who wants to use the database has access to the same store, or cache, of data, even across multiple servers. Although IBM's mainframe DB2 uses shared-cache, the Unix version employs an alternate technology called "shared-nothing," as does Microsoft's SQL Server. In a shared-nothing architecture, the database servers must split up, or partition, the data and hand it off among them rather than sharing it. This can create reliability problems if a server is off-line, making part of the database unavailable. Ellison had a lot of fun with this concept onstage at OpenWorld. "Every single Oracle application will run on multiple servers without changing a line of code," he maintains, because the shared-cache architecture doesn't require partitioning. "IBM and Microsoft [server] clusters can't run anything except benchmarks. We run everything; they run *nothing*," he emphasizes, clenching his right hand into a fist with empty air inside it. Mills says that IBM can set up DB2 as shared-cache or shared-nothing. "Both have usefulness," he says. Shared-nothing is better for situations in which there are lots of requests for information (queries) coming from end users to the server. Shared-cache is better for processing transactions rather than queries.

Mills sees Ellison's pointed attacks against IBM as proof of Big Blue's success. "Being the schoolyard bully he is, Larry is reverting to these tactics out of desperation and sheer frustration," says Mills. Because Oracle is competing on all fronts— with its partners, its customers, even internally—it has no safe harbor anymore. "It's not simply about competing, it's about executing, and this is an area where Oracle continues to fumble," Mills maintains. "If you're going to run a high-testosterone culture, better show up ready for battle. Oracle challenges everybody to a fight. They're vulnerable in virtually every single thing they do." AMR analyst Shepherd sees Oracle surrounded by a sea of enemies, for a host of reasons, including its arrogant attitude toward partners and competitors, its belligerent advertising, and Ellison's unchecked criticism of competitors. "Everyone in the industry hates them," Shepherd says. "It's never a good thing to have that many people in an industry cheering for your demise."

BATTLE OF TWO BEHEMOTHS

Oracle's relationship with Microsoft is classic intragenerational rivalry. The two companies were born in the same era, reached adolescence (went public) in the same week, and now find themselves as mature companies squabbling over how to divide a good chunk of the computing world, as Oracle seeks to expand from the center (the database) and Microsoft seeks to expand from the edge (the PC). Then, of course, there's Ellison's personal resentment of Microsoft founder and chairman Bill Gates (more on that in the next chapter, on Oracle's culture). Despite their leaders' differences, Microsoft and Oracle have actually had pretty similar strategies in the past. In contrast to IBM, which positions itself as a "solutions" company that will put together whatever setup a customer asks for, both Oracle and Microsoft want you to buy from them alone. "With Oracle, everything revolves around the database product," which gives it leverage in selling its applications and application server, says Carl Olofson, program director for information and data management software at market research firm IDC. "It's a sink-or-swim philosophy"—you either buy all Oracle or go elsewhere. "Microsoft is the same with Windows," he adds. "Both Microsoft and Oracle have a core technology, and all their other technology radiates out from it." Even Ellison has grudging praise for Microsoft. "The history of this industry is that one company has done it all, like Microsoft in PC software." In fact, he says, Microsoft's dominance at the PC level with products like Windows and Office is what Oracle is modeling itself on at the enterprise level. "Who else is going to offer the complete applications suite with a database? The enterprise business is ours," Ellison proclaims.

Microsoft and Oracle face similar challenges as they look for future growth. Each dominates a particular segment of computing that is becoming saturated and must seek new markets, which means encroaching on the other's territory. "Oracle's future still depends on their ability to hold the database market," says Canopus Research President Will Zachmann, because the database helps it leverage sales in other areas. However, since database is a mature market, "the chance that they'll gain market share is unlikely. If they're going to get growth, they have to get it outside the database business," he maintains. Likewise, with Microsoft, "its growth strategy is dependent on the success of .NET becoming the IT [information technology] backbone of the enterprise," says Olofson. "They haven't achieved their ultimate objective yet to define that environment." Microsoft's strength has been at the lower levels of the corporate, or enterprise, market, while Oracle's has been at the upper end.

So if Microsoft is tying its push into the enterprise to .NET, then what is .NET? I asked the guy who should know, Barry Goffe, group manager for .NET Enterprise Solutions at Microsoft. First of all, he says, you have to understand why a new technology strategy is needed: it's because of the so far unsolved problem of integration; customers want to tie together all their various applications, from back office to front office, with their database, their Web site, and other software. "Over the last couple of decades, there have been a lot of different approaches to solving integration, and none of those technologies has really been satisfactory," says Goffe. They're expensive, they take a long time to set up, and they have to be redone every time there's a change in any of the connected software. The Internet only exacerbated the problem by making connectivity more fluid, not just among internal applications but also vendor to customer or vendor to supplier. "Where we've ended up is with Web services as a way of solving the integration problem, although it's not the 100 percent solution," he cautions. Web services is the next paradigm of computing, after Internet, client-server, and mainframe. "The incumbents in the Internet computing era [where he concedes Oracle did well] will not necessarily be incumbents of Web services."

.NET is Microsoft's strategy for embracing Web services, Internet-based software that encompasses everything from stock market quotes to package-tracking systems. (Certain protocols known by acronyms like XML and SOAP make this possible.) A lot of Microsoft software aimed at the corporate world will be packaged under .NET, such as its database SQL Server, its Windows XP for mobile devices that want to interact with Web services, and its controversial identification software Passport. This is supposed to provide an environment, or platform, for Microsoft customers to build their own Web services, although not everything that will be part of .NET is yet available. Says Goffe, "It's a long-term vision." He admits that Microsoft hasn't done a good job of explaining .NET or how it solves the enterprise integration conundrum. Nonetheless, that is the positioning.

In fact, Goffe adds, .NET is a step away from the Windows approach and a step toward the solutions approach. "We'll provide you with the capability of making all your stuff work together and with your partners," he says. "We used to go in to customers and say, when you run everything on Windows, the world will be a happy place, your teeth will be whiter." But enterprise customers, which had a lot of existing applications and needed more robustness than Windows-based technologies, balked. "They showed us to the door," Goffe admits. Hence, the new approach based on Web services. "Oracle has a 'rip-and-replace' strategy," he says, but "even if you believe everything Ellison says and go all-Oracle, what about your partners? What if you buy another company? Instead of making the world one homogenous environment, we're saying we believe in playing nicely with others." That's certainly a newly humble approach for Microsoft, and it's questionable, with the federal government's lawsuit resolved, how long that attitude will hold.

Goffe suggests that Microsoft with .NET and IBM with WebSphere have been the "thought leaders" in Web services. Oracle, he says, "has been pretty much absent." But Oracle counters with its combination of the latest database, application server, and 11i enterprise applications suite, although it has not really designated these as a Web services platform. In the past, it has joined with Sun Microsystems in support of Java (with which .NET is not compatible) as the development environment for Web services. However, at Oracle's Open-World conference in December 2001, executives opened the door to possibly also supporting .NET. Thomas Kurian, vice president of the application server line of business, said Oracle would stick with Java for its own development but offer interoperability with .NET when and if it was needed. Canopus Research President Zachmann believes that .NET, as it develops, will make inroads against Oracle, Sun, IBM, and other companies accustomed to dismissing Microsoft at the enterprise level. "For a lot of things that a corporation does, particularly on the Web, .NET will be more attractive, because it will be a way to get there better, faster, cheaper," Zachmann says. That, in turn, will strengthen Microsoft's database entry, SQL Server. Although IBM has been a strong supporter of Java, "it will play both sides and embrace .NET," Zachmann adds, responding to customers that ask for it.

In the stand-alone database market, Goffe believes that SQL Server will make inroads against Oracle regardless of what happens to .NET. "Oracle is getting turfed out," he says. "Our database business is already over $1 billion and catching Oracle quickly." Oracle, he maintains, is trying to rescue itself with enterprise applications and lately has not been as innovative with its core database. He says, "9i [the latest version of Oracle's database] was lipstick on a pig." Although Oracle still leads the market, "they're holding on to that by a tenuous thread." E-services consultant Nance says that while most of his customers currently run on Oracle, they're now starting to consider SQL Server because of the cost differential. In late 2001, SQL Server was about $20,000 per CPU (central processing unit, or microprocessor), while Oracle was $55,000 and IBM was $110,000. That doesn't include services, Nance notes. "Our clients are also looking at the annual support and maintenance costs," where Oracle costs roughly triple what SQL Server does to maintain. "We have a client spending $1.5 million a year with Oracle who is going to SQL Server." Morgan Stanley analyst Phillips says that Microsoft will gain database share from both Oracle and IBM because it can sell SQL Server packaged with its enormously popular

Windows NT operating system, which is the chief competitor to Unix in corporate markets.

Besides bundling SQL Server with Windows and .NET, Microsoft poses another threat to Oracle. It could be positioning itself to move into enterprise applications. At the end of 2000, Microsoft shelled out $1 billion to buy Great Plains, which makes ERP-like software aimed at small and medium-size businesses. Says Goffe, "There is a long-term strategy for how Great Plains will integrate with .NET over time. It hasn't been rolled out yet." He denies that Microsoft is interested in the high end of ERP applications, pointing to its partnership with SAP and PeopleSoft. But given Microsoft's history of partnering, then pilfering, and its purchase of Great Plains, there's speculation that Microsoft could be eyeing enterprise applications. Indeed, in February 2002, it rolled out a CRM package, which would put it in direct competition with the other vendors in that arena, including SAP, Oracle, and Siebel Systems. "Microsoft has the ingredients to cover all the bets," says Dennis Byron, vice president of ERP and industry applications research with IDC. If .NET doesn't take off as expected, "they're just as likely to move up into the enterprise applications market."

MOONING SAP

The most famous anecdote about SAP and Oracle never actually happened, according to SAP's marketing people, although it does have its basis in truth. Like Ellison, SAP's CEO Hasso Plattner is a fan of sailing and has often competed with his applications rival. In a 1996 event off the coast of Hawaii, Plattner's boat, the *Morning Glory*, declared an emergency, with a busted mast and a severe injury to a crew member. While the crew was waiting for help, Ellison's yacht, the *Sayonara*, passed by, followed by its tender boat. "The tender boat circled *Morning Glory* two times without offering to help," as was required by the sailing rules, says Herbert Heitmann, SAP's director of global communications. "Instead, they were videotaping." So Plattner pulled down his pants and mooned the boat. Naturally, this evolved into Plattner's mooning Ellison himself. "Hasso has never mooned Larry. He just showed these people who were taping videos what he thought about their behavior, but it did not involve Larry," Heitmann says. "This has nothing to do with Oracle or Larry. Hasso was upset that somebody wouldn't stick to the international rules." Ellison has denied that his crew behaved improperly. Nonetheless, the incident has become the stuff of legend inside SAP and Oracle and, no matter what really occurred, epitomizes the relationship between the two. Oracle thinks of SAP as an uptight German company overly concerned with rules, while SAP looks at Oracle as an immature competitor that doesn't play fair.

As for their respective applications products, the story is more complicated. While SAP used to be the rigid applications provider demanding that customers conform to its way of doing things, the German company has moved toward the IBM view of the world: offering solutions rather than just software. Meanwhile, Oracle, with its applications suite filled out in 11i, is the one that insists that customers do things its way. In 1992, when SAP released version R/3 of its ERP package, "we believed we could replicate the whole business world in one system and serve all the customer's needs," says Heitmann. SAP rode the coattails of the business reengineering movement, as companies restructured and adopted standard processes. But as the Internet became more important, many of those processes went out the window. "It became obvious that the world has grown more complex," says Heitmann. "Our customers want to have more than one single vendor and a guarantee that these [disparate applications] are not black boxes that don't communicate. So we put our main emphasis on productivity and integration." With 11i, "Oracle is dreaming what we dreamt with R/3," he adds. "But customers don't like to be locked in." By telling customers they can mix and match applications software, "we let them know that they have the freedom to go somewhere else. Giving them that freedom in some cases makes them more willing to use only one vendor," Heitmann says.

Of course, SAP had to reposition itself during the move from client-server architecture to the Internet, which it fumbled. At first, "SAP development thought of the Internet as a bit of a fad with mainly consumer-type applications," says Jeremy Coote, the former president of SAP America. "They decided to sit back and watch how things developed to see how they could accommodate the market. As a result, they earned the reputation of missing the Internet revolution." By contrast, Oracle, thanks to Ellison's pronouncements, gave the impression that it "immediately embraced the Internet," Coote says. Heitmann concedes that, at least on the marketing front, Oracle won the battle. SAP lagged because "it was not obvious what the gain would be in businesses processes," he says. While its developers tried to sort through the new design requirements and develop the browser-based front end known as MySAP, which was introduced in 1999, SAP was quiet about the Internet. "In the two years we spent with redesigning business processes and developing integration, the Oracle marketing department did an extremely good job of positioning Oracle," says Heitmann. MySAP, incidentally, accesses not only SAP's R/3 applications but also those of competitors. "We want the opportunity to demonstrate the values we bring to the table," says Heitmann. "In the end, it's the customer's decision what applications to use."

Oracle resents SAP not only for being the market leader but also because it licensed its database to the German company for a song. Not realizing how big R/3 would become, Oracle gave SAP "a very attractive deal to resell the database," says Coote. "Oracle did not see the ERP revolution coming and at the time was looking for validation of its product." As R/3 began making major inroads into the largest companies, still SAP's stronghold, it brought the Oracle database along with it. "SAP was certainly a huge driver for Oracle becoming the de facto database standard in the *Fortune* 1,000," Coote says. "Later, this became highly contentious in the Oracle field sales teams because SAP could undercut the price of the Oracle database." Oracle tried desperately to change the terms of the agreement, but with other database vendors, notably IBM, coming into the marketplace, SAP refused. To this day, the Oracle sales organization blames the partner alliances group for giving away the crown jewels to its chief competitor in applications.

TOUGHENING UP PEOPLESOFT

In 1999, it was obvious that PeopleSoft was going to have to change radically to survive. Founded eleven years earlier by a notable animal lover, Dave Duffield, who has devoted large sums of money to making the San Francisco SPCA a "no-kill" shelter, PeopleSoft was known as "the nice company" to work for and do business with. It had an in-house rock band; people dressed casually and brought their pets to work; everyone, even Duffield, worked in a cubicle. The epitome of the laid-back company, in stark contrast to aggressive, in-your-face Oracle. But guess what? The nice guys were finishing last. Oracle had seized the Internet turf, while PeopleSoft was still trying to craft an entry. The lack of discipline inside People-Soft was also manifest in its poor collection of accounts receivable, exacerbated by the approach of Y2K, which caused many customers to stop spending for a time. To the rescue— Craig Conway, a former Oracle salesman who had risen to executive vice president but was fired by Ray Lane. Conway ran a couple of start-ups before being tapped by PeopleSoft.

Inside PeopleSoft, the reaction was hardly ecstatic. "Everyone's fear was that Craig would try and make PeopleSoft into a little Oracle," recalls Rick Bergquist, who has been with PeopleSoft since the beginning and is its chief technology officer and senior vice president. At first, Conway seemed to fulfill those fears, as he slashed other projects to focus on development of the Internet suite, PeopleSoft 8. In the first nine months, he lost a quarter of the workforce and 80 of 120 senior managers.[1] But Conway persevered, and PeopleSoft 8, released in September 2000, helped push the company to $2 billion in revenue in 2001. Says Bergquist, "Craig has changed PeopleSoft, and PeopleSoft has changed Craig." Conway brought a needed intensity and a hard-to-match knowledge of the marketplace, especially Oracle, with which PeopleSoft battled to become number two overall in enterprise applications. "Knowing your enemy is a plus," Bergquist notes. But he also believes that Conway took from PeopleSoft "its caring approach to customers," something for which Oracle is hardly known. "Craig has been able to morph together our commitment to our customers with operational excellence. We've become much more effective as an organization," Bergquist says.

Today, PeopleSoft is again a real competitor of SAP and Oracle in enterprise applications, having filled out its offering with the introduction of a well-received CRM product in mid-2001. PeopleSoft supports the best-of-breed approach advocated by SAP and IBM, in part because the younger company was a specialist in human relations software for years and its product line still lacks functionality in some other areas. "PeopleSoft doesn't have the reputation or functionality to compete in manufacturing," says Jennifer Chew, Forrester Research's analyst for E-business applications. "Realistically, they have to integrate with someone else in manufacturing." However, she adds, among the full-throttle ERP vendors, "PeopleSoft has the best reputation for CRM functionality." SAP is a strong second, while Oracle lags. But for large corporations that want to choose just one ERP vendor, "there are only two possibilities," says Chew, "SAP or Oracle. If you're a large manufacturing company, PeopleSoft doesn't have what you need." And with most of these customers already using the Oracle database, even though Oracle doesn't have best-of-breed ERP applications, "for the sake of compatability, they often choose Oracle in spite of the issues around quality."

This means that Conway, and PeopleSoft, still have their work cut out for them. But Conway did bring Oracle's swaggering confidence in his company's technology with him. "PeopleSoft has leapfrogged Oracle and SAP from an architecture point of view," Conway says, praising his company's "pure Web-based product." PeopleSoft 8 is written in HTML, the language of the Internet, so it's accessible with any browser. "Oracle is now losing sales to PeopleSoft," he asserts. Like other Oracle competitors, he believes that Oracle's reputation can be used against it. "To some extent, companies are not dissimilar from people. They have a level of honesty and integrity, professionalism, respect, commitment to fair play. And just like individuals differ in those ways, so do companies."[2] Lane believes that Conway has done a good job with PeopleSoft. "He walked away from Oracle and didn't immerse himself in the politics of Oracle versus PeopleSoft."

Although PeopleSoft must cooperate with Oracle to make its product work on the database, "if any customer comes without a database preference, I'll help them make one," says Bergquist. And it won't be Oracle. "We have partnerships with IBM and Microsoft, and I'm going to recommend someone who doesn't compete against us." That brings him to his favorite story about Oracle. One of PeopleSoft's database technologists was at Oracle one day to test PeopleSoft applications on the database. As he got into the elevator with his PeopleSoft backpack, Ellison strode in, too. "He sees the PeopleSoft backpack, walks out of the elevator, and takes another one," says Bergquist. Thanks to those attitudes, Oracle, he says, echoing Mills, has alienated people who should be its friends. "Every time we sell an application, it's an opportunity for a database deal," says Bergquist. "Here we are making his database work with our apps, and Larry can't be in the same elevator with PeopleSoft."

HOSTILITIES ABOUND

On June 6, 2003, Ellison, who had been talking recently to the press about the need for dramatic consolidation among technology companies, put his money where his mouth was: he announced an uninvited bid to acquire PeopleSoft for $5.1 billion in cash. This came in response to PeopleSoft's intent to merge with a smaller rival in the enterprise applications business, J. D. Edwards, vaulting the combined company past Oracle for number two overall in that market. While market leader SAP took out ads to woo PeopleSoft and J. D. Edwards customers in the confusion, PeopleSoft CEO Conway was livid, describing Ellison's move as "diabolical" and "straight out of Genghis Khan." Ellison wasn't particularly interested in PeopleSoft's 8,200 employees, most of whom he reportedly planned to jettison, nor in its product. It was a market-share play, pure and simple. PeopleSoft's customers would be coaxed/coerced to move to Oracle's E-business suite.

Ellison's move certainly created consternation for PeopleSoft, its customers, and for the technology industry itself, which was largely unaccustomed to hostile takeovers. It was an industry that had enjoyed so much growth that mergers were done on a friendly basis to scoop up needed talent or intellectual property, not necessarily market share. But recognizing that times had changed—technology purchases were shrinking in many sectors, including enterprise applications—Ellison made his stunning bid, based on consolidation of Oracle's place in the enterprise market, nothing more. (You could say that Hewlett-Packard had presaged the move by buying Compaq, but that was a negotiated merger agreed to by both sides.) Says Ray Lane, "If you look at the market shares of the applications business, Oracle has lost so much share they are now just about on an even basis with PeopleSoft. If PeopleSoft bought J. D. Edwards, that would push Oracle down to third or even fourth place," the latter if you count Siebel Systems (see next section), which makes only one kind of enterprise application. Ellison hates being in second place, let alone third or fourth.

Lane says Ellison's viewpoint on mergers was typically that he wanted to win with Oracle's technology, not purchase anything from outsiders. Ellison did at one point consider buying database rival Sybase for market share, "but he could never get the price cheap enough," says Lane. However, Oracle was losing the applications battle, especially as competitors took advantage of the problems it was experiencing with customers (detailed in Chapter 9). Not only that, Ellison was being advised by two former investment bankers in executive vice presidents Safra Catz and Charles Phillips, both of whom supported deal-making. Lane terms the PeopleSoft bid "an act of desperation on Larry's part that basically works. If he gets PeopleSoft, he cements second place." Even he doesn't, Ellison had pushed an important rival seriously off-balance. "He made it very difficult for PeopleSoft to close their (current) quarter," notes Lane, although PeopleSoft later reported second-quarter earnings that had exceeded expectations, in part because customers were rallying to the company's defense. Lane adds that Conway's initial reaction lashing out at Ellison "just plays to Larry's hand."

PeopleSoft and Oracle held dueling press conferences on June 12, 2003, after the PeopleSoft board of directors unanimously rejected Oracle's bid, stating that, "The unsolicited and hostile nature of the offer, combined with Oracle's statements, is designed to disrupt (PeopleSoft's) strong momentum at significant cost to customers." Conway asserted in his teleconference that PeopleSoft customers were "surprised and outraged" by the bid and were rallying to the company's defense. He also raised antitrust concerns, noting that "the (broad-based) enterprise software market would be down to two competitors, SAP and Oracle." About an hour later, at his own teleconference, Ellison retorted that PeopleSoft management was not doing a good job for its shareholders. "Their stock is down 28 percent for the year . . . Their license sales (in the most recent quarter) dropped nearly 40 percent . . . I'm not sure how you can describe going down 39 percent as strong momentum in the market." He added that J. D. Edwards was "in worse shape" than PeopleSoft, so that merger didn't make sense for shareholders. Ellison also disparaged the antitrust issue. About a year ago in mid-2002, Conway had approached Oracle to propose that PeopleSoft acquire Oracle's application business. (Conway confirmed this.) "Conway," said Ellison, "identified himself as the right person to run that business. Now he suddenly perceives that a combination of PeopleSoft and Oracle has antitrust concerns. The only difference is, in our proposal Mr. Conway would not be running the combined company."

The spat got uglier as PeopleSoft and J. D. Edwards both filed lawsuits against Oracle on antitrust grounds, as did the state of Connecticut, a user of PeopleSoft software. Oracle sued PeopleSoft to try to overturn its so-called poison pill provision, which makes a takeover more difficult.

On June 18, Oracle substantially boosted its bid for People-Soft to $6.3 billion, signaling that it was indeed serious about the offer and that Ellison wasn't just playing games. In its revised offer, Oracle got in a customary dig, tracking People-Soft's stock performance since May 24, 1999, when Conway took over as CEO. PeopleSoft was down 9.5 percent (although the NASDAQ exchange overall was down 32.9 percent in the same period), while Oracle was up 115.9 percent. People-Soft's board again rejected the second bid, while the company sped up its acquisition of J. D. Edwards (effectively completed in July) and opened the door for a "white knight," possibly IBM, to come in and rescue it from Oracle.

Both Ellison and Conway, and their respective companies, appeared to be digging in for a protracted battle. PeopleSoft got some support in July when the attorneys general from more than half the states agreed to cooperate in an antitrust investigation of the takeover attempt. Oracle, meanwhile, raised its bid to $7.3 billion, to cover buying J. D. Edwards as well. At a July 9, 2003, meeting with analysts, Ellison reiterated his determination to acquire PeopleSoft, even if it meant trying to gain control of its board during a scheduled election in June 2004. He also tossed off one of those joking ad-libs that make his public relations staff cringe, when Ellison said that Conway was so incensed he "thought I was going to shoot his dog." If Conway and the dog "were standing next to each other and I had one bullet, it wouldn't be for the dog." Whether or not Oracle succeeded with the merger, Ellison had once again demonstrated his ability to shake up the technology industry with his warlike mentality and his refusal to be bypassed by events.

OUTDUELING ORACLE

Tom Siebel left Oracle in 1990, but Oracle has never left Siebel, even though he'd like to believe it has. "Most of what I learned about management I learned at the feet of Larry Ellison. I do exactly the opposite," he insists. Siebel likes to call Ellison "His Larriness," a title coined by late cofounder Bob Miner. "When I left [Oracle], I thought it was a bankrupt culture," says Siebel, once the top Oracle salesman, who followed his mentor Gary Kennedy out the door. "There was no sense of purpose beyond making money. That wears pretty thin. If you're coming to work to make money, you get tired. People want to work for other things, like creating value and satisfying customers." So when he founded Siebel Systems in 1993, Siebel created a company that above all else placed the customer at the center. Salespeople were rewarded based not just on sales figures but on customer satisfaction. He established a culture of accountability, with formal dress, no pets at work, no games in the halls. And yet, even though the core values are different, Siebel Systems is just as much a cult of personality as Oracle, dominated by one individual. Siebel's San Mateo headquarters bears an eerie resemblence to Oracle's just a few miles south. In fact, Siebel is very much like Ellison in his single-minded devotion to his company and his vision. Says Lane, "I've talked to people who have left Siebel [Systems]. They went there because they saw tremendous opportunity, and they left out of frustration with management, just like Oracle."

The competition between Siebel and Oracle is intensified not only by the shared backgrounds of the two founders but by the fact that Tom Siebel used technology similar to what he had developed at his former company to capture a new market—a market that Oracle now avidly wants for its own. While he was still with Oracle, Siebel set up internal software called OASIS (Oracle Automated Sales Information System) to handle lead generation and financial accounting for the telesales group (where he also met his wife, Stacey Brusco). Soon he grew the group, which he'd taken over from Anneke Seley, into the largest revenue producer at Oracle. Seley says she had started OASIS on a limited basis, "but Tom in his brilliant way made it the cornerstone of what he accomplished." He also stirred up fierce internal competition with the direct sales force over the size of deals going to telesales. But Ellison never wanted to sell OASIS externally, and after Siebel left Oracle, he used the concept in sales force automation software that became the foundation of a new market. Siebel vaulted to $1 billion in sales in just seven years, half the time it took Oracle. After an acquisition that brought it customer care software, Siebel Systems is now the market leader in customer relationship management (CRM), a niche that enterprise applications vendors like SAP and Oracle missed because no one thought it would be a particularly huge market. No one except Tom Siebel.

"When Siebel started, SAP wasn't ready to enter this particular area as quickly as necessary," admits Heitmann. "A new company can just focus on a very trendy product and deliver on expectations." Lane says Siebel approached him when he started his namesake company and proposed a deal with Oracle. "I looked at the demo and told him, 'When you have a system, get back to me.' He never did." But Lane says he knew that Ellison would never do a deal with Siebel because he wanted Oracle to develop its own product. "Now Siebel leads this huge category, and he's in Larry's sights," says Lane. Both CEOs have personalized the battle. "Larry doesn't think Tom has a product culture. Tom would say Oracle doesn't have a customer culture." The irony, Lane adds, is that Oracle could have had the market before Siebel was even created. "The first day I was at Oracle, Ron Wohl interviewed me about what we needed to do in things like sales force automation and order management," he recalls. "The application team wanted to know what a sales-forecasting system should have." But when Oracle finally got around to doing CRM, its first release, in 1998, didn't work very well. "Customers would do evaluations against Siebel, and we couldn't even get our demo to run," says Lane. Finally, in 2001, Oracle released a workable CRM product, part of its 11i suite, and analysts suggest that Siebel may be in trouble. "Oracle, PeopleSoft, and SAP are all going to gang up on Siebel during the next round of upgrades. They're going to give away their CRM software to knock Siebel out," predicts IDC's Byron, something the trio can do because they offer more than simply CRM. But Siebel insists he's still in the sweet spot and has no interest in moving into broader enterprise applications. "My goal is always to get the 50 percent share in any market," he says, something that would be impossible in ERP. He claims a 65 percent share in CRM and is now eyeing ERM, or employee relationship management, "the application of communication technology to maintaining relationships with employees." This will be a $26 billion market, Siebel proclaims, and he aims to get his 50 percent share.

WHERE IS ORACLE?

If Web services is indeed the next paradigm of computing, it isn't clear where Oracle fits. In a year of researching Web services, says Ethan Cerami, author of *Web Services Essentials*, "Oracle never came up." He identifies the leaders as IBM; Microsoft, with .NET; and Sun, with its Java-based initiative, Sun ONE. Lane believes that Oracle should move more decisively and become "the premier application provider" for Web services, meaning that instead of delivering a massive integrated package of applications, Oracle offers software on an as-needed basis over the Internet. It's an option already offered by small competitors such as Salesforce.com, founded by Oracle departee Marc Benioff. "I'm a big believer that the enterprise community is headed toward Web services," says Lane. "Developing these apps rapidly and putting them into service is what Oracle should be doing." The barrier, though, will be Oracle's failure on the application server, which delivers Web services. "They're losing out in the positioning in that market, which is going to be the primary tool for development in the future," says Lane.

Oracle was late to the game with application servers, acknowledges Ken Jacobs, a twenty-year Oracle veteran who is vice president of product strategy for server technologies. "We tried to do too much and didn't do it well. We also didn't have the right technology for Java." But with the release of Oracle's most recent application server, called 9iAS, "we have a strong product" that can compete "head-to-head" with IBM and BEA. Jacobs says 9iAS has a built-in market—everyone running the Oracle database. "We're going after the biggest market, which is Oracle. We believe that every one of our database customers is a customer for 9iAS."

Lane is skeptical that Ellison really gets it. Web services, he says, "is about companies working in collaborative fashion with suppliers and customers," developing applications that serve all three. "In a very dynamic business process environment, you want to keep up with changes by writing applications quickly. You want to change business process in real time." Lane, based on his investing as a venture capitalist at Kleiner Perkins, believes there's a huge market building for services that allow for this kind of development. "Microsoft is all over this. IBM sees it as a major market. But I can hear Larry saying, 'That's stupid. What they need is good software engineers writing good lines of code.'" Analyst Olofson believes that Oracle still has a window of opportunity to promote its integrated product line while Web services get sorted out. But it's a limited window. "Oracle needs to take the heterogeneity issue a little more seriously," he says. "They must have a plan that says, at some point in the future, we will shift gears and move into components." Ellison is capable of nimbleness and flexibility, he adds. "I expect that once he has played the hand that he's currently got, he'll cut the deck and deal a fresh hand. Three or four years from now, you'll hear Oracle talking about the importance of interoperability."

While Oracle has shot itself in the foot so many times it appears to be limping badly, it's too early to count the company out. It still has the leading database, which gives it leverage to sell a plethora of other products, including applications, tools, and application server. Its 11i applications suite is gradually getting better, and Ellison appears poised to devote more resources to shoring up Oracle's on-line business that sells products on an as-needed basis. Oracle is the only one among all of its competitors that can give you the database, the application server, and the entire ERP suite. This is appealing, especially for midlevel customers that don't want the hassles of dealing with a bunch of different vendors. These are the same customers that could be attracted by a subscription-based, on-line sales model.

Among database competitors, IBM poses the most serious threat to Oracle because DB2 is close to Oracle 9i in quality, as demonstrated by performance benchmarks. Microsoft's SQL Server is sold mostly bundled with its other products and still falls short of DB2 and Oracle on performance and robustness. Among the ERP vendors, SAP, for all its push to become more flexible, retains the reputation for having long installment periods and requiring adherence to complex business processes. Oracle could counter that by ratcheting up its on-line business and giving customers more choices in products and pricing. PeopleSoft, despite its development of a full-bore ERP suite, and Siebel, which has stuck with CRM, are perceived as best-of-breed buys, so Oracle's competitive positioning is to offer a broader range of products with easier integration. Olofson suggests that Oracle could do quite well in the future by accepting the realities of operating in two mature markets—database and enterprise applications. "They need to set expectations lower and adopt business models that reflect that [maturity]," he says, by cooperating more with partners and toning down their aggressive sales tactics. "That way, it's not double-digit growth or shrink. It's grow at a steady 4 to 5 percent," he says. However, given Oracle's past, its culture, and the personality of the man at the top, it doesn't seem as if Oracle would be able to switch from a "go-go" to a "whoa-whoa" mentality.

12

CULT OR CULTURE

> "I WILL BUY YOU . . . THE GENERAL ELECTRIC
> CORPORATION, WHICH IS QUITE EXPENSIVE,
> AND EVEN DINNER ON FRIDAY."

Oracle's culture is brutal, draining, and filled with potential pitfalls. Success depends upon making sure that either Larry Ellison is unaware of you or he likes you. One former midlevel executive kept moving sideways to avoid moving too far up the ladder. "If you pop your head up above the turf, it's going to get mowed off," he says. Another compared Oracle to the movie *Rollerball*, in which the rules change constantly and part of the game is trying to figure out the new set of rules before you get whacked. But Oracle has produced more executives who have the chops to go off and run their own show than any other company in Silicon Valley. As a result, it's surrounded by competitors and partners who know it from the inside: Tom Siebel of Siebel Systems, Craig Conway of PeopleSoft, Greg Brady of i2 Technologies, Marc Benioff of Salesforce.com, Gary Bloom of Veritas. Then there are smaller ventures led by Oracle expatriates, including Polly Sumner of Alphablox, Robert Shaw of ArcSight, Stephen Kelly of Chordiant, Pete Tierney of MarketFirst Software, Nimish Mehta of Stratify, Ad Nederlof of Genesys, Beatriz Infante of Aspect Communications, Farzad Dibachi of Niku, and George Kadifa of Corio. Other high-ranking executives have also departed, some going into consulting or venture investing, others to new positions or retirement: Jay Nussbaum, Ray Lane, Craig Ramsey, George Roberts, and Jeremy Burton. The list goes on and on.

Oracle's capricious culture flows directly from Larry Ellison and includes extreme combativeness, outrageous arrogance, and visionary intelligence, coupled with laserlike focus on technology and where it's going. The cutthroat politics leaves little room for loyalty or kindness. Oracle is great for individuals who want to scale the mountain and don't care who gets left behind. Ambitious young people like Siebel and Benioff climbed through the ranks and fashioned jobs around their needs and skills. Benioff, who was a master at this, summarized it all in a brief conversation with Luke Little, a former midlevel manager at Oracle. Little had called to ask Benioff what to do about a complex sales deal he was trying to bring together, but no one would give him approval. Recalls Little: "Marc Benioff gave me the best piece of advice I ever got at Oracle. He said, 'Luke, do what you want. Just do what you want.'" Little signed the deal.

This cherished freedom to succeed or fail based on your own decisions has drawn many an entrepreneur to Silicon Valley (and many an immigrant to the United States). It's exhilarating when everything is going right, when the company is growing rapidly and no one questions whether deals were signed too quickly or people were promoted beyond their capabilities. But what happens in tough times—like the early 1990s and early 2000s for Oracle—is that all the executives and managers look to save themselves by casting blame elsewhere. This is the conundrum of doing what you want: freedom can turn sour, and youthful energy can be sapped by second-guessing. That outcome is inevitable when bright, ambitious, strong-willed people are thrown together in an environment that doesn't give them clear goals and guiding principles applied in good times as well as bad. Says former product executive Nimish Mehta, "At Oracle, I didn't have any friends, because you never knew whom you could trust."

Ellison embodies the "do what you want" philosophy, from his sexual dalliances with women who work for him to his outbursts in public forums to his thumbing his nose at authority—whether it's flying his plane into the San Jose Airport after curfew or building a vastly oversized "stately pleasure dome" in Woodside, Silicon Valley's answer to Xanadu. This attitude invariably flows down throughout the company that Ellison founded and runs by fiat. The result is rampant creativity, all too often unchecked by the real needs of customers or partners, along with disdain for competitors and contempt for anyone who espouses a more conservative path. Oracle is a melodrama with an open-ended script.

LARRYLAND, INC.

Whenever Ellison attends an executive committee meeting at Oracle, he plays the reigning guru whose whims must be obeyed. The CEO defines the tone of a meeting by setting up an extreme position, such as "We're moving all the applications to the Internet and terminating support of previous versions." This invites a response from someone else, often Ray Lane while he was there, taking a more realistic view. "Larry initiated the dialectic," recalls George Kadifa, formerly an executive with Oracle Consulting Services. "Ray would stand up and say, 'We can't do this.' Larry would listen, and a new decision would get made. It was very obvious what he was doing. He was a master puppeteer." This was fine when Ellison had executives such as Lane, Robert Shaw, and Polly Sumner, who would stand up to him and present the dissenting view. Ellison would steer Oracle in a new direction, while Lane and like-minded executives kept the company from veering too far off course. But now there's almost nobody left as a moderating influence, and Ellison can be, to put it mildly, erratic when he's the sole decision maker. "Other than [CFO] Jeff [Henley], Larry has now run out of managers who are able to say no to him," says Beatriz Infante, formerly senior vice president of Oracle's Internet and new enterprise software applications. "Larry ultimately can't tolerate disagreement," Infante adds. "That inherently becomes his downfall."

Ellison is a genius at motivation. One time he called Nimish Mehta at home to talk up a researcher at the University of Washington working on the human genome, biomedical research being one of Ellison's passions. The CEO wanted Mehta to write a quick little software application to help the researcher with his work "I said, 'Larry, I'm really busy with this product for Oracle.'" Ellison replied, "What exactly do you do in the morning? You come in at nine, walk over and get your coffee. You have time." Mehta promised to get the application done. "Great answer," Ellison said. The man can sniff out any weakness and exploit it. "He really has a way of getting to you," Mehta says. Many times, Ellison's manipulation of people pays off, for Oracle and for them. Virtually every one of the executives interviewed for this book spoke of the opportunities that Ellison gave them and the ways in which he drove them to heights they might never have achieved on their own. Says Benioff, "Larry knows how to pick people who have the qualities to be a leader, sometimes before they know it themselves. Then he pushes them out of the nest, like he did with Tom [Siebel]. It worked out great for Tom."

But on the flip side there's what Ellison himself has called "management by humiliation." Time and again, he dismisses an idea, a strategy, a presentation by calling it "the dumbest thing I ever heard." Even Benioff, who was a favorite of Ellison's, remembers the gut-wrenching feeling of hearing those words. "Larry makes you feel like the world is ending, and that it's your fault," he says. "That dismissive behavior hurts." Jim Bensman, the former president of SAP America, was hired by Lane as a consultant in 1995–1996 to come up with recommendations on Oracle's struggling applications business. One presentation he gave to the executive committee was supposed to be about the importance of avoiding conflicts between salespeople selling directly to the customer and salespeople who worked with partners such as SAP and PeopleSoft. Bensman just had time to unroll a banner about the issue and tell Ellison, "You're competing against yourself," attempting to explain why Oracle was engaged in self-defeating behavior. Ellison responded, "I don't understand what you're talking about. That's the way I want to run it. Sit down." The rest of Bensman's carefully prepared script went out the window. Another recommendation fared no better. He suggested that the applications business be set up as a separate unit, with its own profit-and-loss statement, accountable executives, and dedicated sales force. "You're trying to compete with companies that are totally focused on apps. You need to do this," Bensman told Ellison. But the latter quickly rejected it, with his patented put-down, "That's the dumbest idea I ever heard." No way would Oracle ever spin out applications, Ellison insisted. It would diminish Oracle too much. On that point, he could be right. Oracle's future growth depends on applications, not database.

On the other hand, it is possible to win Ellison over. He will listen to people whom he respects. "In the five years I worked for Larry, I found that if I presented a logical reason as to why something was important, he would seize on it and support me," says Infante, who helped orchestrate the 1994 acquisition of Digital Equipment's Rdb database. With good reason, Ellison was wary, she recalls. Successful large-scale acquisitions in the software industry are rare because they require merging quirky, talented people who can go just about anywhere they want. "You have to appeal to Larry on technology first," Infante says, and Ellison was impressed with the power of Digital's database for very large systems. Infante and others who worked on the deal convinced Ellison to do the $108 million deal on several counts: bringing Oracle some great technology, expanding market share, fending off rivals such as IBM, and adding a talented development team of two hundred engineers. Infante remembers telling Ellison why he couldn't just hire away those engineers. "Digital was very concerned about that," she recalls, and insisted on writing a noncompete clause into the agreement that preceded any negotiations.

"That was wise on Digital's part," she says, because Ellison did suggest pirating the development team. "Larry is almost amoral, but he doesn't realize it," adds Infante. "It's like the genetic makeup of morality is missing. You've got to explain to Larry, 'This is why something is wrong.' If he respects you, he'll back off."

If Ellison isn't interested in something, like Oracle's applications (until he moved them to the Internet), he ignores the subject. But if he's intrigued by an area, like marketing, his attention to detail can be remarkable, unpredictably so. That's why the top marketing job is one of the fastest revolving doors at Oracle. Jerry Held, who oversaw interactive TV and then the database product in the mid-1990s, remembers working on ads for Oracle 8 with the marketing person and a desktop-publishing expert. "We were over at Larry's house," Held recalls, and the expert was fine-tuning an ad on the computer that featured Oracle's red banner. "Suddenly, Larry says that's not our standard banner," Held said. "He kicks the guy out of the seat and starts fiddling with the computer." Ellison said, "There are three extra pixels here. The Oracle banner is too wide." He had discerned that there was a hair's breadth of extra width on the banner. Held also recalls an earlier incident when he first took a position at Oracle. He was living in Almaden Valley, an hour and a half's drive from Oracle headquarters, and told Ellison he was concerned about the commute. "Larry said, 'There will be a town car every morning to pick you up. It's going to be anthracite gray with a gray interior.' " Says Held, "He'd not only solved the problem, he knew what the car would be like. And sure enough, every day I worked there, a car like that showed up."

Ellison is also capable of pure exhilarating magic in coming up with a new approach or a vision of something that no one has ever thought of in quite that way before. This doesn't involve just Oracle strategy but issues with political and social ramifications such as the national ID card or the network computer. "Some of my most wonderful moments at Oracle were when Larry would come into a meeting and start talking about his latest idea," says Mehta, everything from restructuring the schools to making all buildings wireless. "When you went from that to someone who's a mere process manager, it was a letdown." Adds former head of sales Barry Ariko, "Larry is totally intuitive." Most people move from "A" to "B." With Ellison, "we would start at 'A,' and suddenly we're at 'F.'" No one had worked out how to get from "A" to "F," except if Ellison thought it was possible, then in his mind, it was already done. Ariko compares dealing with Ellison to playing the game of "wrong rock." "Ellison says, 'Bring me a rock.' And you did. He'd tell you, 'Sorry, that's the wrong rock. Bring me another rock.'" And so on and so on. Ellison "would never tell you what the right rock is, just that you had the wrong one," Ariko says.

Executives who fall out of favor for some reason are in limbo, until Ellison finds a way to get rid of them. Says Ariko, "Larry doesn't know how to subtly criticize someone, maybe saying, 'You're doing a pretty good job, but I'd like you to focus more on this issue.' He'd rather just stew on it and then suddenly come out with, 'You're fucking crazy.' He doesn't know how to keep it from exploding." Adds Held, "At the executive level, Larry would churn the positions deliberately. He tends to reach down in the organization and promote people way over their heads, then dump them when they fail." The upshot of all this is that no one is ever certain of his or her position at Oracle, and everyone, as a consequence, competes against one another to curry favor with Ellison. Many times he will say no to something in a meeting and change his mind later after personal lobbying. "You left meetings not knowing whether 'no' meant 'no' or whether it meant he's in a bad mood," Ariko recalls. " Everybody got plenty of power and money at Oracle, but underlying that was this realization that you can't really control your job." Even though young executives like Benioff felt as if you could "do what you want," as they moved up closer to Ellison and attracted his attention, that freedom became heavily dependent on how much the CEO liked them.

PERSONAL DISTRACTIONS

Like many companies in Silicon Valley, Oracle has a long history of employees having personal relationships with coworkers. Tom Siebel married a woman who worked for him; so did Ray Lane; so did Ellison (his third wife, Barbara Boothe, who is the mother of his two children). It's no surprise that in an organization that prizes fierce dedication and long hours, coworkers wind up dating one another. Then, too, the man at the top is well known for hitting on attractive female employees. "There was dating and flirtation all over the company," says Anneke Seley, an early employee who was with Oracle sales through the 1980s. She was acquainted with Boothe, whom Ellison married and later divorced. "She was a lot of fun, very athletic. Everyone knew she was dating Larry," says Seley. However, Seley herself never went out with Ellison. "I'm not at all Larry's type, nor is he mine. In those days, he wanted tall, blonde, athletic women," says Seley, who is petite and fresh-faced, with short-cropped brown hair. Former executive John Luongo remembers that one of his early management challenges was evaluating Boothe for a raise in 1982. "I was running corporate operations at the time and handling personnel," he says. "It came time for her annual review. I wondered, 'How do I evaluate the boss's live-in girlfriend?'" Luongo decided to disregard Boothe's relationship with Ellison. "I recommended the average raise," he says. "Larry was outraged because he didn't want her to get any raise. He wanted her to quit and stay home," which she did not long after.

The most publicized of Ellison's many dalliances with coworkers occurred in the early 1990s, with a marketing assistant named Adelyn Lee. She at first worked for marketing chief Kate Mitchell, who was planning to terminate her as part of a marketing group layoff. But Lee appealed to Ellison for more time, and sales executive Craig Ramsey wound up hiring her as an administrative assistant. As Lee and Ellison, who met during an elevator ride, started dating, they bantered a lot via E-mail exchanges. At one point, Lee wrote, "Would you really consider giving me a loan for $150,000?" Ellison suggested dinner instead. Lee pestered him for an Acura NSX, asking "How about this instead of a watch?" Ellison responded, "Are you sure you are tall enough to drive an NSX?" In another message, he said, "Of course, I will buy you an Acura NSX and anything else you want—a house in Woodside, a Gulfstream jet, a Hope diamond, even the General Electric Corporation which is quite expensive and even dinner on Friday."[1] It was a big mistake, as many subsequent law journals would point out, for Ellison to be so open about the relationship in E-mail messages, for these became public during two subsequent trials involving the pair. The E-mails also summarize the shallowness of a relationship based on Ellison's wealth and Lee's greed.

By all accounts, Lee was not particularly competent at her job. Lane would call Ramsey on the phone, and Lee would pick up. "I remember saying to him, why don't you get rid of her?" Lane says. "She's rude when she greets you, and she has terrible phone etiquette." Ramsey, of course, was in a very difficult position, but in April 1993, he did fire Lee. Then Ellison received an E-mail, ostensibly from Ramsey, saying that he had terminated Lee "per your request." Outraged, he wrote a respond brimming with profanity, then deleted the vulgarities and sent the message: "Are you out of your mind? I did not request that you terminate Adelyn. This is a most bizarre note."[2] Lee subsequently filed a wrongful-termination suit and won a $100,000 settlement from Oracle. However, it was overturned when Oracle was able to prove that Lee herself had sent Ellison the termination E-mail, which was the centerpiece of her case, under Ramsey's name. In 1997, she was convicted of perjury, sentenced to a year in jail, and ordered to repay the $100,000. The two court trials, though, revealed embarrassing details of Ellison's personal life, including the fact that he was dating other women while having a relationship with Lee. During the perjury trial, he insisted he was joking about buying Lee the car, the diamond, General Electric, and so forth. Her attorney suggested that Ellison led women on and "dangled money" in their faces, but that line of questioning was thrown out by the judge. Lee accused him of becoming rough on their last date and trying to force her to have sex. Ellison denied that but conceded they had "some form of sex." He also acknowledged that he knew Ramsey was about to fire Lee but did not tell her.[3]

All this was going on as Ellison was seeking to advance the cause of the network computer and position himself and Oracle upon a national stage. He was often compared to then president Bill Clinton, a personal friend of Ellison's once rumored to be ready to join Oracle's board of directors. Neither Ellison nor Clinton was a stranger to the abuse of power and sex. Says Ramsey, "There's no question that [the Lee case] was distracting. Anytime you're involved in a sexual harassment suit, it's distracting. What she did was wrong, but at the same time, because of the extenuating circumstances of the power issue, I felt real uncomfortable with the sentence she received." He believes that Ellison today would not get involved with someone like Lee. "He's grown up to the extent that he appreciates in this [public] environment, it's very difficult for him to become involved with young women who work there and not have huge exposure." Indeed, Ellison's current fiancée is a freelance writer and novelist, Melanie Craft, who does not work at Oracle. Still, Ramsey has mixed emotions about the sexual permissiveness at Oracle. "The people you meet are people that you work with," he says. "It's a very logical happening for people to date each other. And if you become a manager, it's very likely that the person could work for you." Therein lies the real issue: power. "Sexual harassment is about power and becomes difficult to control," he says. "In the early days, having affairs was a very accepted part of the culture, almost encouraged. I don't think that was healthy."

When Ray Lane joined Oracle and imposed new rules on its loose nature, he found himself in an uncomfortable position as he and his assistant, Stephanie Herle, became personally involved. He had left his estranged wife behind in Texas when he started at Oracle. "I was working long hours, and Stephanie was with me eighteen hours a day," he recalls. They went out to dinner and talked mostly about work. "She loved Oracle, and the last thing she wanted to do was get involved with a married man. I'm old enough to know you don't marry your assistant." Yet they found themselves attracted to each other. Not long after he joined Oracle, Lane attended a customer conference that Herle had helped to organize. Several people talked Lane into hosting an impromptu party at his suite in the San Francisco Marriott. "It was a collection of people I didn't know—employees, their friends, hotel staff," says Lane. Suddenly, Herle, who had driven all the way back to Oracle to get some files that Lane wanted, burst into the room and ordered everyone out. After she'd cleared the room, she told Lane, "Those girls who were sitting there are bimbos. Do you know what this makes you look like?" As she lectured him, Lane leaned over and embraced her. "I knew she was protecting me," he says. "When we hugged, it felt right."

Yet after that incident, they backed off for about a year, feeling as if the relationship would be too complicated. "She was my assistant, and I was still married although separated, heading for divorce," says Lane. More than Herle, he realized the conflicts that could ensue. How would people deal with her as an assistant if they realized she was dating the boss? Even though that seemed to be business as usual at Oracle, "people had come to see me as something totally different," says Lane. "Yes, a lot of people misbehaved at Oracle, but I was like Dad breaking his own rules. . . ." After finalizing his divorce from his first wife, he proposed to Herle. And then he fired her. "I told her, 'If you say yes, there's no job for you at Oracle.'" Herle, who is just as tough-minded as Lane, left unwillingly. "It was a decision made for me," she says. "We argued about it. I had spent a long time at Oracle. These were my friends, my life." Lane and Herle were married in November 1995 and now have two children. Lane bristles at any comparison between his conduct and Ellison's. "There's a big difference between sleeping with your assistant and marrying your assistant. I fell in love with her, and I saw it through," he concludes.

TRASHING BILL

For Larry Ellison, Bill Gates is the exasperating kid who's always just a little bit ahead: younger, richer, and more successful. For all of Ellison's tremendous accomplishments, Gates has bested most of them. He's number one on the *Forbes* 400 list of wealthiest people, while Ellison is number four. Microsoft is the largest independent software company in the world; Oracle is second. The $24 billion Bill & Melinda Gates Foundation is one of the world's largest charitable foundations; Ellison has committed a mere (by comparison) $20 million annually to aging research through the Ellison Medical Foundation. Gates grew up in comfortable upper-middle-class surroundings in the Seattle area and had a close relationship with his mother, who inspired his charitable giving. Ellison was born to an unwed mother whom he never knew as a child and sent away to be raised by distant relatives in a tough part of Chicago; his cold adoptive father regularly bashed his self-esteem. Gates's lone marriage is a lasting one; Ellison has been married and divorced three times. Even though Microsoft is a monopolist, it's Oracle that is considered the pariah company, accused of operating outside the norms of accepted business behavior. Microsoft's database is becoming a threat to Oracle, as is its Web services initiative. If Ellison were to have a private conversation with God, you can imagine him saying, "Dammit, why can't I catch a break for once?" On the other hand, Ellison has more discriminating aesthetic taste than Gates, as illustrated by his stunning collections of Japanese artifacts, and he's probably knowledgeable about a wider range of subjects. Oh, and there's the jock factor: Ellison is a body-conditioning fanatic who flies his own plane, sails maxi-yachts, and once challenged and beat a triathlete. The words *athlete* and *Gates* rarely appear together.

It would no doubt have been illuminating to be a fly on the wall in 1988, when Ellison and Gates met one-on-one at

Ellison's house in Atherton, California. Former Oracle marketing director Pete Tierney set up the secret meeting after "we got wind that [database competitor] Sybase was going to do a deal with Microsoft. I got Bill to agree to come and meet with Larry" en route to another meeting in Silicon Valley. An Oracle employee picked up Gates at the airport and was preparing to drive him to Oracle headquarters, but there was no Ellison to be found. Finally, his assistant was able to reach him at home. "Have Bill come to my house," Ellison told her. Tierney was sick with worry at this change in plans. "Larry's favorite trick was to say, 'Meet me at my house.' You'd drive up to the gate, push the buzzer, no answer. He would keep you waiting at the gate. Then it would open up. This was his way of showing his power. We knew this would be a disaster." Sure enough, recalls Tierney, "Larry keeps Bill waiting in the driveway for something like forty-five minutes before he lets them in." Gates and Ellison talked privately for a very brief period. Tierney says Ellison was prepared to undercut Sybase to do a deal with Microsoft for the Oracle database. "Bill came back out to the car in about two minutes and said, 'Let's go.' The speculation is that he told Larry he wouldn't do it." Tierney says Ellison has always refused to talk about what happened at that meeting. Obviously, this was one session in which Ellison didn't prevail, since Microsoft did license Sybase's technology.

Ten years later, there was a public confrontation between Gates and Ellison. Ray Lane remembers attending the prestigious World Economic Forum in Davos, Switzerland, in 1998. At a session involving the world's most powerful CEOs of software, hardware, and telecom companies, the late Michael Dertouzos, MIT's technology visionary and cochair of the forum, had structured a program in which each table was supposed to come up with a topic of discussion and a chairperson to present the thinking. Ellison's table happened to be next to Gates's, and naturally, both were chairmen. Ellison stood up and announced, "We talked about the death of the PC and the fact that one man, Bill, cannot own the Internet. One man, Bill, cannot own all the information." (This was the period when Ellison was trumpeting the network computer.)

Gates stood up and retorted, "We talked about the economics of the industry and why databases are too expensive. We need a low-cost database. We need a 90 percent price drop." Out of turn, Ellison jumped up again: "Why don't you make it fucking free and put us out of business like you did Netscape?" Says Lane, "Larry never got invited back [to the forum]."

Then there was the infamous garbage incident. In mid-1999, Oracle hired a Washington, D.C., detective firm, International Group International (IGI), to find out how Microsoft was trying to influence public opinion in its antitrust fight with the U.S. Justice Department. Several newspapers, including the *Wall Street Journal*, later revealed that IGI obtained information about Microsoft's funding of pro-Microsoft groups by rifling through its trash. In one publicized incident, IGI reportedly even offered cash to a cleaning crew in exchange for office trash from a company acting on Microsoft's behalf. Ellison acknowledged authorizing the budget for IGI but claimed to be unaware of how it was obtaining its information. (IGI's revelations that Microsoft had paid groups linked to criticism of the government's antitrust effort did prove embarrassing to that company.) "Some of the things our investigator did may have been unsavory," Ellison said. "Certainly from a personal hygiene point, they were. I mean, garbage . . . yuck!" But when asked what he would do if Microsoft were to go through Oracle's trash, Ellison joked, "We'll ship them our garbage. We'll send them all our garbage."[4] Lane says Ellison made the decision to hire IGI on his own. However, Lane adds, the executive committee did approve of Oracle's providing information to the Justice Department in the antitrust suit. For example, when Digital Equipment Corporation made a decision not to do a particular kind of chip that could have been used in set-top boxes and the NC, "we suggested it was because of a threat from Microsoft," says Lane. "Anything like that we had, we would help. We felt very strongly that Microsoft was using monopoly power and that it should be penalized or broken up, although we had some trepidation that many Microsofts might be worse than one."

Oracle's competition with Microsoft escalated in the mid-1990s, first with the interactive-TV effort and then with the network computer. "The NC was really focused against Microsoft," says Lane. Oracle's traditional competitors had faded, "and there was only one enemy. It was Microsoft doing interactive TV, video streaming, the Internet. Larry started spending a lot of time obsessing about Microsoft." The NC became his "bully pulpit." The result, recalls Benioff, who was involved in one of the anti-Microsoft initiatives at Oracle, was products devoted to bypassing Microsoft's stranglehold on the desktop. "Larry would come up with huge marketing initiatives around the NC. They called it NCA [for network computing architecture], but it should have been called the NMW strategy, for no more Windows," he says. Adds Ariko, "Larry didn't want to do anything that helped Microsoft, even if it helped Oracle, too." As his outburst in Davos demonstrated, Ellison was determined to move computing away from the PC-centric world dominated by Microsoft toward the free, flexible Internet browser popularized by Netscape, running on an NC. But for all of Ellison's efforts, he was never able to destabilize Microsoft nor loosen its hold on the desktop. Today, the titanic battle with Microsoft continues, infusing Oracle with competitive energy. Says Lane, "You have to have someone to hate, and Microsoft was the natural target."

Although Gates himself has remained above the fray, other executives at Microsoft profess that there's no love lost with Oracle. "You can't spell Larry Ellison without the letters *l*, *i*, *a*, and *r*," notes Microsoft group manager Barry Goffe. Referring to Ellison's campaign surrounding a national identity card, he quipped, "Would you trust a guy to manage national ID who was caught rummaging through our garbage?" Goffe proclaims, "When Bill gets up and does a keynote at an industry conference, he talks about the industry, trends, and technology. Larry bad-mouths IBM or Microsoft. Microsoft is motivated by changing the world. Oracle is motivated by knocking Bill Gates off the map." Canopus Research President Will Zachmann says Oracle has good reason to fear Microsoft, because it offers lower pricing and more flexible technology.

He suggests that Ellison has taken the battle to a personal level because he can't win on technology alone.

HAMMING IT UP

Ray Lane came in to change Oracle's arrogant approach and discipline its business practices, but like everyone who comes to Oracle, he was also changed. He imposed new processes that brought maturity to Oracle's operations and, for a time, a kinder, gentler face to the customer. But Lane was at the same time absorbed by the theatrics inside Oracle. Even though he was the resident "adult," there was something inside him that succumbed to the urge to get up in front of a crowd and act out a particular fantasy. In Lane's case, it was presentations based on the dramatic, epic movies he loves, like *Braveheart*, *Apollo 13*, the Indiana Jones series, and *2001: A Space Odyssey*. This all surfaced when Lane initiated global management meetings in 1995 and decided that he needed a theme to rally the troops. "The company was getting so big, I wanted to have the management team all in one room to reprogram for the next year," he says. Some five hundred sales managers from around the world usually attended the cheerleading sessions.

In the first year, Lane was captivated by *Braveheart*, which he had just watched in his hotel room. He got up onstage and tore into Microsoft. The reasoning went like this: *Bill Gates is taking money out of your pocket, and that money is to buy food for your children, so Bill Gates wants your children to starve. The way to beat Bill Gates is to band together and give up everything for the cause.* "We were the Scots," says Lane, "and Microsoft was the evil king of England." Mike Hagan, a manager who attended the meeting, remembers the huge slides that Lane used in the presentation, with letters around thirty feet tall. One slide featured a single word, *COMMIT-MENT*. Recalls Hagan, "Ray drew an analogy around Braveheart, who gave his life for what he believed in. Ray said, 'If you think this isn't important to you, you're sadly mistaken. If we can't sell software, you're not going to have a job. Then you can't feed your family.'" Recalls Hagan, "It was a great rallying cry. You were either with us or against us."

Another event that stood out in a number of managers' recollections was the video that served as the sales kickoff for fiscal 1998. A clip from *2001: A Space Odyssey* showed the scene in which one ape discovers how to use a bone as a weapon for the first time. The video then cut to Lane, sitting at his desk with a bone in his hands, which he used to smash a plastic PC. "We're less than a thousand days from the beginning of a new millennium," Lane said. "The opening film clip you've just seen seems ageless but serves as a reminder to us as we face the new millennium that societies have always developed based on the use of new tools, and of course, the owners of these new tools established themselves as leaders in the new society." Lane went on to drum up support for Oracle's initiative that year around network computing and the Internet. "I would say that going into the next millennium, we've got the bones," he said. Today, Lane is a trifle sheepish as he remembers these presentations. You certainly can't imagine him doing anything like them at the straitlaced venture capital firm for which he now works. "I did it because it was Oracle," he says. "I wanted a high-impact ending so they would go away remembering the message."

That effort extends beyond Lane. Contractor Rod Mickels has orchestrated a number of big-budget Oracle events, like keynote sessions at its OpenWorld trade conferences, with themes ranging from *Blair Witch* to the *Rocky Horror Picture Show*. Ellison is usually the star, coming onstage to do the demo for whatever product Oracle wants to show off that year. In one demonstration, at Radio City Music Hall in New York, Ellison walked onto the stage amid blue light and smoke, wearing a black shirt and suit. As he put his hand on the table, the computer slid off and exploded. Ellison calmly walked to another table to demonstrate that Oracle's database isn't dependent on one computer but only on the network. "It was all planned," says Mickels. "We had a breakaway table and a computer rigged to explode." Sometimes other executives will do the honors, especially if the show goes on the road. For example, Mickels recalls, in 1999, Oracle did a product tour promoting its new E-business suite. At the hotel conference room in Washington, D.C., fake smoke burst out of the wall and everyone was told to please leave the room. When they returned, the presenter, Oracle sales manager Todd Beamer, had a new slide up: "Agenda, post fire," talking about how the E-business suite was a total departure from the past.

Sadly, Beamer was killed two years later on United flight 93, which crashed in western Pennsylvania on September 11, 2001, evidently forced down by passengers like him. His last words, in a telephone conversation with a GTE operator, were, "Are you ready? Let's roll." He personifies the best of Oracle's culture. Enlisted in a worthy cause, the mantra—*Do what it takes to get the job done, no matter what the cost*—can elicit courageous and meaningful action. Unfortunately, as the unfolding scandal depicted in the next section reveals, Oracle far too often succumbs to simple greed in making the numbers, as it did in the infamous "go for the gold" era of the late 1980s and, in the absence of Lane and other leaders who imposed a higher standard of maturity, seems to be doing again.

CALIFORNIA NIGHTMARE

In 2002, Oracle got caught in what for a corporation could only be called the "perfect storm." First, in difficult economic conditions, sales slumped in both its major lines of business, and so did Oracle's stock price. Second, high-ranking executives continued to defect. Finally, pressure to make a sale landed Oracle in the middle of a high-profile public scandal involving a $95 million contract with the state of California. In a no-bid contract signed on May 31, 2001, just in time for the end of Oracle's fiscal year, the state agreed to buy licenses for 270,000 end users, 40,000 more people than it actually employed. And thousands of state employees have no reason to use the Oracle database or software. An Oracle partner, Logicon, negotiated the deal with state officials, even as it advised those same officials on why the deal would be beneficial for California. The scandal reached all the way into the governor's office when it was revealed that a key technology aide to Democratic governor Gray Davis had accepted a twenty-five thousand–dollar check from an Oracle lobbyist, which was sent to Davis's reelection campaign. Most of this detail poured forth in front-page newspaper articles in early to mid-2002, as the California auditor and a legislative committee launched investigations. The auditor's office concluded that the deal could leave the state with $41 million in unneeded software, and Davis moved to cancel the contract. State Assemblyman Dean Florez, a Democrat who headed the legislative investigation, charged, "Every agency head involved in this fiasco abdicated their duties, to the detriment of taxpayers and to the benefit of the corporate interests." He added that the contract probably would never have been signed had Oracle not begun "pulling strings" and wielding political influence.[5]

While the state was certainly a chump in the way it handled the deal, the scandal once again highlighted how Oracle's do-whatever-it-takes mentality is damaging the company. "Their whole business model is predicated on closing deals at the end of the quarter," says Laurie Orlov, research director for business applications at Forrester Research. While other companies also seek to bring in revenue as a quarter closes, few are as aggressive as Oracle. As the end of the quarter or fiscal year approaches, Oracle boosts its discount, sometimes dramatically, and wears down the buyer. The state of California, without any scrutiny, ended up signing a ridiculous contract, notes Orlov. "It's 50 percent complicity by the buyer, 50 percent by Oracle." Indeed, E-mails released by the state in its investigation showed that Oracle salespeople and Logicon representatives sought to withhold certain details about how the state's projected savings on the deal were calculated. "Too much information can only be a bad thing," read one E-mail from Logicon to an Oracle salesperson.[6] The Oracle salespeople also hoped to block competition by establishing its database as the state of California's standard, eliminating IBM and Microsoft as options.[7] As all this came to light, officials at other government entities, including the city of Toronto and the states of Ohio and Georgia, also rescinded or renegotiated deals with Oracle. "The pressure was on in the California deal because Oracle wasn't making its numbers on government sales," says Lane. "Oracle was being too creative with the [California] contract, but you have to have a customer to buy into it. If the government wants to buy without going out to bid, I would sell to them all day long." He says Oracle shareholders should be concerned that the company gave up too much to close the California contract without soliciting competitive bids. "I'm sure they gave a 90 percent discount to avoid bidding." However, that point is moot because the state has since canceled the contract.

Oracle's gamesmanship has caught up with it. A decade ago, the winning strategy for software companies from Microsoft to Oracle to AOL was to get market share no matter what, even if that meant temporarily sacrificing the bottom line. *Market share* was the rallying cry of the 1980s and 1990s, not profitability, not strict adherence to accounting principles, not restraint. But in the new millennium, the rules have changed. Oracle is no longer a feisty start-up fighting to reach the top of the heap in the evolving database market. It's the dominant player, and what was once merely aggressive now looks like bullying, or worse. Oracle's culture remains stuck in the twentieth century. Neither Ellison nor the sales force appears capable of adapting to the reality of slower growth and partnership with the customer. And its competitors are taking merciless advantage of Oracle's weakness, just as Oracle would do with them.

OPPORTUNITY LOST

Despite everything that Oracle has achieved, nearly all its executives express a sense of frustration over missed opportunities. Oracle's culture does some things really well: it allows talented people to carve out their own space and develop entrepreneurial abilities that enable them to go off and lead other companies. In its worship of technology, it attracts skilled, highly energized engineers and salespeople who are caught up in the vision of creating and selling innovative products. Ellison's gurulike presence galvanizes employees into devoting their lives to the company, giving their all to make Oracle great. And yet Oracle executives must devote so much time to political infighting, to what it takes for them to succeed, that they're often not very focused on the best strategy for the company. As Beatriz Infante remarks, "Oracle wastes tremendous intellectual capital competing with itself. If it spent a fraction of that energy on its competition, it would be twice the size." The conflicts among departments and executives that Ellison deliberately sets up are, in the end, counterproductive, for they suck up energy that could be used in defeating Microsoft or SAP or IBM. Says former executive vice president Gary Bloom, now CEO of Veritas, "Oracle was always a culture of missed opportunities. If we'd executed better, we might have been substantially more successful."

Oracle should have become the market leader in both enterprise applications and application servers, vaulting Ellison closer to his cherished goal of running the most important software company in the world. Taking the combined revenues (about $7.5 billion) of the leaders in those two segments, SAP and BEA Systems, and giving a good portion to Oracle would put it a lot closer to being the world's largest, most valuable software company. Barring some very unlikely drastic action by the government against Microsoft, it seems improbable now that Oracle will ever displace it. Rather, Oracle is going to have to fight hard just to maintain its positions as the leading database vendor, the number-two software company, and a major player in enterprise applications. And it all falls upon Larry Ellison to helm Oracle's course in an increasingly choppy sea. For he has thrown overboard most of the other people who might have helped him.

13

ON THE EDGE

[ORACLE PEERS OVER THE PRECIPICE]

At the close of 2001, Jay Nussbaum, the executive vice president of Oracle who oversaw sales, marketing, and consulting in the services industries, left to join the consulting firm KPMG Peat Marwick. "Jay built and leaves us with a deep management team that is well prepared for additional responsibilities," Larry Ellison felt compelled to write in an E-mail to employees announcing the departure.[1] In fact, Oracle's management team is woefully depleted. With the exception of Jeff Henley, virtually all members of the senior team who participated in Oracle's turnaround and tremendous growth during the 1990s have left the company. They include Gary Bloom, Ray Lane, George Kadifa, Polly Sumner, Randy Baker, Pier Carlo Falotti, Robert Shaw, Jeremy Burton, George Roberts, and many, many more. Sandy Sanderson, who had been filling the void that Lane left as Oracle's customer-facing executive, took a medical leave in August 2001 and wasn't expected to return. Henley himself is questionable. Rumors have swirled on occasion that the chief financial officer was leaving, causing Oracle's share price to plunge. Although Henley steadfastly denies any intention to resign, he has sold his house in Silicon Valley and lives in Santa Barbara, commuting up to Oracle every week.

This leaves Ellison with the tricky task of running Oracle without a net of strong executives beneath him. "Oracle has moved from a team of B players led by A players to a team of C players led by B players," Sumner says. Ellison now depends heavily on Executive Vice President Safra Catz, a onetime investment banker who acts as his chief of staff and is about as much of an enigma as her boss. She has shunned the limelight, even though Lane and others describe her as Ellison's "hatchet man" in carrying out what he wants done. But she has no experience running a company on her own and no public persona, hardly qualifications to be CEO. No one else inside Oracle leaps to mind, either. Ellison adamantly refuses to name a second-in-command, saying he's going to wait until it's apparent that he needs one. So Oracle's stakeholders—customers, partners, shareholders, and employees—are at the mercy of a nearing-sixty CEO who indulges in high-risk behavior and whose interest in his company is fitful. In late 2002, Ellison spent weeks at a time anchored off the coast of New Zealand, while the eighty-foot yacht that he paid for, *Oracle*, participated in the America's Cup trials. Early on in the trials, Ellison was a crew member, but the captain, Chris Dickson, yanked him for a more veteran sailor. Ironically, Ellison had elevated Dickson to captain to replace someone else. The Oracle head capitulated meekly to being thrown off the boat, conceding that the captain must prevail.

Even if Ellison's energy level and commitment to being CEO remain high, no lone executive, no matter how capable, can single-handedly run an operation as complicated as Oracle and also focus on how to reposition the company for the future. While competitors like IBM and Microsoft smoothly transitioned their leadership from, respectively, Lou Gerstner and Bill Gates to Sam Palmisano and Steve Ballmer, and built up teams around them, Ellison coyly toyed with executives like Lane and Bloom. Although some observers still see Bloom, the CEO of high-flying Veritas, which makes software to store and protect data, as a possible outside successor to Ellison, Bloom proclaims that he's going to build Veritas into another Oracle and doesn't need to come back. "Before

Larry's ready to step down, I have an equally good chance of making Veritas a similar-size company," says Bloom. "I want Veritas to have all the prestige and respect Oracle gets."

In late 2002, Oracle wasn't getting a lot of respect. For more than a year, sales and earnings had failed to meet expectations. It was only after Henley guided the Wall Street estimates down a couple of times that the company managed a quarter that wasn't worse than expected. In its fourth quarter of fiscal 2002, ended May 31, Oracle reported a 16 percent decline in sales and a 23 percent decline in net income. But those otherwise dismal results were slightly better than what had been forecast. Finally, in the first half of fiscal 2003, Oracle managed to grow new database sales—by 4 percent— but application revenue continued to decline, as did overall revenue. Between 2001 and 2003, Oracle's revenues shrank by more than $1 billion, from $10.9 billion in the fiscal year ending May 31, 2001, to $9.5 billion in the year ending May 31, 2003. Even by 2004, revenues were still projected to be below the high-water market of $10.9 billion in 2001. While Ellison and Henley continued to blame the poor economy and the collapse in corporate spending after September 11, 2001, that reasoning was wearing thin. It was becoming obvious that most of Oracle's problems were internal, related to its loss of management at the top, its alienation of everyone from customers to partners, its conflict-ridden culture that sucks energy into the black hole of corporate politics and last but not least, the flawed personality of the Oracle himself, Larry Ellison.

SETTING SUN?

If there's any company whose destiny parallels Oracle's, it's Sun Microsystems, a fellow Silicon Valley pioneer founded in roughly the same time frame and led by another iconoclast, Scott McNealy. Sun is the market leader in Unix workstations and servers, by far the most common hardware underneath Oracle's database and applications. While Sun has mulled buying a database company, it never did so because of its close relationship with Oracle. Not only do the two companies often negotiate deals together, but they've been staunch allies in the anti-Microsoft coalition. Ellison and McNealy are regular keynote speakers at each other's trade shows. Ellison's idea of the network computer paired neatly with Sun's development of the Java programming language as an alternative to Windows. Even when the NC failed to take off as expected, Java and its related technologies became the foundation for the browser-based Internet architecture that Ellison embraced and continues to champion. Oracle's 11i application suite is a major utilizer of Java technologies, while Microsoft's .NET is an effort to replace Java as the center of the emerging Web services market. Both Sun and Oracle aided the Department of Justice in its antitrust action against Microsoft, which was settled in late 2001 in a fashion disappointing to critics who wanted the company broken up.

Sun and Oracle are both product companies stressing technology rather than solutions companies (à la IBM) stressing customer needs and wants. This leads to a mind-set in which technology leadership becomes all-important, especially as the rest of the world migrates to more ubiquitous platforms such as Microsoft's Windows NT and .NET. Sun and Oracle had better be the best at the technology they offer, because that is their primary edge, along with switching costs that customers face in moving to other platforms. "We've been working together since the earliest days of Sun [founded in 1982]," says Michael Bohlig, senior director for the Oracle Business Unit at Sun. "We share a lot of common DNA between the two companies: the spirit of innovation, new technology that we bring to market, the commitment to investing in our own intellectual property. We drive change through our technology rather than replicate other people's intellectual property." The last is a reference to the fact that much of the rest of the world has migrated to Microsoft operating systems on Intel microprocessors. Sun has its own chip, its own hardware, and its own operating system. Oracle, although it has a database for Windows NT, runs largely on Sun. About two-thirds of its database sales are on Unix servers, which Sun dominates, while 70 percent of Sun servers are shipped with the Oracle database.

Recently, however, cracks have appeared in the partnership. Oracle's new "cluster" strategy, which allows its database functionality to be divided among a lot of computers, undercuts Sun. Rather than an expensive, high-end Unix server like Sun's offerings, the Oracle database can utilize much cheaper Compaq or Dell servers. Oracle announced a brand-new alliance with Dell at its OpenWorld conference in late 2001. This also involves having the Oracle database running atop the low-cost Linux operating system on an Intel microprocessor rather than atop Sun's proprietary Solaris operating system on its own chip. Meanwhile, Sun forged an alliance with Oracle rival Siebel Systems to comarket and sell the Siebel software on Sun hardware. Sun also is using Siebel internally for at least part of its customer relationship management (CRM) needs. Finally, Sun and Oracle are competing directly against each other in the application server market, although both are bit players behind IBM and BEA Systems.

Oracle is actually in a better position to distance itself from Sun than vice versa. "Sun needs Oracle far more than Oracle needs Sun," says a former Sun executive, who notes that Sun's hardware market is rapidly becoming commoditized by competitors such as Dell. "Oracle has a defensible position in database, but it must deliver on the broadest platform, which means Intel rather than Sun." To that end, Oracle has intimated that it will at least connect to the .NET world, although it is at the same time ostensibly committed to the Sun ONE alliance, which trumpets Java as the centerpiece of Web services. Ellison obviously is trying to keep a foot in both camps without alienating McNealy. The bond between the two has been strong, as McNealy was one of the few executives to back Ellison's call for a national ID card. For an example on the business front, in mid-2000, IBM was enticing other members of the Java alliance to pull out in favor of WebSphere, Big Blue's new product for Web services. McNealy got in touch with Ellison, who was on his boat in Aruba, and told him that he'd heard Oracle was considering joining the WebSphere group. "Larry called back in five minutes and said, 'It's taken care of,'" recounts a former Sun executive familiar with the interchange. Oracle did not join the WebSphere alliance. Adds Bohlig, "If we're trying to compete against IBM and Microsoft, we're better off doing it together."

Juan Jones, vice president of the system platforms group for Oracle, which manages the Sun relationship, says that Sun/Oracle "has moved to a new level of maturity." Translation: both companies are in trouble and both are striking out to broaden their markets, even if it means revamping the existing partnership. "The fact that Sun has iPlanet [its application server] is not the one we're worried about. .NET is clearly the enemy," Jones maintains. Interestingly, Microsoft's Barry Goffe agrees. "Having people who want to crush us is a motivating factor for us to do a better job," he says. "Sun and Oracle are rocked back on their heels right now. No one is under the illusion that this [Web services] is a playing field where one vendor is going to completely dominate. There will be multiple platforms. We are in a new market and a new era, and we want to get our fair share." So do Sun and Oracle, which means that, increasingly, they may find themselves at odds. Oracle has enough problems without trying to shore up Sun. To put it coldly, Ellison has to worry about his own house first in the hurricane. "Oracle is incredibly important to Sun, which is dependent on every move it makes," says Lane. However, "Scott [McNealy] can't control Larry. Larry feels vulnerable to Sun, so he's opened up new fronts to other vendors, which scares Sun. But Larry's right to do that."

SUPREME DICTATOR

As Lane's power receded at Oracle, other people became more prominent, first Gary Bloom and then Safra Catz. One of Lane's direct reports, Barry Ariko, remembers Ellison's paring responsibilities from Lane. "Applications was where the friction started. Then it got into things like managing expenses,"

Ariko recalls. Ellison would ask Lane to cut marketing or support expenses in half, and Lane would question what the impact would be on the business or the customer. Then Ellison would criticize Lane for not trying to cut costs enough and use that as a wedge to reduce his authority. Gary Bloom picked up many of the responsibilities that Ellison was taking away from Lane. Bloom says he and Lane were allies until the last eighteen months or so of Lane's tenure, when Ellison set them up against each other. "Larry moved pieces of Ray's organization to me," recalls Bloom, including marketing, education, and support. As that happened, "there was a collision between Ray and me. We didn't agree on how these should be approached." Then Bloom grew disillusioned about his prospects to become the top dog at Oracle while Ellison was still there, and he left, too. Says Ariko, "Larry views everybody as disposable." Ellison often tells his executive staff, "Oracle's like the navy. Admirals come and go, but Oracle goes on." Except, of course, for Ellison, who remains indispensable.

Dave Roux, formerly head of corporate development at Oracle, says the disagreements between Ellison and Lane "almost always came down to a discussion of prioritizing 'now' versus 'the future.' Ray lived in the present: making the quarter, keeping the customers happy. Larry's job was worrying about the future. If what he was doing two years out caused a problem, who cared?" That was an unusual division of power. In most companies, one executive—typically, the CEO—becomes the outside, public face for the company, while another senior-level executive is the operational, inside manager. For example, at Sun, McNealy was Mr. Outside to Ed Zander's Mr. Inside. "Mr. Outside is very quotable, while Mr. Inside makes the trains run on time," Roux observes. "With Larry and Ray, you had two guys who were very comfortable being Mr. Outside." In effect, each could be Mr. Outside and Mr. Inside, with Lane presiding over sales and operations and Ellison over development and both being quoted frequently in the press. But that split was bound to cause problems because of overlapping goals. "You'd always have the future at odds with the present, because it was a different guy making the trade-offs," Roux says.

Catz, an investment banker who once dated Ellison, came into the company in mid-1999 and swiftly became a power broker. "The division between Larry and Ray widened when Safra showed up," says Dennis Bonilla, recruited in early 1999 to run Oracle's educational unit under Bloom. "Larry was depending more and more on her for advice and strategy. She became his right-hand person much more than Ray." And Bloom wasn't happy, either. "As Gary saw Safra get more and more responsibility, that's when he got out," Bonilla says. "She's always in the background. No matter where Larry is, Safra's there." Adds Lane, "I don't think the chef in the cafeteria could plan a menu without Safra's OK." Bloom notes that when management coaches would come in to pitch for Oracle's business, "I would explain the working relationship with Safra, and they'd say they'd never seen that before. It's clearly one of the odder management structures."

Catz was initially chief of staff, whom Ellison would dispatch to look into situations inside the company and report back to him. "Over time, that manifested itself into being a funnel of communications into Larry. Virtually all communication from all executives to Larry went to Safra," Bloom says. "Larry would let Safra know what he wants, and she'd go back to the executives." He found that grating because top executives need the CEO to interpret his own decisions directly, but the insulation by Catz doesn't allow it. She doesn't question Ellison but reflects what he wants. "When your right-hand person reinforces many of your extreme thoughts as being good ideas, it's difficult to challenge those thoughts," says Bloom. Lane compares Catz to Rasputin, the sinister power broker in early-twentieth-century Russia. "She's in Larry's mind," he says. "There are two things he can't resist: a woman and a high IQ."

Catz's emergence is yet another example of Ellison's power to fall in love with someone (in a nonsexual way) and elevate that person beyond his or her depth. Bloom concedes that Catz is smart and politically savvy but has no experience managing an organization. "The reason she moved into such a powerful position so quickly is because she's so close to Larry," he says. "But ultimately, she's a staff person who doesn't have people reporting to her." Catz is useful in getting Ellison to focus on what needs to be done, he allows, but her rapid ascension and her seemingly absolute power over Ellison stir resentment among the rest of Oracle's executives. "Larry has labeled her as heir apparent. It's lost on me how somebody can be heir apparent who doesn't manage anything except Larry," Bloom says. Catz herself, in rare public interviews, has denied any interest in such a role, perhaps recognizing that expressing that ambition would alienate her champion Ellison.

Ellison is now alone at the top with no one to challenge him or replace him. Only Jeff Henley, a respected presence inside and outside the company, has the stature to take on that role. "Our departure [of Lane and Bloom] allows Jeff to be the senior statesman and communicate to the marketplace," says Bloom. "It's really his time to shine." But Henley is the same age as Ellison and thus too old to be considered a probable successor. And his career has been spent on the financial side, so he has little experience in sales, engineering, or product strategy. Besides, Henley has definitely signaled his intention to step away from Oracle as soon as the waters have calmed and has shown no interest in rocking the boat in the meantime. Bloom believes that Oracle's midlevel management, at the vice president and senior director levels, remains strong, "but clearly, at the higher levels, there has been a continual bleeding of leadership. So Larry is now dealing with that lower level more directly." That means Ellison is stretched too thin, even for him. "There should be a set of two to three individuals in a company of Oracle's size who stand out as thought leaders," says Bloom, whom Ellison can bounce crazy ideas off and have them refined by sharp questioning. "The problem is that when you look through the window, you can't see who those two or three are. It's not clear they even exist," Bloom says.

This is troubling for shareholders, customers, employees,

and anyone else whose future is tied to Oracle. "Clearly, Oracle has lost some great players," says applications customer Lisa Harris. Going forward, "my biggest concern is senior management stability. What you don't want to see is more executives leaving." Long-term, she adds, "I don't believe Larry can possibly stay on this job. At some point, he's going to say, 'I want to go play on my boat.' " Besides sailing, biotech investing is another avid interest that could pull Ellison away from Oracle. He once spent a vacation doing research into molecular biology at Rockefeller University and has been pouring millions of dollars into antiaging research. Ellison told the Oracle AppsWorld 2001 conference that if he had to do it over again, he'd probably go into genetic engineering rather than computing. After three generations of computing—mainframes, client-server, and Internet—"there will be no new architecture for computing for the next 1,000 years," he says. "The computing industry is about to become boring."[2] Scarcely encouraging words from a CEO whose company right now is extraordinarily vulnerable to his whims.

WHITHER ORACLE?

Two primary scenarios could play out at Oracle, each with differing ramifications. The first is if Ellison, for whatever reason, were to leave unexpectedly in the near term. The second is if he stays for the longer term. It's unlikely that Ellison would ever be forced out of Oracle, since he owns one-fourth of the stock and has a relatively weak board of directors. But given his propensity for fast jets, fast cars, and sleek yachts, some kind of accident is possible. Once, Ellison almost died in a surfing accident off Hawaii. Or he could decide that Oracle has become boring and simply leave to start a biotech company. It is just those kinds of scenarios that cause the CEOs of most major companies to do succession planning. Not Ellison. One wonders if he can even conceive of Oracle's existence without him. Other people wonder, too. "If Larry was incapacitated, the cult would dissolve," says former executive

Marc Benioff. "It's unclear if Oracle is a sustainable enterprise without Larry because his personality is so firmly entrenched." If Ellison went with no warning, definitely chaos would ensue at Oracle. "They aren't prepared at all if he walks out suddenly," says Lane. "It's better for him to stay in the short term because there's somebody with a vision." Former board member Arnold Silverman agrees. "Without Larry, Oracle would go through a difficult period. There would be a lot of arm waving and flapping around. Maybe somebody would come in, grab the reins, and stabilize it." Maybe, but who that would be is a mystery. Lane says he'd go back if Ellison were out of the way, because Oracle would need a proven leader. "It would have to be somebody with a very, very different style than Larry. I'd do it because Oracle is an incredible asset that's being destroyed," he says. But other insiders tell me that Lane may have burned his bridges at Oracle by speaking out publicly against Ellison and by addressing the trade conference of competitor SAP, so returning as CEO is problematic. Of course, the many ex–Oracle executives who head other companies, like Bloom (Veritas), Craig Conway (PeopleSoft), Greg Brady (i2 Technologies), Marc Benioff (Salesforce.com), and so forth, would be candidates, but whoever did it would face monumental challenges. He or she would simultaneously have to fix a troubled company, overhaul a counterproductive culture that has been a quarter century in the making, and fill the shoes of one of the most high-profile corporate leaders in the world.

In Ellison's absence, the other possibility would be a merger. A number of observers suggested that a Sun/Oracle combination could make a lot of sense, giving the new company ownership of everything from the server to the database to applications. Since significant competition exists at all those levels, it's doubtful that antitrust concerns would derail such a combine. Sun's McNealy is a charismatic CEO with a demonstrated ability to lead an unconventional company with a maverick approach. Sun and Oracle have the same enemies and the same essential strategy: focusing on products instead of solutions. Says Lane, "Sun could be Larry's exit path."

Together they can fight the other two integrated competitors: IBM and Microsoft." Naturally, neither Sun nor Oracle would officially comment on this. Laughs Sun's Bohlig, "I'm sure some analyst every year is saying that's a possibility. We don't see it."

If Ellison continues to lead Oracle, as seems most likely, the outlook for Oracle is murky. "If he stays, Oracle doesn't change," says Lane. "He's a very capable leader in terms of putting together a product strategy, expressing vision to the marketplace, and telling people what to do. But there's also a lot that's missing, like management style. There's no team underneath him. It's basically a dictatorship, and everybody works in the hope that they'll get rich." If Oracle continues to falter, the board might exert more pressure on Ellison to bring in strong managers beneath him, as he did in the early 1990s with Lane and Henley. "What people are looking for today from senior leadership is not simply vision," says Gartner Group analyst Betsy Burton. "Oracle is out of balance. The yin has left, and only the yang remains." But given Ellison's track record of running through executives, it might not be as easy for him this time to attract the best people. Even if Ellison were to step down as CEO and remain chairman of the board, as some scenarios have suggested, "I don't think top-notch people will go to Oracle," says ex–board member Silverman. "Who would want to be CEO with Larry still involved? Anybody qualified to do it won't do it."

With no new initiatives on the horizon, Oracle faces tough battles in expanding its core database market, which accounts for nearly all its profits, and in making applications a viable line of business by winning back wary customers. The database business is especially critical, since its hefty profit margins enable Oracle to support applications and application servers. "If I were sitting in Larry Ellison's chair, the first thing I would focus in on is, How do I regain my control of the database market?" Burton says. However, that may mean sacrificing price for volume. Worrisome for Oracle is the movement toward cheaper databases, a trend augmented by its own clustering technology. In 2002, Oracle's low-end product, called Standard Edition, accounted for half of its database license revenue, up from about 15 percent just two years previously. "The SE product was designed to compete with Microsoft on price, which it does well, but Oracle never anticipated it would grow to half of its database revenue," says analyst Charles Phillips, of Morgan Stanley (who later joined Oracle). The hope for Oracle is that customers will upgrade to the high-end product, Enterprise Edition, but Phillips says that migration path is not guaranteed. "The SE product is sufficient for even large customers" in many instances, he says. Although Oracle doesn't appear to be losing existing customers to IBM and Microsoft, those two "are certainly winning their share of new business," Phillips adds. "Oracle still has the leading product that can span from very small to very large applications with the market's most reliable database." But count on more pricing pressure, both from competitors and from reluctant customers that have become more price-sensitive in a slower economy. Phillips forecasts that, at least in the near term, Oracle's growth will be flat and profit margins will depend on controlling expenses.

On applications, Oracle has been losing market share to PeopleSoft and SAP, due to the quality issues that surfaced with the early release of 11i. Phillips believes that Oracle has fixed the technical problems but has a long way to go to repair the damage to its reputation from having mistreated customers. Jennifer Chew, analyst for E-business applications at Forrester Research, says that any of the three leading ERP vendors can meet functionality and business process requirements and they are fairly equal on service. That means the decision comes down to intangibles, like with whom would you rather work, and there Oracle has hurt itself. "Attila the Hun looks kind compared to Larry," she says. "Oracle needs to abandon the 'all-Oracle, all the time' message." It can still fashion a winning strategy on applications since it's able to bundle so much more than SAP or PeopleSoft, she says. "Because Oracle has so many other products, like database, toolset, and services, they can afford to discount very heavily on applications and still know that over the life cycle, they'll get plenty of money out of the customer."

Where does Oracle position itself in the emerging Web services world? So far, it hasn't spelled out much of a strategy. "Can Larry take it to the next step?" asks former board member Joe Costello. "I understand what the next step is at Microsoft, but there is no articulated vision at Oracle." Recently, Ellison has talked about moving into hosted applications. Instead of buying a suite of software that they have to install, customers would pay Oracle monthly fees to provide and maintain what they need from its own data centers. "Guaranteed, you will never have to pay for another upgrade. You will never pay for another piece of software. You will never pay for another piece of hardware," Ellison says, predicting that this could be a $1 billion business for Oracle in a few years.[3] Cliff Godwin, senior vice president of applications technology, says Oracle has more than two hundred customers using its Oracle.com hosted solution. "We believe in hosting as a strategy and in software as a service," Godwin says. "We will be putting out a lot of new hosted offerings. We want to build an economy around that and have other partners come in with value-added services, such as those with expertise in retail or banking."

So far, however, the hosted business has proved only a drop in the bucket for Oracle, and smaller, nimbler competitors like Benioff's Salesforce.com are already there. "It's a pipe dream," says Lane. "It's not in Oracle's DNA to work that way, delivering a service month after month. Software development is very different than operating the applications for a customer." He recalls a conversation he had with Ellison in 1999, when the on-line business was getting started. Lane told Ellison he needed to put a strong operational person in charge to make sure customer problems got solved. Ellison retorted, "We'll put an NC on-site with a customer," running the same applications. "If a customer calls in, we'll tell him to walk over to the NC. If the application's working there, go call your network provider. It's a network problem." It's doubtful that many companies would want to entrust their ongoing software needs to a company whose CEO has attitudes like this.

"Oracle has had its best days," maintains Canopus Research President Will Zachmann. "There's no way they can grow like they did in the 1990s. More likely, they will go into a decline." He's not as concerned as other observers about the succession problem. "Larry doesn't seem to be going anywhere, so I don't think the cult of personality is the big issue. It's how they respond to challenges from Microsoft and IBM. If they lose their core [database] business, the rest of it will crumble." Zachmann adds that Ellison's aggressive, expansionist management style "works as long as you're winning. It remains to be seen how well it works in a defensive mode where they're not leading a market. There are no more quick victories."

THE ORACLE'S END

Can Ellison come up with another breakthrough concept such as developing the network computer or moving applications to the Internet? Perhaps, but given his grouching about how boring computing has become and the lack of any new architecture, it doesn't seem as if he has anything yet. To be sure, the hostile takeover bid for PeopleSoft showed that he's not to be counted out, but that move was hardly visionary or indicative of a technology breakthrough. Rather, it was a defensive move, a brilliant one but still defensive, intended to shore up Oracle's position in an existing market rather than inaugurate something new. So, assuming that the playing field is unlikely to change dramatically in the near future, the focus has to be on Ellison and his leadership. His tragic flaw is his inability to connect with people or regard them as anything other than disposable commodities. With the complexity of the technology world and the unavoidable requirement to forge interrelationships with partners, customers, even competitors, does Ellison's shortcoming now become a fatal flaw?

Lane's answer is emphatically yes. "Larry's destroying the

company," he maintains, comparing Ellison to the former CEO of Digital Equipment Corporation, Ken Olsen. Although he was a formidable technologist and entrepreneur, Olsen couldn't embrace changes in either management or technology that would have kept DEC competitive. It was eventually absorbed by Compaq, itself now part of Hewlett-Packard. "Larry is like Ken Olsen, in that Olsen didn't listen to what was going on around him. Larry dismisses a lot of things the same way," says Lane. The only way out is for the board to compel Ellison to name a successor from the outside and convince Ellison to become chairman. "The last time Larry was alone, in 1990, he blew it," says Lane. "He's blowing it again."

Former journalist and longtime Oracle observer Alex Vieux agrees with Lane that Ellison's and Oracle's destiny may end unhappily. For one thing, Oracle is a cannibal company that has devoured many of its best soldiers. "If I had a question for Larry, it would be 'Where is your heart?'" Vieux says. "Larry stands out for his achievements, his talents, his brilliance, his ability to pull people together, and his ability to rip them apart." Ellison compels people to cross a "profound chasm" for him, and then he pushes them into it. "When you live a life of tragedy, you finish tragically," Vieux says. "The story of Oracle and Larry is a very uneven, unstable relationship. For six months, he's involved, then he's on his boat or he has a girlfriend. It would be inconsistent that such an epic relationship ends up smoothly. You have to say that one day something terrible will happen. Larry is the tragic king of the computer industry."

Don't make the mistake of counting Ellison out too soon. As even Vieux acknowledges, "He manages the unexpected. He came out of that hole in 1990 when they thought he couldn't." But today, coming out of the hole into which Oracle has put itself may depend on Ellison's voluntarily relinquishing power. "Oracle's the largest public company I know that's privately held by an individual," says former executive Polly Sumner. "It was built on the back of Larry's charisma." Whether Oracle goes the way of DEC or succeeds in overcoming the intergenerational transfer of power like IBM or

Hewlett-Packard is largely in Ellison's hands. "The normal dynastic transfer process happens through a well-thought-out partnership with someone who shares your cultures and values," notes Sumner. But that's hardly Ellison's forte. He's a narcissistic loner who thrives on being the center of attention and power. When leadership consultant Rich Hagberg drives by Oracle's towers, "I tell my kids that's where Darth Vader lives." Ellison has gone over to the dark side of the Silicon Valley infatuation with power and wealth. Because his world is solipsistic, the one thing he can't do is to admit the possibility of his own mortality, and naming a successor would imply that. With people like Ellison, "their identity is so tied up with their achievements that they don't have any identity beyond that," says Hagberg.

Oracle is going to have to come perilously close to running aground, as happened in 1990, before Ellison even considers relinquishing the helm or the board of directors gets up enough backbone to pry him from it. He gave up the wheel voluntarily in the Sydney-to-Hobart yacht race, but only because lives, including his own, were in jeopardy. It may be that he's no longer capable of letting go of the company that he formed and that now defines his very being. Sums up Jane Kennedy, the wife of ousted sales leader Gary Kennedy, "Larry is the saddest creature that I know. He's never had anybody he could trust, and he doesn't trust anyone, not even himself." Ellison looks in a mirror and no doubt sees the glittering facade of Oracle. If Oracle were to disappear, what would he see then? He must somehow find within himself the strength and will to separate himself from Oracle, for that is the only way his grand creation survives him. Otherwise, Oracle is in danger of imploding.

As Shelley wrote,

> *"My name is Ozymandias, king of kings:*
> *Look on my works, ye Mighty, and despair!"*

But all that is left of Ozymandias is a shattered stone visage in the middle of a desert.

Nothing beside remains. Round the decay
Of that colossal wreck, boundless and bare,
The lone and level sands stretch far away.

One day, students of the technology industry's history may regard Ellison as the Ozymandias of a bygone era never to be duplicated, when someone like him could fashion a company in his own image. He is a far more colorful, intriguing, conflicted figure than those who will come after him and perhaps remake Oracle. That's why the ancient Greeks wrote tragedies in which the flawed heroes invariably get whittled down by more ordinary individuals. We watch with open mouth as Ellison zooms ever closer to the edge, waiting for the moment when he goes over. For he has been a wildly entertaining performer, and we applaud him for that, even as we mourn how much more he could have been.

interview with Larry Ellison for the PBS series *Betting It All*. Taped October 20, 1999, at Oracle headquarters in Redwood Shores, Calif.

4. Ibid.

5. Ibid.

6. Leibovich, "The Outsider."

7. Ibid.

8. Malone, unpublished transcript.

9. Ibid.

10. Mike Wilson, *The Difference Between God and Larry Ellison* (New York: Quill, 1997), 34.

11. Ibid., 38.

12. Daniel Morrow, excerpts from an oral-history interview with Larry Ellison for the Smithsonian Institution, October 24, 1995, published on smithsonian.com.

13. Malone, unpublished transcript.

14. Morrow, excerpts from oral-history interview.

15. Leibovich, "The Outsider."

16. SiliconValley.com, on-line edition of the *San Jose Mercury News*, September 24, 2001.

17. Larry Ellison, "Digital IDs Can Help Prevent Terrorism," *Wall Street Journal*, October 8, 2001, A26.

18. Michael Maccoby, "Narcissistic Leaders: The Incredible Pros, the Inevitable Cons," *Harvard Business Review*, January–February 2000, 69.

19. Ibid.

[3] THE EARLY YEARS

1. Michael R. Leibowitz, "Now Comes the Real Battle at Oracle," *Upside* magazine, May 1991, 33.

2. Daniel Morrow, excerpts from an oral-history interview with Larry Ellison for the Smithsonian Institution, October 24, 1995, published on smithsonian.com.

3. Ibid.

4. Ibid.

5. Michael S. Malone, unpublished transcript of videotaped interview with Larry Ellison for the PBS series *Betting It All*. Taped October 20, 1999, at Oracle headquarters in Redwood Shores, Calif.

6. Morrow, excerpts from oral-history interview.

7. Ibid.

NOTES

INTRODUCTION

1. Richard Karpinski,, "Oracle Strikes Back over Dat[Market Numbers," *InternetWeek.com*, May 8, 200[

[1] DAYS OF THE DEPARTURES

1. Lee Gomes, "Oracle Ex-President Criticizes Forme[Employer," *Wall Street Journal*, August 24, 2000,[
2. Michelle Quinn, "Ex-Oracle Exec Sues Company,"[*Francisco Chronicle*, November 1, 1994, D3.
3. Michael S. Malone, unpublished transcript of vide[interview with Larry Ellison for the PBS series *Bet[Taped October 20, 1999, at Oracle headquarters i[Shores, Calif.
4. Pat Dillon, "Money Changes Everything," *Fast Co[1997, 79.
5. Rich Niemiec, "Rich Niemiec Interviews Bruce Sco[*Magazine* (International Oracle User Group maga[January–February 2002.
6. Daniel Morrow, excerpts from an oral-history inter[Larry Ellison for the Smithsonian Institution, Oct[1995, published on smithsonian.com.

[2] WHO'S LARRY?

1. Michael R. Leibowitz, "Now Comes the Real Battl[*Upside* magazine, May 1991, 33.
2. Mark Leibovich, "The Outsider, His Business and [*Washington Post*, November 30, 2000, A1.
3. Michael S. Malone, unpublished transcript of vide[

8. Rich Niemiec, "Rich Niemiec Interviews Bruce Scott," *Select Magazine* (International Oracle User Group magazine), January–February 2002.
9. Ibid.

[4] ON THE ROPES

1. Michael S. Malone, unpublished transcript of videotaped interview with Larry Ellison for the PBS series *Betting It All.* Taped October 20, 1999, at Oracle headquarters in Redwood Shores, Calif.
2. Ibid.

[5] SAVING ORACLE

1. Michael S. Malone, unpublished transcript of videotaped interview with Larry Ellison for the PBS series *Betting It All.* Taped October 20, 1999, at Oracle headquarters in Redwood Shores, Calif.
2. Kathy Williams and James Hart, "Getting Oracle Back to Basics," *Strategic Finance*, April 1999, 36–41.
3. Michael Maccoby, "Narcissistic Leaders: The Incredible Pros, the Inevitable Cons," *Harvard Business Review*, January–February 2000, 69.

[6] REMAKING ORACLE

1. Ian Mount, "Attention Underlings, That's Mister Conway to You," *Business 2.0*, February 2002.
2. Melanie Austria Farmer, "Exec Sues Oracle for Age Discrimination," *News.com*, May 12, 2000.

[7] BECOMING A HOUSEHOLD NAME

1. Richard L. Brandt, "The Triumph of Showmanship," posted on *Upside.com*, September 1, 1996.
2. Peter Behr and Rajiv Chandrasekaran, "Oracle Chief Weighing Apple Takeover Effort," *Washington Post*, March 28, 1997, GO3.
3. Associated Press, "Apple Chairman Scoffs at Oracle Chairman's Takeover Musings," Associated Press, March 28, 1997.
4. Associated Press, "Oracle Chairman Suspends Plans to Try to Buy Apple Computer," Associated Press, April 29, 1997.

5. News briefs, "Anti-Microsoft Front Cracks as Netscape and Oracle Quarrel," *Financial Post*, October 3, 1996, 18.

[9] MEMO TO ORACLE

1. Lee Gomes, "Oracle Spars with Gartner Group, Sees Bias in Consultant's Reports," *Wall Street Journal*, August 28, 2001, B4.
2. Lee Gomes, "For Big New Product, Oracle's Pitch Smacks of Wishful Thinking," *Wall Street Journal*, August 6, 2001, A1.

[10] GOING FOR THE JUGULAR

1. Peter Loftus, "Ellison Sees Big Shakeout Coming in Silicon Valley," *Dow Jones Newswires*, April 1, 2003.
2. Mylene Mangalindan, "Oracle's Larry Ellison Expects Greater Innovation from Sector," *Wall Street Journal*, April 8, 2003, B1.
3. Shelley Pannill, taped interview with Mark Jarvis, conducted in February 2001 for *Forbes ASAP*. All Jarvis's comments in this chapter come from her interview.
4. Shelley Pannill, taped interview with Craig Conway, conducted in February 2001 for *Forbes ASAP*. All Conway's comments in this chapter come from her interview.
5. Stuart Lauchlan, "Oracle Staff Policies in the Dock," *Vunet.com*, August 21, 2000.

[11] UPHILL BATTLES

1. Carleen Hawn, "Now, for My Next Trick . . . ," *Forbes*, January 21, 2002, 90–92.
2. Shelley Pannill, taped interview with Craig Conway, conducted in February 2001 for *Forbes ASAP*.

[12] CULT OR CULTURE

1. Benjamin Pimentel, "E-mail Trial Reveals Billionaire's Lifestyle," *San Francisco Chronicle*, January 20, 1997, A17.
2. Ibid.
3. Ibid.
4. Ted Bridis, Glenn Simpson, and Myelene Mangalindan, "Oracle Took Out Microsoft's Trash in Software Feud," *Wall Street Journal Europe*, June 30, 2000, 25.

5. Noam Levey and Ann E. Marimow, "Senator Rips Politics behind Oracle Deal," *SiliconValley.com* (*San Jose Mercury News*), June 17, 2002.

6. Noam Levey, "E-mails Reveal Companies' Effort to Hide Details in State's Oracle Deal," *SiliconValley.com* (*San Jose Mercury News*), May 14, 2002.

7. Ann E. Marimow and Noam Levey, "Oracle Hoped California Deal Would Block Competition," *SiliconValley.com* (*San Jose Mercury News*), June 4, 2002.

[13] ON THE EDGE

1. Wylie Wong, "Top Oracle Sales Executive Quits," CNET *News.com*, November 30, 2001.

2. Wylie Wong, "Ellison: Computers Are Bunk, Biotech Is Where It's At," *ZDNet*, February 21, 2001.

3. Jim Kerstetter, Steve Hamm, and Andrew Park, "Larry Ellison's One-Man Show," *BusinessWeek On-line*, March 25, 2002.

ACKNOWLEDGMENTS

I would first like to commend Ray Lane, the former president of Oracle, for his integrity and candor during the many hours he spent with me talking about subjects that could be painful to remember. I'm also grateful to other former Oracle executives, including Gary Kennedy, Marc Benioff, Craig Ramsey, Polly Sumner, Robert Shaw, Dave Roux, Barry Ariko, Geoff Squire, Kate Mitchell, Jerry Held, and many others too numerous to mention, for agreeing to interviews. Thanks must also be extended to Oracle's customers, competitors, and partners, and to outside experts on database and business software who shared their thoughts with me. And to Eric Nee, my former colleague, who, as always, provided keen insight and editing advice. Without all of them, this book would not have been possible. Finally, I appreciate the hard work of my agent, Daniel Greenberg, in landing me this contract. I thank Random House/Crown Business for having the courage and conviction to publish this book, especially my editor there, John Mahaney, for helping me make the story of Larry Ellison the best it can be.

INDEX

ABOUT THE AUTHOR

KAREN SOUTHWICK is an experienced journalist who has worked for several magazines, including *Forbes ASAP* and *Upside*, and metropolitan daily newspapers, including the *San Francisco Chronicle*. She has covered subjects ranging from nuclear power and biotechnology to software. She has a B.A. in communications from Brigham Young University and an M.B.A. in finance and policy from the University of California at Berkeley. She has published three previous books on the business side of technology, including *Silicon Gold Rush, High Noon: The Inside Story of Scott McNealy and the Rise of Sun Microsystems,* and *Kingmakers: Venture Capital and the Money Behind the Net.* She is currently at work on a book about best practices in corporate philanthropy.